THE
BATTLE *of* BRITAIN

IMPERIAL WAR MUSEUM

OSPREY
PUBLISHING

THE
BATTLE *of* BRITAIN

KATE MOORE

First published in Great Britain in 2010 by Osprey Publishing,
Midland House, West Way, Botley, Oxford OX2 0PH, United Kingdom.
44-02 23rd St, Suite 219, Long Island City, NY 11101, USA.

E-mail: info@ospreypublishing.com

In association with the Imperial War Museum
www.iwm.org.uk

A CIP catalogue record for this book is available from the British Library

ISBN: 978 1 84603 474 9

Page layout by Myriam Bell Design, France
Index by Alan Thatcher
Typeset in Bembo
Originated by PPS Grasmere Ltd, Leeds, UK
Printed in China through Worldprint Ltd

10 11 12 13 14 15   10 9 8 7 6 5 4 3 2 1

For a catalogue of all books published by Osprey please contact:

ACKNOWLEDGMENTS

With grateful thanks to the IWM Sound, Photo, Art, Documents and Printed Books
Departments and with particular thanks to Nick Hewitt, Terry Charman, Abigail Ratcliffe
and Madeleine James for their careful check of the manuscript and page proofs, and whose
advice was gratefully received. The wonderful collection of art and photographs contained
with the IWM are well known, but it is only in recent years that the treasures of the Sound
Archive have been brought to the public's attention. The several hours I spent listening to
the interviews of Battle of Britain veterans was truly inspiring and the collection is without
a doubt a national treasure. Thanks are also owed to the wonderful team at Osprey
especially Ruth Sheppard and Emily Holmes whose kind support and hard work made the
book happen. Any mistakes are entirely the responsibility of the author.

Particular thanks are due to Mr Nigel Cameron for granting permission to quote from his
childhood wartime diary and Mr Hans-Ekkehard Bob for the use of extracts from his
papers held by the IWM. Mr Piers Mayfield and and Mr C. Morris were also kind enough
to grant permission for the use of extracts from the diary of Rev. Guy Mayfield and the
unpublished memoirs of Air Commodore E. J. Morris. I would also like to especially thank
Mrs Edith Kup (neé Heap) who was kind enough not only to grant permission for the use
of copyrighted material but also to write to me regarding personal recollections of the
Battle as well as her fianceé Denis Wissler.

A special thanks also to my friends and family, especially my husband Edward, for their
support and patience during the preparation of this volume.

DEDICATION

For my father, Ron Flintham, who inspired a love of history.

IMPERIAL WAR MUSEUM COLLECTIONS

The vast majority of the photos in this book come from the Imperial War Museum's huge
collections which cover all aspects of conflict involving Britain and the Commonwealth
since the outbreak of the First World War. Many of these rich resources are available online
to search, browse and buy at www.iwmcollections.org.uk.

In addition to Collections Online, you can come to the Visitors Room where you can explore
over 8 million photographs, thousands of hours of moving images, the largest sound archive of
its kind in the world, thousands of diaries and letters written by people in wartime, and a huge
reference library. To make an appointment, call (020) 7416 5344 or (020) 74165333 for
photographs, (020) 7416 5294 for film or email collections@iwm.org.uk.

Imperial War Museum www.iwm.org.uk

Front cover: *Battle of Britain*, by John Nash. (IWM Art LD1550)

Back cover: Spitfires of No. 610 Squadron flying in three 'vic' formations on 24 July 1940.
(IWM CH 740)

Endpapers: Squadron Leader Douglas Bader DSO (front centre) with some of the Canadian
pilots of the 242 (Canadian) Squadron at their home station of Duxford. (IWM CH 1413)

Title page: Three Spitfires of No. 19 Squadron grace the skies in 1939 shortly before the
outbreak of war. Reportedly one name for the aircraft considered by Supermarine was
'Shrew', which would not have done the elegant aircraft justice. (IWM CH 20)

CONTENTS

PREFACE 7

INTRODUCTION 9

FIGHTER COMMAND 19

THE LUFTWAFFE 55

BLITZKRIEG: GERMANY'S LIGHTNING STRIKE 83

SPITFIRE SUMMER: THE AIR BATTLE FOR BRITAIN 97

AFTERMATH 181

NOTES 188

APPENDICES 191

BIBLIOGRAPHY 195

INDEX 197

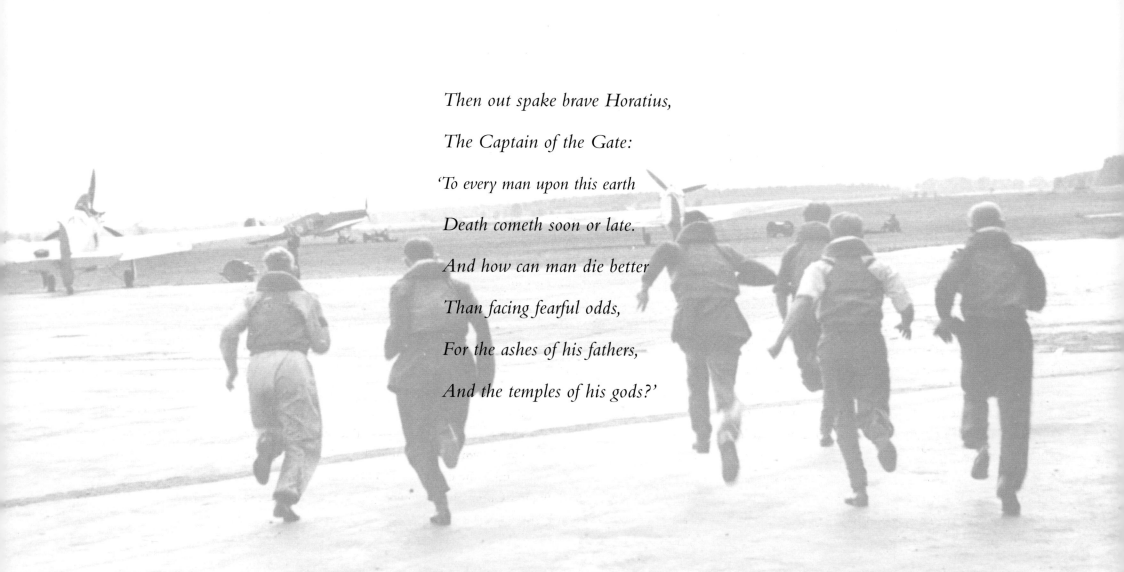

Then out spake brave Horatius,

The Captain of the Gate:

'To every man upon this earth

Death cometh soon or late.

And how can man die better

Than facing fearful odds,

For the ashes of his fathers,

And the temples of his gods?'

Thomas Babington Macaulay, *Lays of Ancient Rome*
Memorized by Winston Churchill at age 13

PREFACE

NOW, AT LAST, his hour had come. For years, he had haunted the corridors of power but as the Nazi juggernaut continued its unassailable assault on France, Belgium and the Low Countries, Winston Churchill was summoned to see the king and asked to form a government. A mere fortnight later, his War Cabinet braced itself for the worst military defeat in British history. Even with Churchill at the helm, nothing could prevent the disastrous retreat of the British Expeditionary Force (BEF) as it fell back towards the Channel ports. The 220,000 Tommies waited on the Dunkirk beaches in the hope of salvation, which seemed destined not to come. The king and the House of Commons were warned that they would be lucky to save a tenth of the force. The call went out for vessels of all shapes and sizes to assist in the evacuation and a strange armada of ships started to gather. From all along the Thames, from Kent and Essex, pleasure craft and trawlers, tugboats and rowing boats, gathered alongside the Royal Navy. Even today what follows seems miraculous. In a brilliantly executed Royal Navy operation which lasted nine long days 338,226 British and French soldiers were successfully evacuated from the port of Dunkirk, most directly onto the 42 British destroyers and other Royal Navy vessels, with many of the exhausted soldiers ferried directly from the beaches to the waiting destroyers by the fleet of civilian manned 'little ships'.

But, as Churchill rightly pointed out, 'wars are not won by evacuations' and as the nation braced itself, only the Royal Air Force's inexperienced Fighter Command could prevent the seemingly inevitable invasion from being attempted. As Churchill electrified the nation with his soaring oratory, strengthened the resolve of the embattled British people and gave them hope, it was a rather different character who would conduct the nation's defence. Taciturn, prickly and politically inept, Air Chief Marshal Hugh Dowding was everything Churchill was not. And yet, they shared some crucial qualities. Both had recognised the danger that Nazi Germany had posed from the start and had done everything in their power to prepare for what they felt was an unavoidable conflict. Now Churchill would allow Dowding to conduct the defence he had so carefully planned for and as the enemy gathered at the gate, the men and women of Fighter Command, outnumbered but defiant, braced themselves for battle.

Opposite:
Pilots scrambling for their aircraft on 25 July 1940. (IWM HU 49253)

INTRODUCTION

> 	" *War is horrible, but slavery is worse, and you may be sure that the British people would rather go down fighting than live in servitude.* "

Winston Churchill to the *New Statesman* journalist Kingsley Martin in January 1939

On 1 September 1939, Hitler unleashed his armies and raced into Poland. Europe had been floundering towards war for months, but Britain, together with France, had continued to attempt to negotiate a settlement that would appease the German dictator. Their attempts had failed and instead 56 German divisions, nine of them armoured, had crossed the Polish borders under the cover of darkness in the early hours of the morning. The Anglo-French governments, despite their alliances with Poland, failed to immediately declare war. As the Siegfried Line stood virtually defenceless, manned by a mere ten divisions, the Allies baulked at the thought of yet another world conflict. Instead, Paris and London expressed their willingness to negotiate should Hitler withdraw his forces from Poland. The Führer had no intention of doing so. As the realization slowly dawned throughout the course of the day that war was unavoidable the British Prime Minister sent for Winston Churchill. The Member of Parliament for Epping had been a virtual pariah for most of the decade, accused of warmongering and troublemaking. But in recent months his star had been in the ascendant. The Munich Agreement of 1938 had rapidly proven to be a red herring. With the growing disillusionment of the British people, the press had clamoured for Churchill's return to government. Now Chamberlain asked him to become a member of his War Cabinet when it was officially formed. But war had not yet been declared. While Chamberlain's government delayed the inevitable, the Panzers had continued to roll into Poland. Within Britain itself blackouts were declared and gas masks distributed to everyone, but an air of unreality prevailed, the Football Association declaring that there was no need to cancel any games, just as sandbags went up round London's monuments and government buildings.

This sense of unreality continued within the government. Despite Hitler's continued rejection of Anglo-French calls for withdrawal, Lord Halifax, the Foreign Secretary, persisted in his negotiation attempts, assuring the Italian Foreign Minister that no ultimatum had been issued and that the role of the British government was simply that of a mediator, despite Britain's mutual defence treaty with Poland. Churchill's hands were tied. He had been invited to join a War Cabinet that did not yet exist, but the acceptance of the post meant that he was reluctant to openly criticize the government.

Opposite:
Prior to the official declaration of war, the evacuation of children from the East End of London was begun on 1 and 2 September 1939, amid growing fears of the destruction that would be caused by German bombing raids. (IWM HU 36238)

He did not need to do so. The groundswell of public and parliamentary opinion was turning against Chamberlain. The House of Commons met the delaying tactics of the Prime Minister and Foreign Secretary with horror, and in a revolt of conscience Chamberlain's own Cabinet repudiated their leader. Chamberlain realized that he could delay no longer and formally issued an ultimatum to Germany. The deadline came and went. At 11.15am on 3 September 1939, Chamberlain addressed the nation over the radio, officially announcing that Britain was once again at war.

Edith Heap was 21 and still living at home when she first heard the announcement. Like most people, she expected the declaration to be immediately followed by a stream of German bombers:

On 3rd September, a beautiful autumn day, we listened to the fatal broadcast with dismay but not surprise. We expected to be bombed at once, and were quite surprised to wake up the next day to an equally beautiful, peaceful day.[2]

She was not alone. Fighter Command immediately sprang into action. Edward Morris was a pilot with No. 79 Squadron and later recalled how they were instantly scrambled:

Immediately after the Prime Minister's announcement we were ordered to Cockpit Readiness. When we had strapped in and switched on the R/T we were ordered to start engines and Stand By. We sat for what seemed ages with the engines getting hotter all the time until the

Squadron Commander called Operations and told them either we had to take off or close down the engines before they all boiled. Rather reluctantly they agreed to stopping our engines but we had to remain at Cockpit Readiness.[3]

Britain seemingly expected an imminent attack and her armed forces were willing to defend her, but would the youth of 1939 rally as enthusiastically as that of 1914? Churchill had been predicting war for six long years. Now he would have to inspire the British people and her armed forces to fight, as the road ahead would be both long and arduous. The following day he addressed the House of Commons. Churchill was the fourth speaker of the day, and the House was growing restless, but he gave his audience a taste of the electrifying oratory that was still to come. Churchill had realized instinctively that the violation of a treaty alone was not enough to inspire the British people, declaring:

> This is not a question of fighting for Danzig or fighting for Poland. We are fighting to save the whole world from the pestilence of Nazi tyranny and in defence of all that is most sacred to man. This is no war of domination or imperial aggrandisement or material gain; no war to shut any country out of the sunlight and means of progress. It is a war, viewed in its inherent quality, to establish, on impregnable rocks, the rights of the individual, and it is a war to establish and revive the stature of man.[4]

Churchill was now once again a member of a Cabinet at War, appointed First Lord of the Admiralty as he had been in 1914. Despite the Dardanelles fiasco in 1915, in many ways he was a naval

Chamberlain waves to the crowds gathering outside 10 Downing Street on the day war was declared. An experienced politician who had been a member of Parliament since 1918, Chamberlain had sought to contain Hitler's ambitions through gradual and limited concessions, including the annexation of Sudetenland, then part of Czechoslovakia, by Germany in 1938, through the Munich Agreement. Six months later Hitler would defy the terms of the agreement by invading the remainder of Czechoslovakia. Chamberlain's attempts to secure peace had failed. Less than a year after Munich Britain was once again at war. (IWM HU 5538)

Fearful that the British population would not rally to the nation's defence as willingly as they had done in 1914, a series of posters were designed throughout 1939, with the intention of driving up recruitment through a mixture of patriotism, inspiration, cajolement and fear. (IWM PST 13959, IWM PST 14818)

England expects

NATIONAL SERVICE

FREEDOM IS IN PERIL DEFEND IT WITH ALL YOUR MIGHT

man: he spoke the same language as his admirals, had spent years studying German naval developments and could easily recite from memory the specifications of British and enemy classes of ships. He had condemned the Anglo-German Naval Agreement of 1935, which had reined in Britain's control of the seas, but he retained his confidence in this, the senior service. Despite the batterings the Royal Navy received from U-boats almost immediately there were some isolated successes against the Kriegsmarine. What really worried him was not in his remit, and that was the air force.

Nearly two thousand German aircraft had annihilated the Polish Air Force as it lined up on its runways. Then fleets of Junkers 87 Stukas, the dreaded dive-bombers of the Luftwaffe, had screamed down on the massing Polish armies and decimated them. The Poles actually had 250,000 more men under arms than the invaders. But this was modern warfare, with every plane and tank worth more than an entire regiment of men. Churchill was right to fear the Luftwaffe.

For three weeks the Poles resisted. However on 17 September Russia invaded from the east, fulfilling their terms of the secret alliance between the Nazi and Soviet states. Pockets of resistance could still be found in the first week of October, but eventually the Polish government was forced to flee. One hundred thousand Poles escaped, often making their way first to France, then, when she too fell, on to Britain where they would eventually fight as Free Poles. Polish destroyers made their way to Scotland and joined the Royal Navy, and 146 Polish pilots would fight in the battle to save Britain herself in the summer of 1940.

A strange disquiet followed Poland's collapse. Churchill, true to form, christened it the 'sinister trance', but for eight months the British public called it 'The Bore War'.[5] In fact Hitler had hoped to launch his offensive in the West as soon as possible, calling on his army chiefs to propose plans for an all-out assault. But the weather intervened and the plans were halted. Hitler was not disappointed. The proposals for the assault had been unimaginative and far too traditional for his liking. The long, unusually cold winter gave some of the more gifted generals time to plan. In the February of 1940, General von Manstein presented his strategy for a massive sickle-cut manoeuvre, through the Ardennes and to the sea. It was approved with a launch date set for May, once spring had arrived.

In the meantime, a small sideshow had been taking place after the conquest of Poland and her division between Germany and Russia. Russia had attacked Finland to secure Finnish territory that was judged critical to ensure her defence of Leningrad (modern St Petersburg). This had remained outside of the sphere of the main European conflict. However as the winter thawed the world's attention was suddenly drawn towards the Scandinavian peninsula. The German war effort was dependent on Swedish iron ore transported through Norwegian territorial waters and the port of Narvik. Concerned about potential Royal Navy interference, Hitler ordered the invasion of Norway on 9 April 1940. The war, as much as the weather, was hotting up. Ironically the British had just begun

their cautious efforts to mine the waters and deny them to the Kriegsmarine when Hitler launched his bold offensive. At first it seemed like events might play into British hands. By nightfall the Germans had seized every important Norwegian port, leaving valuable warships bottled up and short of fuel. Now they would have to defend them against the might of the Royal Navy. The Kriegsmarine suffered heavily throughout the operation and was virtually crippled. But the Royal Navy had not reckoned on the destructive power of the Luftwaffe. In contrast to the well-coordinated German attacks, the British counter-landings, often composed of newly called-up Territorial Army reservists as the professional army was already in France, were poorly organized. The deciding factor in the fate of Norway was the superior performance of the German air services. With the Royal Navy anti-aircraft guns

The view from a Luftwaffe Junkers Ju 52 bomber with the outskirts of Warsaw ablaze below. (IWM HU 3218)

unequal to the task, and the British landing forces unprotected against Luftwaffe air attacks, both took a pounding from the 317 German bombers present. To supplement the forces of Coastal Command, four squadrons from Fighter Command were also deployed. Operating independently of any air defence system and, at times, forced to improvise airfields from frozen lakes the 36 fighter planes were obviously no match for the might of the Luftwaffe. With poorly equipped troops, an operational plan thwarted by interference from Whitehall and the Luftwaffe's control of the air the Allied effort in Norway was doomed from the start. On 28 April the War Cabinet ordered the withdrawal of the British expeditionary forces, but fighting continued in Narvik.

The press and Parliament began to clamour for Churchill as the conflict in Norway ground to its inevitable conclusion. In the meantime the greatest army Germany had ever amassed was gathering prior to their assault on the Low Countries and France. The Blitzkrieg in the West was about to begin.

At the outbreak of war, the French General Maurice Gamelin had declared to his own airmen that 'There is no such thing as the aerial battle. There is only the battle on the ground.'[6] If the Allies had learnt anything from the fiasco in Scandinavia it was that control of the skies could determine either victory or defeat in any major military operation. The Royal Air Force's contribution to the campaign had been minimal. Now the rival air forces would be deployed in strength against each other. It remained to be seen who would win the command of the skies.

Three posters associated with wartime propaganda, including possibly the most famous one of the war, which has come to symbolise the success of Fighter Command during the Battle of Britain. In fact, it was a bomber crew who posed for the image and Churchill's oft-quoted statement referred to the RAF as a whole. (IWM PST 14972, IWM PST 14982, IWM PST 14842)

The following chapters look at the origins and preparations of the two rival air forces. Aerial engagements had, of course, been fought during the First World War, but the Battle of Britain was the first large-scale aerial battle the world had ever witnessed, and one in which victory or defeat would have far-reaching implications. The origins and development of the opposing air forces would have a direct impact on how the Battle was ultimately fought. Born out of the Royal Flying Corps' (RFC) experiences during the First World War, throughout the 1920s and the early years of the 1930s the RAF placed far greater significance on the development of Bomber Command. In fact, RAF bombers would be able to perform only limited attacks against Britain's adversary during the course of the Battle and suffered high losses, which far outweighed any gains achieved. This was a defensive battle that could be fought only by the forces of Fighter Command, and one that the force was uniquely prepared for. Years of preparation had gone into the development, not only of the fighter aircraft themselves but also an elaborate defensive screen masterminded by the Commander-in-Chief of Fighter Command, Hugh Dowding, and relying on the

latest technological developments, most notably radar. In contrast, the Luftwaffe was born in secret. Banned from having an air force following her defeat in the First World War, even prior to Hitler's ascent to power small bodies of pilots were secretly trained in preparation for a national air force that did not yet exist. These pilots would later provide the experienced core of the Luftwaffe. More than anything the Luftwaffe was 'Hitler's Air Force' and was uniquely tied into the political and strategic aspirations of the Führer. It was developed as an attacking force of both bombers and fighters for a resurgent Nazi Germany, with combat-experienced and tactically superior fighter pilots thanks to the Luftwaffe's early forays during the Spanish Civil War.

The rival forces were first arraigned against each other in strength following the launch of Blitzkrieg in May 1940. This was a crucial opportunity for both sides to assess their rivals' strengths and weaknesses, refine tactics and, for Fighter Command, gain much-needed combat experience. The deployment of Fighter Command during the Battle of France is also crucial to the story of the Battle of Britain because it could have so easily led to the

Right:
A view of the German destroyer *Hermann Kuhne* on fire during the Royal Navy's attempt to retake Narvik. The photograph was taken from a Fleet Air Arm aircraft. The Allied failure to control the skies over Norway guaranteed the eventual German success despite the high losses of her Kriegsmarine. The unqualified triumph of the Luftwaffe seemed a portent of things to come. (IWM A 36)

Far right:
Pilots and ground crew gather around the fuselage from No. 87 Squadron's first kill, a Heinkel He 111 shot down by Flight Lieutenant Robert Voase-Jeff on 2 November 1939. Pilot Officer Dennis David, who damaged another Heinkel on the same day, autographs the trophy. Watching on the right is a new member of the squadron, Pilot Officer Roland Beamont (in flying helmet), a future ace and famous post-war test pilot. (IWM C 457)

wholesale destruction of a large number of British fighters and pilots if Dowding had allowed a greater number of squadrons to be committed to the Battle. That he so valiantly resisted sending more squadrons ensured that there were adequate reserves to defend Britain once France fell.

From July until October, the daylight bombing raids over Britain constituted the Battle of Britain. The clear summer weather ensured that only on a few days could Fighter Command rest easy in the knowledge that the Luftwaffe would be unable to attack. Instead it became an endless, exhausting battle of attrition for both sides as they struggled for mastery of the skies. This was a battle fought between rival pilots and air crews when individual decisions could make the difference between success and failure, life and death. Throughout the book, their own words, drawn almost exclusively from the Imperial War Museum's own archives, are used to bring these events to life.

The remnants of the contribution of the RAF to the campaign in Norway. With minimal aircraft committed, mostly obselete Gladiator biplanes such as this, and lacking the benefits of an early warning system, far from their home base and without any airfields, the British pilots could contribute little to the Allied attempts to retake Norway from the Nazis. (IWM HU 2873)

FIGHTER COMMAND

> *You came into big things as an accident of naval power when you were an island. The world had confidence in you… Now through an accident of air power you will probably cease to exist.*

Churchill ruminating to a friend on the fate of the British Isles after the first flight at Kitty Hawk by the Wright Brothers in 1903

THE ORIGINS OF FIGHTER COMMAND

The Royal Flying Corps was first deployed in battle at the start of the First World War. It was a small force of three squadrons or just 60 aircraft.[7] This alone was nothing short of extraordinary considering that the first recorded flight had taken place a mere 11 years previously. The growth of this arm, however, was exponential and Britain concluded the war with almost 23,000 machines, and a new service – the Royal Air Force – to rank alongside its older, more illustrious sister services of the Royal Navy and the army. Post-war it was recognized that the somewhat amateurish, albeit courageous, nature of the air force would need to be formalized. As such, in 1920 Cranwell, the world's first military air academy, opened its doors to new recruits. Churchill, then Secretary of State for War and Air, wrote in the first issue of the college magazine in September 1920: 'Nothing that has ever happened in the world before has offered man such opportunity for individual personal prowess as the air

fighting of the Great War… It is to rival, and no doubt to excel these feats of your forerunners in the Service that you are now training yourselves and I, for one, look forward with confidence to the day when you are not at the College and will make the name of the Royal Air Force feared and respected throughout the world.'[8] Churchill, despite his initial concerns, embraced the phenomenon of air power with the realization that here lay the best means of defence for his island nation. Cranwell combined the spirit of the First World War aviator with the professionalism and technical nuance of the new world order. A Technical Training School was also established in 1920 at RAF Halton, which would provide skilfully trained specialist ground crew for the next 70 years. Two years later these establishments would be complemented by the creation of an RAF Staff College at Andover.

The RAF itself offered a somewhat unique experience to the sister services and not just because of the exposure to the then still risky business of regular flying. Rather, it was because of its distinctly more egalitarian spirit. All entrants to both pilot officer and technical

Opposite:
Flying practically wingtip to wingtip, an impressive formation of No. 111 Squadron Hurricanes photographed in January 1938. Their flying skills were later matched by their fighting ability as they pioneered the effective but gut-wrenching tactic of head-on attacks on enemy formations. (IWM HU 68334)

training had to show real aptitude and were rigorously tested in mathematics, experimental science and English. As a result there was less of a distinction between RAF officers and other ranks, and many apprentices at Halton were later accepted for flying training. Indeed, the three best apprentices per year at Halton were offered cadetships at Cranwell and in 1921 it was announced that flying training would be offered to all candidates from the other ranks if they demonstrated suitable ability. It was envisaged that they would then serve as pilots for a period of five years before returning to their own trade, with the added distinction of promotion to sergeant. Although they did not become officers, it was a remarkable concept for its time, and one that would ensure that when war did break out Britain would have a pool of skilled, technically knowledgeable NCOs alongside their pilot officers.

In an effort to supplement the underfunded, and therefore undermanned, RAF, Lord Trenchard, the first Chief of Air Staff, encouraged the development of university and auxiliary squadrons. The former would serve as ideal officer candidate material, with the hope that the offer of flying lessons would entice many students who might otherwise have been tempted to join the other services. University Air Squadrons were successfully established at Oxford, Cambridge and in London, with many graduates of such schemes later serving within the ranks of Fighter Command throughout 1940. The concept of a territorial branch of the RAF was first mooted in 1919 and was eventually formalized in 1924. Not surprisingly, these auxiliary squadrons were more elitist than the RAF itself, as they consisted almost exclusively of wealthy amateurs who could afford the luxury of either their own aircraft or private flying lessons prior to joining.

Despite such efforts, by the close of the decade the RAF still consisted of only 25 home-based regular squadrons, supplemented by 11 auxiliary and reserve units, drastically short of the figure of 52

A photograph of five new recruits to the post-war RAF taken in 1921, a year after the world's first military air academy opened at Cranwell. (IWM HU 41572)

squadrons that had been set as the required number for home defence as early as 1923.

As the 1930s dawned and the extremism of Fascism and Soviet Communism continued to darken the European continent, only Churchill, now a mere MP and virtual political pariah, continued to argue forcefully for strategic rearmament across the board and a growth in strength for the RAF. Finally in 1934 the government voted for a five-year general expansion plan for the RAF and in 1936 the service was divided into four key commands: Bomber, Fighter, Coastal and Training. In July 1936 Hugh Dowding was appointed as Air Officer Commanding-in-Chief of Fighter Command and would have direct control over the fighter force, anti-aircraft and balloon commands as well as the Observer Corps. Significantly at this time Fighter Command was regarded as of secondary importance in comparison with Bomber Command.

A formal group portrait of four RAF flying officers and sergeants together with 20 student cadets from the Oxford University Air Squadron standing in front of their Avro 504N training aircraft. (RAF Hendon, PC98/173/5099/7)

A First World War recruiting poster for the youngest of the services. The glamorous appeal of flying would continue during the Second World War, with both sides adopting a 'knights of the air' attitude, and pilots wanting to emulate their boyhood heroes. (IWM PST 5277)

A portrait of Hugh Trenchard painted at the General Staff Headquarters in 1917 by Sir William Orpen. Trenchard was typical of the adventurous spirit of the early aviators. He had served as an infantry officer during the Anglo-Boer War of 1899–1902, where he survived being shot. He commanded the Royal Flying Corps in France between 1915 and 1917. Post-war he oversaw the formal creation of the independent RAF and was known as the 'Father of the Air Force', although he was critical of the expansion of Fighter Command prior to the outbreak of war. (IWM ART 325)

THE BOMBER WILL ALWAYS GET THROUGH

Following the First World War there was undoubtedly a growing belief that air power was the future but that the bomber was the key. Trenchard, as Commander in Chief and a former First World War fighter pilot, was convinced of the war-winning potential of strategic bombing campaigns. His contemporary the Italian military theorist General Giulio Douhet authored the seminal work *The Command of the Air*. In it he argued that the essence of aerial defence was that it was virtually impossible and that the only true defence was a strong offence. Moreover, strategic bombing would invariably result in victory because it would destroy armed forces on the ground, key centres of the opposing government and industry, and ultimately break the willpower of civilians, forcing their representatives to sue for peace.

This bleak picture rapidly gained official endorsement by the leaders of fledgling air forces throughout the world. In Britain, this military viewpoint was further endorsed by the government with a keynote address by past Prime Minister Stanley Baldwin in 1932. The speech was entitled 'A Fear for the Future' and as Baldwin addressed the House of Commons he sounded a pessimistic warning for the public at large: 'I think it is well ... for the man in the street to realise there is no power on earth that can protect him from bombing, whatever people may tell him. The bomber will always get through. The only defence is offence, which means that you have to kill more women and children more quickly than the enemy if you want to save yourselves.'[9]

This was not just pure hyperbole. At the time, thanks to their multiple engines, bombers enjoyed a superiority of performance over fighters, and without the later benefits of radar it was hard to envisage at this stage what kind of defence could be adequately deployed. The events of the 1930s undoubtedly confirmed their destructive power with the Italian use of gas bombs in Abyssinia in 1935, the Japanese attacks on Shanghai and Nanking and notwithstanding the British use of terror bombing to quell tribal warfare in Iraq in the previous decade. But the bombing of Guernica in 1937 by the German 'volunteers' of the Condor Legion, as well as more damaging carpet-bombing raids on Barcelona the following year, provoked particular horror in Europe as they were seen as deliberate attacks on unprotected European civilians.

Therefore Dowding, as Commander-in-Chief of Fighter Command, was swimming against a powerful tide if he hoped to

Unlike the Royal Air Force Volunteer Reserve, which consisted of former members of the RAF, the Auxiliary Air Force squadrons were manned entirely by civilians who wished to pursue their passion for flying. Prior to the outbreak of war there was often an elitist nature to the AAF, thanks to the expensive nature of their hobby, but this soon faded away amid the rigours of war and as replacements were drafted in from all walks of life. This wartime image is of No. 601 (County of London) Squadron, once known as the 'Millionaires' Club'. The picture shows the 'A' and 'B' flights during the height of the Battle of Britain. The original caption reads 'Weekend Pilots now Fighter Aces'. In many cases this was quite true. (IWM CH 1623)

General Giulio Douhet, former head of Italy's Central Aeronautical Bureau and later author of *The Command of the Air*, which shaped much of the strategic thinking about air power throughout the 1920s and early 1930s. (IWM HU 44232)

convince any parliamentary lobby that the meagre funds for defence should be diverted from Bomber Command. It is ironic, therefore, that he finally found a political ally in the man who has since come to embody the weak-willed, morally and politically misguided appeasement governments of the 1930s – Neville Chamberlain. When Chamberlain assumed the office of Prime Minister in 1937 he was horrified by Baldwin's stark view that the only means of defence was the deaths of thousands of innocent civilians. He searched for an alternative and found one with Dowding's plans for fighter defence. From 1937 onwards, the priorities of air armament were altered and Dowding would have the fighters he so urgently needed.

THE DOWDING SYSTEM

Following Dowding's appointment to Fighter Command in 1936 he began to implement and refine a defensive screen, which would later be known as the 'Dowding system'. Fighter Command itself was divided into four operational groups numbered as 10 through to 13. No. 10 Group consisted of a handful of squadrons and their area of operations was the south-west. No. 11 Group held the south-east, which would be the frontline throughout the Battle, and to the north of London was No. 12 Group. No. 13 Group controlled a vast swathe of area from the north of England to the outer limits of Scotland but again was manned by only a small number of squadrons. This disposition of forces reflected the reality of an aerial defence that

Britain could be expected to mount. London was, naturally, a primary target, while many of the key industrial targets, in particular aircraft factories, were also concentrated in the southern half of Britain. Moreover, it is a peculiarity of the island itself that the southern weald, that body of land between the North and South Downs with its gently undulating landscape and lack of strongpoints, is virtually indefensible. This would be the main disembarking point for any invading fleet and it was over these Kentish villages, Essex suburbs and London itself that the majority of dogfights would be fought.

The Groups were part of a complex defensive system, with each Group having its own headquarters that sent out orders to individual sector stations based at key airfields. At the heart of the defensive structure, however, was the Fighter Command Headquarters at Bentley Priory near Stanmore on the outskirts of London. This manor house and its surrounding grounds had been a royal residence, failed hotel and all-girls' boarding school by the time the RAF acquired it and its suitably eccentric past seemed fitting for its somewhat eccentric new commander. This non-flying RAF base would serve as the nerve centre for Fighter Command. Dowding established a Filter Room at Bentley Priory to which all information on incoming raids would be relayed from radar stations around the coast and Observer Corps posts throughout the country. Once a raid had been identified as 'hostile' and aircraft flight paths had been determined as best as possible this information was relayed to the operations room. Here the information would be laid out on a large plotting table overlaid with a map showing the boundaries of the various sectors within a Group, each indicated by an alphabetical list. The information would then be relayed to the relevant Groups and sector operation rooms where it also appeared on their situation maps. Essentially Bentley Priory acted as a disseminator of information. The great beauty of the system was that Group commanders were allowed a certain freedom to decide which of their sectors to activate, while Sector Station commanders were responsible for the final decision on which squadrons to put in the air to meet the threat.

All the plotting itself was done by members of the Women's Auxiliary Air Force (WAAF). By the outbreak of war the RAF was suffering an acute shortage of manpower, especially as the fighter defence system was so rapidly expanded. Women, with some initial opposition, began to supplement and then replace roles that would normally have been denied to them, including radar operators and plotters. Rosemary Horstmann was 19 in the spring of 1940 and she served for three months as a plotter at RAF Filton:

We sat round, or stood round, a large map table of the area, in the operations room. And with the aid of long sticks, like billiard cues, we pushed little symbols around on this table – showing enemy aircraft coming in, our aircraft going up to intercept them, and that sort of thing. We were hooked up by headphones to Observer Corps stations, and the Observer Corps people would telephone in to us with information about plots. There might be an unidentified something or other, and they would give us a grid reference, and we would put a little symbol on to that grid reference, and gradually the information would build up.[10]

Each wooden block would have numbers allocated alongside it to indicate both the strength of the raiding party and the number of this particular enemy force, together with an arrow to indicate the

Bomb damage in the city of Barcelona in 1938 after a raid. The effectiveness of the bomb attacks by the Nationalist forces struck fear into the hearts of governments throughout Europe. The Republican forces produced a poster (left) to inspire the local populations to resist and to educate the wider world about the true horrors of a bombing campaign waged against a civilian population. (IWM PST 8661, HU 33155)

AIR CHIEF MARSHAL HUGH DOWDING

Dowding was born in 1882, the son of a schoolmaster. He attended the Royal Military Academy, Woolwich, and was commissioned as an officer in the Royal Garrison Artillery. After graduation he had a number of overseas postings including Gibraltar, Ceylon, Hong Kong and India. An enthusiastic skier and polo-player, on his return to England he found the idea of idea of flying immediately attractive. The Royal Flying Corps had been established in 1912 and anyone who could fly was instantly accepted with the added incentive of the reimbursement of the costs of the initial private tuition. Dowding, using powers of persuasion that are not generally associated with his character, convinced the flying school to teach him on credit until he was accepted into the RFC and he received his refund. The independent flying school did not have to wait long – Dowding received his 'ticket' after a total of just one hour and 40 minutes in the air. Following a further three months' tuition at the Central Flying School at Upavon, Dowding officially received his wings. Just weeks later Britain was at war with Germany. Until that point, many army officers had pursued an interest in flying just as actively as they had pursued a variety of sporting interests. With the declaration of war, however, all military pilots were immediately required to report to the RFC. Dowding was already a senior officer by this point, and this combined with regular combat throughout his deployment in France ensured that his rise within the fledgling RFC was meteoric. He was appointed Squadron Commander of No. 16 Squadron in 1915 but he reportedly clashed with Trenchard, overall commander of the RFC, about the need to rest pilots exhausted by non-stop duty – a fear that would continue to plague him throughout the Battle of Britain. In 1915 he was posted back to Britain to Training Command and his frontline position given to Cyril Newall, the future Chief of Staff of the RAF.

Dowding became a career officer in the post-war RAF and gained experience in departments of training, supply, research and development with a promotion to the rank of Air Marshal in 1933 and an appointment on the Air Council. As the Air Council representative for Supply and Research Dowding was responsible for two key decisions. First, he ruled that wood must no longer be the structural base of fighter aircraft and would oversee the development of monoplanes with stressed-metal features, the Hurricane prototype flying in 1935 and the Spitfire a year later. Although this would later seem to be natural technical progression, in fact there was

a strong opposition from the biplane lobby, who could reasonably argue that the wooden biplane was far more manoeuvrable than the earliest metal monoplanes. Secondly, it was on his authority that Robert Watson-Watt began his research into the early development of radar. Significantly, following Dowding's appointment to

An official photograph of Hugh Dowding taken by the Ministry of Information during the war. (IWM D 1417)

Fighter Command, he took the radical step of assuming that Watson-Watt would deliver a functioning radar system, and based his entire defence system on this one premise.

When Dowding was appointed to Fighter Command in 1936 it was not envisaged that fighters would play such a crucial part in Britain's defences. By this stage Dowding had already alienated a number of key members of the Air Council with his uncompromising viewpoints and relentless pursuit of what he felt were key components of defence. Dowding had tragically lost his wife in 1920 after just two years of marriage, leaving him to bring up his infant son alone. Many date his social ineptitude and lack of patience from this point. Certainly his inability to charm or convince both politicians and his fellow members of the Air Council to his way of thinking rapidly became detrimental to his career prospects. After two years at Fighter Command he rightfully considered himself a candidate for the position of Chief of Staff, the most senior position in the RAF. Instead Cyril Newall, who was junior to him in both age and experience, received the promotion.

Now would begin a relentless attempt to remove the thorny Dowding from the side of the Air Council. In August 1938 he was told that he would retire in June 1939, three years prior to the required retirement age of 60. However, following the Munich crisis and the worsening situation in Europe, Newall wrote to Dowding again in March 1939 and asked him to remain in his position until the following year. This was just the start of a stream of correspondence as retirement dates were suggested, then postponed, and Dowding grew increasingly frustrated with the process. Dowding's undoubted knowledge of the defence system he had personally created ensured that in reality his position was never in doubt whilst the war clouds gathered and during the course of the Battle itself. However, it was expected that the postponement of Dowding's retirement would last only as long as Britain's defences remained the primary need. Once Britain's position was secured, Dowding would have to step aside as Bomber Command's role increased in importance with greater attacks on Germany, and a commander was found for Fighter Command who was more suited to an offensive strategy. In reality, Dowding's final days in command were marred by fractious infighting between his Group Commanders and his eventual enforced dismissal occurred with little notice. It was a shameful, unnecessarily rushed ending to what had been a dedicated and successful career, during which Dowding could undeniably claim to be the architect of Britain's defences in that fateful summer of 1940. After his retirement from Fighter Command he was sent briefly to America, tasked with obtaining aircraft and supplies from the United States government. Once again his diplomatic skills failed him. He eventually formally retired from the RAF in 1942. He was nominated for a baronetcy and chose the title 'The Lord Dowding of Bentley Priory'. In his later years he grew increasingly obsessed with spiritualism and even attempted to contact the spirits of dead pilots through various mediums. It was a strange occupation for a man who had been so passionately involved with the hard realities of war. He married an active animal-rights campaigner and together they championed many causes through the House of Lords. He died in 1970 at the age of 87 and his ashes were laid to rest in Westminster Abbey. The opinion of him among the serving men and women of Fighter Command never wavered. He was held in great affection and was commonly known by the nickname 'Stuffy'. Christopher Foxley-Norris, a Hurricane pilot with No. 3 Squadron and a post-war Air Marshal himself, referred to him as a 'father figure'.[11] Elizabeth Quayle, a plotter at Bentley Priory, later recalled the following almost five decades after the end of the war:

We all admired our 'Stuffy' enormously. We had great loyalty to him – I think you might call it affection ... I don't know what there was about him but it inspired loyalty. He was very remote but if you met him, he was always a gentleman. We thought of him as an extremely able and dedicated officer. And quite frankly we felt that he saved Britain.[12]

direction of the raid. Each operations room included a clock, which timed five-minute sectors with a coordinating colour code in red, yellow and blue. The direction arrows would reflect the colour from the most recent five-minute segment, in other words when the information was last updated. Thus a glance at the table would indicate the most current available information to within minutes.

Jean Mills was an 18-year-old WAAF plotter based at RAF Duxford in 1940. She later recalled how the information was received by the plotters:

It took quite a lot of getting into because when you hear unfamiliar voices coming in over the headset, coming in at quite a good speed, you have to concentrate fairly hard until you're familiar with it. It came over like Northwest B for Bertie – that would be the name of the large square, the configuration of it and then it would be, say, one-nine-two-three, 1923, 20 at 10, which would be 20 aircraft at 10,000 feet.[13]

Diana Pitt Parsons had been an art student before the war but she soon found herself performing the more taxing scientific role of a radar operator:

The operations room at Fighter Command HQ was initially situated in the former ballroom of the stately mansion house. A mezzanine floor, or balcony, was constructed so that it was easier to look down on the giant map of Britain, which was placed at the centre of the room and on which incoming raids would be displayed. (RAF Hendon, PC71/19/336/17)

The receiver hut at Ventnor Chain Home radar station on the Isle of Wight. The flimsy structure of many of these buildings meant that they and the staff who worked in them were particularly vulnerable to attack. Ventnor itself was hit several times during the Battle of Britain. However, the open-frame construction of the radar masts themselves was remarkably difficult to destroy and could often absorb the blast from bombs without long-term damage. (IWM C 1868)

You have a transmitter station, which sends out a signal that hits the aircraft, and the signal comes back to the reception area. You have a means of calibrating the distance, finding the distance in between, which you then display on a display unit. So you can judge how far away the aeroplane is and you have, in those days, a pretty rough idea of its height and its azimuthal position. If you picked an aeroplane up at a very far range, you knew it must be pretty high because of the way radio waves – what they called the polar diagram – went out, which meant that it must be high or you wouldn't be seeing it, because the waves go upwards, owing to the curvature of the earth. They go straight out. So that was the sort of thing we worked on to begin with. It was a complicated business.[14]

The system was entirely dependent on radar so it is ironic that it is the Germans who should lay claim to its invention. It had been a German scientist who had first demonstrated how radio waves reflected off solid objects shortly before the end of the 19th century. Later, it was again German researchers who pioneered the idea that this technology could be used to detect ships at sea and in 1934 the first signal of a ship was picked up during a naval exercise in Kiel harbour. British researchers were also aware of the possibilities of radio beams and it was a member of Dr Robert Watson-Watt's team at the National Physical Laboratory who suggested that this technology could be used to track aircraft. Just a year after the idea had first been mooted they were able to achieve detection ranges of 50 miles. Radar itself is an American term, as well as a contraction of the original 'radio detecting and ranging'. Within Britain throughout the 1930s and the Battle itself it was more commonly known as 'Radio Direction Finding' – RDF. This initial success with radar had persuaded the Air Ministry to commit the funds for a series of transmitter-receiver stations along the coast. These were code-named as Chain Home (CH) and the total of 18 stations that were built were capable of detecting and tracking approaching enemy aircraft at distances of more than 100 miles.

However, a series of training exercises revealed that the equipment was unable to track aircraft that approached below 5,000 feet. As such, a new set of stations known as Chain Home Low (CHL), capable of detecting aircraft that flew at 2,000 feet, was also established. CHL had a shorter range finder of only 35 miles but together the stations complemented each other perfectly.

However, there were two serious flaws as different types of aircraft could not be distinguished by radar alone and it would be difficult to track enemy aircraft once they were inland. This would then fall to the Observer Corps. Originally set up during the First World War to attempt to combat the Zeppelin raids, the Observer Corps was formally established in 1929 and in 1940 was commanded by Air Commodore A. D. Warrington-Morris. As such, an RAF officer was in command and it fell directly under the operational control of Dowding himself. However, it was manned almost exclusively by volunteers. The citizen force largely trained themselves in aircraft recognition and height estimation. By the outbreak of war they numbered some 30,000, with 1,000 observation posts scattered throughout the country. They were supplied with a grid map, coloured markers, height estimators, a telephone and, of course, the facilities to make tea to sustain them during their long shifts. These 'spotters' would phone through sightings, which were collated at the Observer Corps Centre and then passed on to Bentley Priory. There was a large element of human error in Observer Corps sightings and it was nearly impossible to give accurate readings of height, but its contribution to the attempt to complete the intelligence picture should not be undervalued.

RAF wireless interception stations were also established. These would take advantage of the poor radio discipline of German pilots during the forthcoming Battle and would help to confirm the range and destination of enemy raiders. For this, fluent German speakers were required and many were found in the ranks of the WAAF. Rosemary Horstmann was one such WAAF recruit who found herself 'volunteered' for this service:

One day a notice was put on our Orderly Room notice board, asking anybody who could speak German to report to the adjutant. Although my German wasn't good, I went along and said I could speak German. The adjutant turned out to be a very good German speaker and he shamed me by putting me through a very searching interview, at the end of which he said, 'But you told me you could speak fluent German!' I blushed somewhat, and he said, 'Never mind. It's nothing to do with me, I have a

railway warrant for you to go to the Air Ministry for an interview. Here you are. Have a 33-hour pass, go to London and enjoy yourself.' So I got on a train, went up to London and was interviewed by a board of brass hats who decided my German was acceptable for the Y Service.

In the Y Service there were a dozen of us WAAFs who took it in turns to sit in a little suburban house off the perimeter of Hawkinge aerodrome and listen to the radio conversations of the German fighter and bomber pilots. We had to be taught how to operate our receivers, how to search the band until we picked up a conversation and how to tune in carefully. Then we had to write down what the pilots were saying to each other and to the ground station. When there was a pause we would write a translation underneath. I was an official eavesdropper.[15]

A view of the plotting table, which was the operational heart of Fighter Command. From Bentley Priory information would be filtered out to Group Headquarters and from there to sector stations. (RAF Hendon, PC71/19/124)

THE WOMEN'S AUXILIARY AIR FORCE

The Women's Auxiliary Air Force was formed in June 1939 and in that first year recorded approximately 1,700 members. By 1943, at its greatest height, it would number 180,000. It was not an entirely new creation: the Women's Royal Air Force had existed at the end of the First World War but the establishment of the WAAF was in an entirely different league. From plotting the course of incoming raiders, to packing parachutes, manning the barrage balloons and other aerial defences, to cooking and telephone duties, there were a variety of roles available to the new recruits. Some of the more challenging roles were not initially thought acceptable to women. Dr Robert Watson-Watt had first found that women were particularly adept at the difficult task of radar interpretation and championed their recruitment despite much initial scepticism. Certainly during the Battle of Britain the contribution of women as radar operators and plotters was regarded as something unique. Petrea Winterbotham, one of the first female recruits for the operations room at Bentley Priory, later recalled her lengthy recruitment process and feeling something like a 'sideshow':

> I had a lecture on how serious this was and how we were never going to be allowed to say what we were going to do. At this point I got rather scared because I had visions of being dropped into French countryside until my brothers pointed out that my French was absolutely awful and nobody would understand me anyway. Then I went for several more interviews and was eventually accepted, and we went off to Leighton Buzzard to be trained as plotters. We were the first women to go on watch in the operations room at Stanmore. They thought that women always chatted and that we couldn't keep secrets... It was a difficult thing to do and you had to be very quick and very accurate. We rather fancied ourselves doing this because everyone said, 'How marvellous.' Of course, everybody in the operations room tried to take us out to the local nightclub, so really it was rather fun.
>
> People came and went, including King George VI and Winston Churchill and everyone else, because we were a bit of a sideshow, I think, because we were the first girls doing this amazing thing. And not only not chatting but plotting![16]

The Women's Auxiliary Air Force actively recruited from the outbreak of war and throughout the early years. It was generally perceived to be one of the more glamorous branches of service and these recruiting posters helped to convey that impression. In fact, the work could often be both tedious and dangerous in equal measures. (IWM PST 2831, IWM PST 3096)

SERVE IN THE WAAF
WITH THE MEN WHO FLY

The knowledge that they were breaking new ground certainly added an element of attraction to the WAAF. Diana Pitt Parsons, another young recruit, recalled that her fellow WAAFs could be somewhat 'snooty' and looked down on the ATS, who had to perform somewhat less glamorous roles.[17] It was not, however, quite as glamorous as the Wrens, who were, of course, given silk stockings to wear. Petrea Winterbotham recalled that when she and her fellow early recruits first arrived on station they were initially treated 'like Duchesses'[18] and handled with kid gloves but that this didn't last long. For many girls aged just 18, it was an incredibly exciting period of their lives, allowed, for the first time, to live independently and earn a wage. Naturally the temptations of the bright lights of London were all too enticing for those stationed in No. 11 Group.

> 'Stuffy' Dowding ... would look at his girlies, as he called us, nauseating but sweetly meant, and say, 'That one looks absolutely exhausted.' Well, she was probably exhausted. She hadn't been to bed the night before because she'd been dancing in London. It was rather nice being so near London. I think we did burn the candle at both ends a bit.[19]

Operating at the heart of Fighter Command was not without its dangers, however, particularly once airfields became Luftwaffe targets. Initial fears that women would not react well when under enemy attack proved unfounded, and a number of women received gallantry medals for remaining at their posts beyond when it was safe to do so. Throughout the course of the war a number of WAAFs were killed while on duty. There were also the psychological dangers. A cool head was required while plotting the course of an incoming raid when it was directly over the homes of friends and family:

> We used to plot the raids and see the raiders go over our own homes. I heard many a girl say, 'God, there's poor old Ma up again, last night too, and that was pretty awful', and that made us realize that we had to be utterly accurate because it was so easy [to make a mistake]. The table was divided into big squares, which were letters, and then 10 squares again, which were numbered, so it might be A B 1212, and you plunked your plot down. But if you took the next square you would get everybody undercover who needn't be and the people who should would be bombed.[20]

Wireless operators had a particularly difficult role to fulfil as they monitored the radio conversations of German and British pilots. Many would overhear a German order for an attack, knowing that an unsuspecting RAF pilot was below and with no means of warning him. It was worse still for those that had formed an attachment with a pilot and were then forced to listen to a dogfight in which he was participating, hearing the shouts of triumph of a successful attack or the screams of despair as flames engulfed a cockpit.

Not all recruits could handle the pressure but the overwhelming majority served with distinction no matter the dangers. The WAAF operated throughout the course of the war and was officially renamed the Women's Royal Air Force in 1949. In 1994 it finally merged with the RAF.

Above:
An aerial view of Bentley Priory taken in 1946. (RAF Hendon, PC71/19/518)

Right:
An official portrait of Sir Robert Alexander Watson-Watt, Scientific Advisor on Telecommunications at the Air Ministry and widely regarded as the 'founding father' of radar. (IWM CH 13862)

The role of Ultra was the one final piece in the jigsaw of intelligence that would be collated for Dowding at Bentley Priory. By the time of the Battle of Britain secret intelligence was being supplied from decrypts of Luftwaffe 'Enigma' traffic, which helped to build up a clearer strategic understanding of the German objectives. Frederick Winterbotham, an RAF officer who worked in Hut 3, Bletchley Park as part of the Special Liaison Units who distributed the vital information:

> One had to be able to get information quickly to Dowding, and I had a direct line from Hut 3 put in to Fighter Command. That was taken by a WAAF at the other end who had that sole job. They had two or three of them at the job of taking the Ultra signals and delivering them to the Commander-in-Chief. So Dowding was right on the ball.[21]

The use of Enigma was highly classified as 'Ultra Secret' and was known only to a select few. Radar was more widely used but was another closely guarded secret. Not everyone had a real understanding of how radar worked, how it contributed to the overall intelligence picture, or indeed how the various parts of the fighter defence system fitted together. The entire process was shrouded in secrecy. Jackie Moggridge was just one of many WAAF radar operators who were trained to reveal nothing:

> They told us that on no account were we to say who we were, what we were and what we were doing, and if anyone asked, we were cooks![22]

Edward James Morrison, who joined No. 79 Squadron in 1939, later recalled testing the radar system and the utter secrecy that surrounded its ongoing development:

to be th
fashione
quick te
Hurrica
frame i
easy to
later m
mechar
more o
would k
to be re

Left:
An example of a Chain Home Low station, this one at Hopton-on-Sea, photographed in 1945.
(IWM CH 15183)

Bottom right:
The Chain Home station at Poling, Sussex. On the left are the 360ft steel transmitter towers with the 240ft wooden receiver towers on the right. (IWM CH 15173)

Top right:
With war imminent a permanent underground operations room was constructed at Bentley Priory, with the same structure of the original room duplicated over 40 feet below ground. The WAAFs in the operations room received information of incoming raids via their headsets and used billiard-style cues to move the unit symbols on the situation-map table and update the picture for the commanders seated around the balcony above. (IWM C 1870)

all-metal stressed skin and the elliptical wings. These famous wings were what gave the machine its unique shape. Mitchell had been driven by a desire for a wing as thin as possible to ensure the high speeds, but which was also strong enough to fulfil the demand for the required number of machine guns. An orthodox wing could not achieve this. The ellipse was the ideal shape as it created the least amount of drag. It also ensured that it had the required strength to hold the guns and the retractable undercarriage, as an elliptical wing tapers slowly initially and then more rapidly towards the tip. In contrast a straight-tapered wing is much weaker from the moment it leaves the root (i.e. the fuselage).

Mitchell himself did not live to see the first Spitfire Mark Is roll off the production line and their delivery to No. 19 Squadron in August 1938. However, his design would live on, seeing service throughout the war in a series of variants and even actively flying until 1952. It inspired love amongst its pilots. One American pilot describing flying it as being so instinctive it was like 'pulling on a pair of tight jeans'.[28] George Unwin was a pilot with No. 19 Squadron during the Battle of Britain and enjoyed many years' subsequent service with the RAF flying a variety of jet fighters but never got over his love affair with the Spitfire:

> It was a super aircraft, it was absolutely. It was so sensitive on the controls. There was no heaving, or pulling and pushing and kicking. You just breathed on it and when you wanted, if you wanted to turn, you just moved your hands slowly and she went... She really was the perfect flying machine. I've never flown anything sweeter. I've flown jets right up to the Venom, but nothing, nothing like her. Nothing like a Spitfire.[29]

Top:
The Spitfire prototype, K5054, which first flew on 6 May 1936. The first production Spitfire I would not have its maiden flight until a full 26 months later. (IWM MH 5214)

Bottom:
Despite the presence of two policemen, this clandestine photo was snapped during the Spitfire's official debut with No. 19 Squadron in 1938 when it was still a highly guarded secret. (IWM HU 55033)

Just as Mitchell's airframe design for the Schneider Trophies of 1929 and 1931 resulted in the Spitfire, the engine used in the competition was also the forefather of the Merlin, the engine that would eventually power the iconic fighter as well as the Hurricane. Rolls-Royce created a V-shaped, inline 12-cylinder design, which could fit neatly inside the sleek fuselage of the new generation of fighters. Originally designed and funded exclusively by Rolls-Royce, Air Ministry funding was granted from 1933 onwards and from then on it was known as the Merlin engine. Like the Spitfire and Hurricane, the Merlin would go through various stages of refinements until eventually being replaced by the Griffon engine in 1942. The most common variant used during the Battle of Britain was the Merlin III, which powered the Spitfire Mark I. The Merlin XII, capable of 1,150hp, powered the Spitfire Mark II (shown on the left) but there were fewer of these available in the summer of 1940. Factory workers (shown on the right) worked on the various component parts that were required to create the intricate engines at the production plant in Derby. The engine in flight gave the Spitfire its legendary throaty roar. A sturdy engine, it was not as revolutionary as the fuel-injected Daimler-Benz DB601, which powered the Me 109 and performed better at higher altitudes. (IWM ATP 10397G, IWM D 12099)

THE PILOTS

RECRUITMENT

From the young aristocrats who formed 601 Auxiliary Squadron after a meeting at the exclusive club Whites, to apprentices turned pilots such as George Unwin, the son of a miner, Fighter Command consisted of a disparate group of young men from a variety of backgrounds. But all shared a passion for flying. It is easy to forget how relatively novel the concept of flying still was before the outbreak of the Second World War. Throughout the 1920s and 1930s many aviators were hailed as celebrities.

Alan Cobham, Charles Lindbergh and Amy Johnson were familiar names to all and helped establish the aeroplane as the symbol of technological progress and the pilot as the hero of the modern age. Young boys thrilled to the stories of their adventures, and this coupled with the folklore of the 'knights of the air' during the First

World War ensured that when the RAF embarked on its expansion plan it had a steady stream of recruits who regarded it as their opportunity to fulfil a childhood dream. Certainly that was how Geoffrey Page, later a Hurricane pilot, regarded his youthful ambitions to emulate the famous pilots of the First World War:

> All I wanted was to be a fighter pilot like my hero, Captain Albert Ball. I knew practically all there was to know about Albert Ball; how he flew, how he fought, how he won his Victoria Cross, how he died. I also thought I knew about war in the air. I imagined it to be Arthurian – about chivalry ... death and injury had no part in it.[30]

While some wished to emulate a previous war's heroes, others, such as Richard Hillary, saw flying as an opportunity to escape the horrors of the trenches, to fight a war on one's own terms:

> In a fighter plane, I believe, we have found a way to return to war as it ought to be, war that is individual combat between two people, in which one kills or is killed. It is exciting, it's individual and it's disinterested. I shan't be sitting behind a long-range gun working out how to kill people 60 miles away. I shan't get maimed: either I shall be killed or I shall get a few pleasant putty medals and enjoy being stared at in a night club.[31]

Hillary's memoir was written after he had fought in the Battle of Britain, and his pre-war convictions had tragically been proved wrong. It was hard to remain disinterested following the deaths of one's closest friends, and he was horrifically maimed himself when trying to escape from his burning Spitfire.

But that was all to come. Prior to joining the RAF few recruits had ever set foot inside a plane or regularly seen one in the skies apart from at special shows such as the Empire Air Day events at RAF Hendon, which ran throughout the 1930s, or a visit from Alan Cobham's 'Flying Circus'. Cobham was a long-distance aviation pioneer who created National Aviation Day Displays. These toured throughout the country and consisted of 14 aircraft including

everything from monoplanes to airliners. They gave many future pilots the taste for flying:

> I started off like quite a lot of chaps – I had a flight with Alan Cobham who used to come round to towns and cities in the United Kingdom, giving rides for five shillings. You did a trip round the airfield and back again. I sat in a little Gipsy Moth. I was in the air for about five minutes. You never saw an aeroplane in the sky unless you happened to live near an airfield or Alan Cobham came to town.[32]

There was an undeniable glamour to becoming a pilot. Rupert Parkhouse, later a Squadron Leader in the RAF, recalled as a schoolboy seeing two pilots at the Hendon Air Show with their girlfriends and thinking, 'This is one way to get your girl.'[33]

Some were motivated by a sense of patriotism, although many of Hillary's Oxford compatriots would have sneered at the word. Certainly, an opposition to Nazism was a very real factor for others. However, the majority of recruits who joined prior to the Munich crisis or the declaration of war had little understanding of the political situation. In the words of George Unwin, the RAF was 'just a happy flying club'.[34]

Whatever their motivations for joining, their differences of class and wealth, even the distinction between regulars and volunteer reserves, were not as acutely felt as they would have been had war not broken out and bound them together in their common cause.

FOREIGN AND COMMONWEALTH PILOTS

Despite the RAF's best efforts to expand Fighter Command, there was still a chronic shortage of skilled pilots in the latter half of the 1930s. Luckily Fighter Command could look to the Commonwealth for additional manpower. The largest Commonwealth contingent to serve with Fighter Command during the Battle of Britain was from New Zealand. The RAF had begun recruiting there as early as 1936 and the first pilots, among whose number was Alan Deere, began arriving the following year. Just behind the Kiwis was a large group of Canadian pilots. The Royal Canadian Air Force was small and with few vacancies, so many were tempted to cross the Atlantic and try their luck with the RAF. This ad hoc relationship with a number of Commonwealth

A Gloster Gauntlet of No. 17 Squadron attracts a large crowd at an Empire Air Day at Kenley airfield in May 1939 (top). Air shows were held throughout the country and were an excellent way to recruit, as seen in the bottom left picture, with the crowds of boys around the RAF recruiting van at a subsequent Empire Air Day just a year later. (RAF Hendon, PC98/173/5780/12 and PC98/173/5838/12)

countries would be formalized with the outbreak of war and the creation of the British Commonwealth Air Training Plan. One of the results of this was the formation of No. 242 (Canadian) Squadron in 1939. This squadron would suffer devastating losses during the Battle of France but would be rebuilt by the charismatic, somewhat controversial Douglas Bader and see active service once again during the Battle of Britain. They were joined by No. 1 Squadron (Canadian) who arrived in June of 1940 and were at the heart of the Battle throughout the summer months. More pilots came from Australia, South Africa, Rhodesia (modern Zimbabwe), India and the West Indies. All these pilots were volunteers and made their own way to Britain to join the RAF. Most Commonwealth pilots had been reared with the general idea that they were 'children of the Empire' and were motivated by a sense of patriotism for the 'Mother Country'. Alan Deere felt a strong draw to the British cause:

> In my generation, in the 30s, as schoolboys, we always thought of this as the home country, always referred to it as the Mother Country. That was the old colonial tie if you like... I was, I think, one of the very lucky New Zealanders who was in the air force at the time of the last war and the Battle of Britain in particular. I consider myself privileged to have been there, to fight for this country... I'd a hectic round, so to speak, but it was all worthwhile.[35]

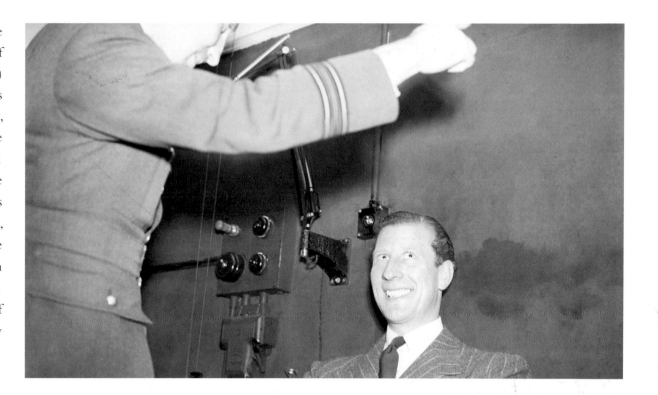

Top:
Pilot recruits were put through an exacting medical before being accepted for training. Here a pilot undergoes a simultaneous eye-movement and hearing test. The latter involved using three tuning forks of different pitch to determine the frequency range of the recruit's hearing. Other tests included blood pressure and sense of balance, as well as more intensive eyesight and hearing tests. The original wartime caption reads 'Yes – a man has to be perfect to become a Royal Air Force pilot ... ' (IWM CH 119)

Bottom:
Commonwealth countries provided urgently needed ground crew as well as pilots throughout the course of the war. Here a group of armourers and wireless operators from the Royal New Zealand Air Force celebrate their arrival in Britain to serve with the RAF. (IWM CH 1224)

Commonwealth airmen were joined by refugees from Poland, Czechoslovakia, Belgium, France and other countries that had fallen during the Blitzkrieg of early 1940. Here a group of Polish airmen undergo physical training with an RAF instructor. (IWM CH 1141)

strange Englishmen. I was the only coloured person from the colonies. I was very proud of what I'd achieved.

And these English people said, 'You're mad! You're a bloody fool! If we'd been born in Jamaica, we'd still be there now! What an idiot!' It destroyed all my ideals of what I believed the whole thing was about. I was so proud of what I'd achieved and they said, 'We'd do anything to get away from the bloody war and you say you come all this way and you tell us that story.' They thought it was completely weird.[36]

Remarkably, few pilots from the colonies experienced any kind of official racism or discrimination. As long as they could fly and passed through all the training requirements they were posted to an active squadron, a testament to the spirit of egalitarianism within Fighter Command.

Not all foreign pilots were from the colonies. Several Americans defied their country's neutrality and travelled to Britain to serve in the RAF. Among their number were Vernon 'Shorty' Keough, Andrew Mamedoff and Eugene 'Red' Tobin. They were three colourful characters. Keough, despite his diminutive height, had been a stunt parachute jumper before receiving his pilot's wings. He was initially refused by the medical board owing to his short stature but he persevered and was eventually accepted, becoming a member of No. 609 Squadron. However he did have to be given a leg-up to clamber aboard his Spitfire and was forced to fly sitting on a cushion, much to the amusement of his British colleagues. He was joined at No. 609 Squadron by both Mamedoff and Tobin, and all three swore their allegiance to the crown, effectively forfeiting their American citizenship. But it seemed a fair trade in their eyes to become members of the 'best flying club in the world' and have a chance to pilot a Spitfire. All three survived the Battle and in the September transferred to the first Eagle squadrons – entirely American-manned RAF units that became operational in early 1941. Tragically, all three would also be dead before the end of that year.

Another famous American pilot was Billy Fiske. The former American Olympian was a member of Britain's high society thanks to his marriage to the former Countess of Warwick and he suitably

William Strachan from Jamaica felt a similar patriotic fervour. He later recalled radio broadcasts calling for support for the war effort from all those 'loyal to the crown'. Unfortunately for William, just 18 and fresh out of school, he had no means of paying for a cross-Atlantic voyage so that he could sign up. Eventually he persuaded a fruit shipping company to offer him a heavily discounted ticket, which he managed to afford once he had sold his bicycle and saxophone. He was thrilled when he eventually succeeded in signing up for the air force although he found the attitude of some members of the public dampened his patriotic zeal:

I was joined up in 4 Elementary Flying Training School. On the Tuesday morning, I was in the RAF, in uniform, kitted out, in a group of 50

decided to join No. 601 Squadron, the Auxiliary Squadron commonly known as the 'Millionaires' Club'. He was motivated by his hatred of Hitler and had already declined to participate in the 1936 Olympics on those grounds. His involvement in the Battle of Britain was all too brief. He was shot down on 16 August and despite managing to nurse his stricken Hurricane back to RAF Tangmere he died later of his injuries. A memorial to him was unveiled in St Paul's Cathedral by Winston Churchill on 4 July 1941, likely done to garner publicity and American support for the war effort. However, the sentiment of the inscription – *An American citizen who died that England may live* – is accurate enough for all foreign-born volunteers.

As the countries of Europe quickly collapsed in the face of the Nazi onslaught, a total of 276 Continental pilots managed to escape and make their way to the RAF. With 146 pilots in Fighter Command, the Poles formed the largest foreign contingent. Despite their short-lived stand against the Nazi war machine, Poland had a proud and successful history of aviators. The Polish Air Force had been small and had carefully hand-picked its recruits. Its training programme was at least as thorough as the RAF's but without modern fighters they did not stand a chance against the Luftwaffe. Dowding was initially nervous about introducing pilots to Fighter Command whose English was poor and whose reputation, already, was rather wayward but eventually overcame his misgivings. When the first Polish squadrons were activated in late August 1940 his trust in this unknown quarter was quickly vindicated as the Poles racked up victory after victory. The Poles were joined by 88 Czechs, among whom was the highest-ranking ace of the Battle, Josef Frantisek. They too earned a reputation as phenomenal pilots and aggressive fighters. The first Polish and Czech recruits were individually absorbed into regular units once their English was deemed sufficient. However as their numbers quickly swelled the RAF realized that a

Three American pilots who forfeited their American citizenship to serve in No. 609 Squadron: Pilot Officers Andrew Mamedoff, Vernon Keough and Gene Tobin. In early 1941 they transferred to the first Eagle Squadron made up entirely of Americans. All three would be killed before the end of the year. (CH 1439)

more effective way to integrate them was the creation of their own squadrons with British Squadron Leaders and Flight Commanders with Polish/Czech equivalents. Johnny Kent was one of the first flight commanders of No. 303 (Polish) Squadron when it was formed, and initially was reluctant to take command of a group of men who had previously been defeated. He was quickly proven wrong. Equipped with modern fighters, they would be more than a match for the Luftwaffe. Indeed, they were so eager to engage in battle that a Polish fighter out on a training flight that stumbled upon some German bombers actually shot one down:

> The sight of these enemy machines was too much for Flight Officer Paszkiewicz of 'B' Flight and he broke formation and shot down a Dornier 17, following it right down on the ground to ensure that it crashed. This was the squadron's first victory and the Poles were absolutely cock-a-hoop over it. Ronald Kellet [Squadron Commander] was so pleased with the way they had behaved that he immediately asked for permission to declare the squadron 'operational'. This was granted and the squadron was placed on 'Readiness' for the first time the following morning, 31 August, just a year after the German attack on their country.[37]

Irish, Belgian and Free French pilots also joined Fighter Command and participated in the Battle of Britain. Nor should one forget that the commander of No. 11 Group, Keith Park, was a New Zealander, while Quintin Brand, the commander of No. 10 Group, was South African. Indeed, this most British of battles could not have been fought without the contribution of many men who had not been born on British soil.

Years after the war most Battle of Britain veterans could still recall the feeling of sheer exhilaration the first time they took to the skies. Many did so thanks to the former long-distance flight pioneer Alan Cobham's Flying Circus, which toured the country offering a quick flip for a small fee, after which some were determined to make a career of it or at least learn how to fly. At the time the RAF offered one of the best ways to receive the training necessary to become a pilot and to be able to fly on a regular basis. (© South Lanarkshire Libraries and Community Learning. Licensor www.scran.ac.uk)

Two unnamed Polish pilots of No. 303 Squadron together with Flight Lieutenant Johnny Kent (centre). Commanded by British RAF officers, the Poles of 303 earned a fearsome fighting reputation and it was the unit with the highest number of kills during the Battle of Britain, a feat all the more remarkable considering that they only became operational at the end of August. Pete Brothers later recalled, 'They didn't give a damn whether they were killed or anything else... I think a lot of them felt that they had nothing to live for anyway and their great idea was to kill as many Germans as they could...' (IWM Sound 10218) (IWM CH 1531)

Czechoslovak ground staff re-arm one of No. 310 (Czechoslovak) Squadron's Hurricanes on 7 September 1940 at the height of the Luftwaffe's day offensive against London. (IWM CH 1297)

TRAINING

Prospective pilots received their initial training at a handful of civilian-manned Elementary and Reserve Flying Training Schools (E&RFTs) before future officer pilots were accepted into RAF Uxbridge. It was no easy matter being accepted for either course. Rupert Parker was just one of hundreds of recruits for Cranwell during the 1930s who had to endure the experience of five days of written exams and a round of interviews conducted by at least 14 civil servants and RAF officers as well as the anxious wait until the list of those that had passed was published in *The Times*. The biannual intake was 30 cadets per intake, much lower than the Royal Military Academies at either Sandhurst or Woolwich, or indeed, the Royal Naval Colleges at Dartmouth and Greenwich. It was a good thing that the selection process was so rigorous because even training to become a pilot was a dangerous occupation. In 1937 the RAF suffered 156 training fatalities and in 1939, 218, at an average of one per 5,000 training hours.

Flying training included blind flying, a particularly challenging task whereby the trainee pilot had to rely exclusively on his basic instruments. Cyril Bamberger later recalled learning how to master this difficult skill:

> I went to 9 Flying Training School at Hullavington where I trained on the Hawker Hart. The Hart was a biplane with a fixed undercarriage but it was light on the controls. I did instrument flying where you flew the aircraft from the front cockpit and pulled a canvas hood over so you couldn't see and were just left with your basic instruments. You had to learn to put trust in your instruments. You might be flying alone at night or in bad conditions when suddenly you would feel as though you were leaning out of the side. You'd look at your instruments and they told you that you were straight and level – but still felt as though you were leaning and you'd try and correct it. I'm sure many, many pilots killed themselves that way.[38]

The RAF was all too aware of the acute differences between being able to master the increasingly obsolete biplanes used in training

A map showing RAF Fighter Command Sector and fighter airfields in south-east England during the Battle of Britain. Dowding's defensive system divided Fighter Command into four operational groups numbered 10 through to 13. No. 11 Group manned the vulnerable south-east which would be at the frontline of the Battle, and was bordered by 10 and 12 Groups. No. 13 Group is not depicted on the map as it controlled the north of England and Scotland.

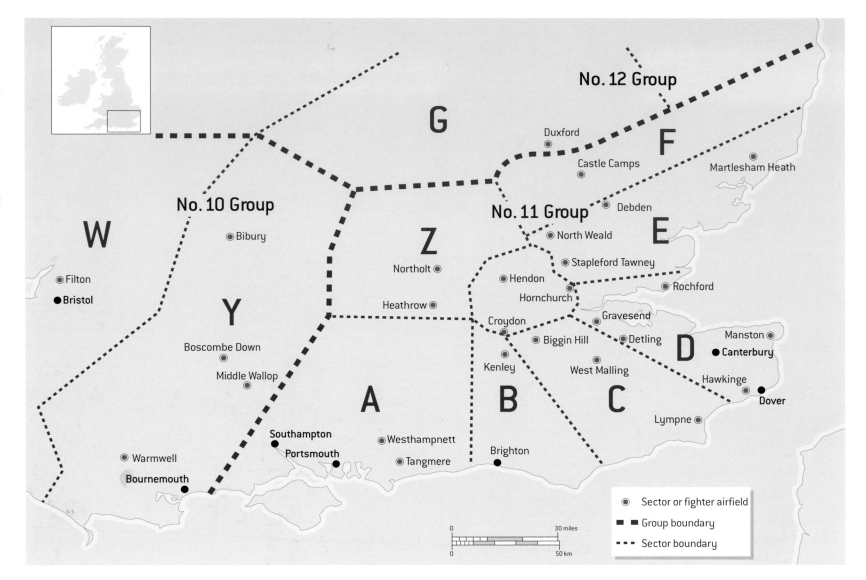

and the Hurricanes or Spitfires that awaited the future fighter pilot once he was posted to his squadron. Gradually the old training planes were replaced with more Harvards as well as the new Miles Master; the latter particularly was capable of faster speeds, and could offer an experience more akin to the new fighters. The RAF also established Group Pools in 1939, where pilots could experience a couple of hours of flying time on either a Hurricane or Spitfire prior to being posted to operational squadrons equipped with the new fighters. With the outbreak of war the E&RFTSs were formally brought under the control of the RAF and renamed Elementary Flying Training Schools (EFTSs). After training here, novice pilots would progress to the Service Flying Training Schools (SFTSs), which rapidly almost doubled in number from six to 11. But the Group Pools suffered as there were few pilots which could be spared to teach the additional training scheme and there was also an acute shortage of fighter planes themselves. The Group Pools system would be replaced with the Operational Training Units (OTUs) and the Air Ministry instructed Fighter Command to ensure that sufficient fighter types and pilots were made available to Training Command to guarantee its success. In reality this was only achieved once fighter production had increased towards the second half of 1940 and the stresses of battle meant that combat-weary pilots had to be posted out of the frontline for rest with a temporary posting to Training Command.

The flying training throughout the pre-war years had been particularly thorough and it was inevitable that the same standards could not be met during wartime. Throughout 1940 training times were drastically cut and many a pilot would be thrown into the frontline having had little time on a modern fighter. Alan Deere, himself an experienced pre-war fighter pilot, recalled one such incident where relative novices were posted to his squadron in the thick of the fighting in the early summer and how the squadron itself was forced to implement some rudimentary training:

We were getting pilots who had not been on Spitfires because there were no available conversion units...They came straight to a squadron from their training establishment. Some of them did have a few hours on the Hurricane, a monoplane experience, but not on the Spitfire. For example, we got two young New Zealanders into my flight...They were trained on some very obsolete aircraft in New Zealand. They were given, I think, two trips or something on a Hurricane and then they arrived at the squadron. So, as we were pretty busy, we gave them what was known as a cockpit check. We had by that time a Miles Master, which was a monoplane. We'd give them one trip up in that. One of the pilots had taken them up to see their handling and brief them on a Spitfire. They'd go off for one solo flight and circuit and then they were in battle. The answer, of course, is that they didn't last. Those last two lasted two trips and both finished up in a Dover hospital.[39]

If the pre-war pilots were excellent at flying, it did not, however, make them indestructible fighter pilots. The major deficits in RAF training were the lack of focus on gunnery skills, and the rigid formation-style flying that was better suited to an air show at Hendon than combat. The 1938 Training Manual outlined six basic patterns of combat flying known as Fighting Area Attacks and this became the required drill for all squadrons. The standard RAF fighter formation was the V-shaped 'vic' of three aircraft. A squadron of 12 aircraft would be split into two flights, A and B, which were in turn made up of two sections, or 'vics', of three aircraft identified by an individual colour code of either red, yellow, blue or green. A full-strength battle formation would therefore have all 12 aircraft grouped together in four sections of three fighters. The squadron CO or a senior flight commander would ideally lead the formation with the other 'V' formations following in line astern. This flying technique had been created with the idea that the squadron of fighters would be attacking unprotected bombers and was therefore perfectly suited to launching successive waves of attacks. This was not an illogical assumption. Bombers posed the greatest danger in terms of destructive power and, moreover, with France as an ally it was

The original 'V' or 'vic' formation (left) consisted of a section of three aircraft each and was duplicated for the entire flight. This rigid formation ensured that only the lead aircraft could scan the skies for the enemy as the other pilots had to ensure that they were still flying in formation correctly alongside each other. This was perfect for display flying but disastrous in combat. With the outbreak of war this rigid formation flying was amended to allow for 'weaver' aircraft to the rear (right), who would zig-zag across the sky. However, such 'tail-end Charlies' were frequently picked out as easy targets by Me 109 pilots.

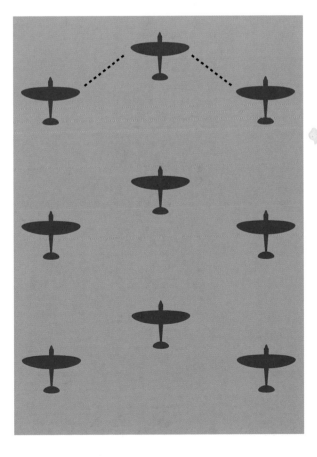

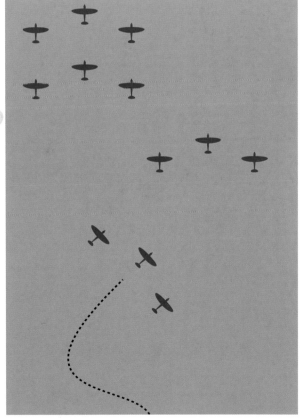

generally assumed that only bombers would have sufficient range to reach British shores.

The primary fault with tightly grouped Fighting Area Attacks was that they required nearly all the pilots to watch the plane immediately in front or alongside. Only the leading plane had a clear view of what lay ahead and all were vulnerable to attack from the rear.

Of course, as many a British pilot would discover to his detriment, the rigid RAF flying formations were particularly vulnerable to attack by the German fighters who escorted the bombers, and who could easily attack undetected from a position of height or from the rear. Indeed, the German pilots soon referred to the 'vic' formation as the '*Idiotenreigen*' – literally, 'row of idiots' – as they provided such easy pickings. Many RAF squadrons would hastily rethink these tactics after their first taste of combat with the German fighters but the formal training would take much longer to catch up and the costly Fighting Area Attacks would continue to be part of the official training programme until late 1941.

Aerial gunnery was part of the official training and all squadrons were expected to attend an annual camp at one of the armament training stations to ensure live-fire practice. But in reality gunnery training was often overlooked, with some pilots having little or no experience of firing at a target before the war, and shortages soon meant that any opportunities decreased just as Fighter Command prepared for its greatest battle. Squadron Leader Johnny Kent later recalled his brief foray into gunnery training as consisting of firing the eight machine guns on his Hurricane once at a ground target. After a half-second burst his guns jammed and on his return to base he was told that there were no more bullets to spare. George Unwin,

Top:
A flight of Hawker Hart aircraft from No. 57 Squadron in 1934. The Hawker Hart, originally designed in the 1920s, was a two-seater light bomber. However it was increasingly used for training purposes in the late 1930s. (IWM H(AM) 217)

Bottom:
An informal photo of a group of fighter pilots at RAF Duxford in 1938. Just over a year later they would be fighting for their own and their nation's survival. (IWM HU 27847)

a sergeant pilot with the crack No. 19 Squadron, did, however, receive training from the experienced flight commander Harry Broadhurst prior to the war:

There were no [gunnery] instructors in those days but he emphasized that the key to shooting was to get in close. And the closer you got the more chance you have of hitting him. I mean, one of the weaknesses of all fighter pilots when the war started was that no one had been taught how to shoot properly and the range or the estimation of range was the biggest weakness.

...All we fired at was the drogue being towed along at a 100 miles per hour and he emphasized the size of the drogue in your gunsight giving you the range, which of course you then transferred, when the time came, to enemy aircraft.[40]

It was sound advice although judging range in combat would prove to be somewhat more difficult. Enemy planes were travelling at far greater speeds than 100mph, there was more than one target and even more enemy aircraft, which could attack from a number of blind spots. Broadhurst was right to predict that getting in close was the key factor. However, the official pre-war thinking was to fill the air with 0.303-in bullets from the guns of the Hurricanes and Spitfires at a range of 400 yards. This was not nearly close enough to cause effective damage and the squadrons who wished to ensure 'kills' would harmonize their guns at 250 yards.

Of course, real skill in dogfighting and in surviving the terror of aerial combat could not be taught; it could only be learnt in the air, during each pilot's personal baptism of fire. However, the RAF did put in some effort to ensure that First World War veterans would lecture new recruits to try to impart some wisdom on how to survive and win in a dogfight. The young Flying Officer Peter Brothers recalled some such advice when he encountered his first Messerschmitt 109 during the Battle of France:

I think one of the things that, if you like, was a saviour in my life in a lot of respects, was that when I first joined the air force we were lectured by a chap called Taffy Jones who was a First World War ace of some renown but who stuttered terribly. And Taffy warned us that there was going to be a war and that we were going to be in it and I make no apologies for his language, this was how he put it. He said, 'W-w-when you get in your f-f-first f-f-fight, you'll be f-f-fucking frightened. N-n-never forget that the chap in the other cockpit is t-t-twice as f-f-fucking frightened as you are.' And that was a pretty good morale booster ... And I was really frightened and I thought that that poor German must be even more frightened than I am.[41]

It was sage advice. Peter Brothers shot down that first Me 109, several more during the Battle of Britain and survived the war. Many other more experienced pilots would not be so fortunate.

An RAF trainee pilot from one of the Elementary Flying Training Schools climbs into the rear cockpit of the Magister training aircraft, capable of speeds of up to 145mph. The dual controls and full standard instrument panel in both cockpits ensured trainee pilots could always hand over to their instructors if necessary. There was no opportunity for this in the far more powerful Spitfires and Hurricanes. (IWM CH 1250)

THE LUFTWAFFE

> ❝ *My Luftwaffe is invincible… And so now we turn to England. How long will this one last – two, three weeks?* ❞
>
> Hermann Göring, June 1940

THE ORIGINS OF THE LUFTWAFFE

At the outbreak of war in 1914, Germany was one of the few real air powers and her foresight would rapidly be rewarded as aircraft played a decisive reconnaissance role in the early months of the war. However, as the frontline stagnated, a new role would need to be found for the German flying forces. Both sides had already made tentative steps towards converting part of their air arms to bomber fleets but it was the Imperial German Air Staff who truly pioneered the concept with the creation of a dedicated Zeppelin (airship) bombing unit. As she would be a quarter of a century later, London was the primary target. The first raid killed 28 people and injured a further 60. Other cities throughout the British Isles would also be targeted during the course of the campaign and a total of 550 civilians would be killed by Zeppelin raids throughout 1915–16. The bombing itself did not in fact cause any large-scale destruction or severely interrupt the British war effort despite the loss of life. However, the psychological effect on the population was severe.

There were widespread instances of panic, and factory workers temporarily abandoned their posts at the munitions plants, which were often the intended target of the raids.

The German Air Staff soon began to realize that the Zeppelin itself was not best suited for the campaign. Although at the time it was the only aircraft within their fleet capable of the necessary range and weight load, in reality it was a temperamental creature and highly susceptible to accidents caused by poor weather conditions or strong winds. The potential destructive power of bombing raids, however, had been recognized. By the autumn of 1916, the German air arm – the Luftstreitkräfte – had been rewarded with its own commander-in-chief and general staff headquarters who would also assume responsibility for the fighter and bomber developments that would result in the creation of a twin-engined bomber, the Gotha G IV, in 1917. The Gotha raids were on a vastly different scale to the Zeppelin raids, with entire fleets of bombers forming up and attacking in a coordinated effort. Once again, the terror caused by the Gothas far outweighed any material advantage. Panic-stricken factory workers once again abandoned their posts, and some RFC squadrons were

Opposite:
A formation of Heinkel He-111 aircraft. Originally designed to serve as a fast medium bomber it could not outrun the Spitfires or Hurricanes of Fighter Command. (IWM MH 6547)

recalled from the frontline to patrol British skies. However, fewer than a thousand people were actually killed in the raids and a number of the Gothas were lost due to technical faults.

The Luftstreitkräfte of the First World War had been at the forefront of developing a bomber fleet capable of attacking an enemy at a great distance and striking terror into the hearts of civilian populations. True, the losses suffered had almost outweighed the gains, but the Luftstreitkräfte had glimpsed the future, and the later Luftwaffe would seek to create a bombing force equal to none. Germany had also created a professional, hard-hittting fighter force capable of great successes throughout the war despite a growing discrepancy in terms of numbers and resources. Such successes, in the face of overwhelming opposition and the crumbling defences of her navy and armies, ensured that Germany's air force would continue to be highly regarded by the German public, despite the nation's eventual defeat, and would be viewed as a critical component of her post-war defences by the military.

But as the ink dried on the Treaty of Versailles in June 1919, it confirmed what everyone had already known for several months, on paper at least: Germany was now a spent force on the European continent. By the terms of Part V of the treaty, Germany's army was restricted to a force of no more than 100,000 men; her navy was limited to a mere 15,000 men, just six out of date battleships, a few worthless torpedo boats and no submarines; and the Rhineland became a demilitarized zone to be policed by an international body. Her air force, meanwhile, had ceased to exist. The creation and use

Top:
Field Marshal Paul von Hindenburg, Chief of the German General Staff (front right), looks at a Gotha G IV bomber during a tour of inspection of Bombengeschwader No. 3 shortly before the first Gotha bombing raid on Britain in May 1917. (IWM Q 108838)

Bottom:
The substantial Junkers plant at Dessau in Germany with an inset of the founder himself, Professor Hugo Junkers. Junkers would design both the Stuka dive-bomber and the Ju 88 medium bomber, both of which were used extensively during the Battle of Britain. (Bundesarchiv Bild 183-R14718)

of any military aircraft was strictly forbidden by the terms of the treaty and on 8 May 1920 the Luftstreitkräfte was officially disbanded. This was not, however, the end of Germany's role as a major player in the aviation world. Indeed, on the morning of the 11 November 1918, the very day that the Armistice was signed and the war concluded, Professor Hugo Junkers, a leading German aircraft engineer and manufacturer, called a senior staff conference to plan the switch to the manufacture of civilian aircraft. This was a revolutionary step, as at the time no large-scale form of civilian aviation in the modern sense existed, barring small sports planes owned by the wealthy few. Junkers, together with several other pioneering German manufacturers, would rapidly help to change that and when a German air force once again existed, it could draw on this wealth of expertise to create an operational fighting force with an inordinate amount of speed.

The role of Lufthansa is crucial to the story. It was formed in 1926 and three years later Erhard Milch, a former protégé of Junkers himself and a First World War Squadron Commander, became Chief Executive. Milch, unlike Junkers, was sympathetic to the new Nazi party. Under Milch's tutelage Lufthansa built extensive airport links, established signal and meteorological networks and thoroughly trained its pilots in long-range navigation as well as blind flying so that when the time came many Lufthansa pilots could easily convert to the bomber arm of the Luftwaffe. Milch reportedly even refused to charge the Nazi party for official hire of Lufthansa planes as they canvassed support throughout the early years of the 1930s. More significantly, a full year before Hitler seized power in 1933, Germany could rightly claim to be one of the world's leading air powers, without infringing any of the terms of the Treaty of Versailles.

In the aftermath of the second German daylight Gotha raid on London, crowds watch as smoke pours from the roof of the Central Telegraph Office, struck by a 100lb bomb on 7 July 1917. The raid, carried out by 21 bombers, left 65 dead and some 250 injured, with anti-German riots occurring in the East End of London later that day. The destruction caused by these early bombing raids would be one of the motivating factors behind the creation of a strategic bombing arm for the Luftwaffe early in the 1930s. (IWM Q 65535)

The Nazi party and Milch alone cannot claim credit for the rejuvenation of German air power. Colonel General Hans von Seeckt was a post-war commander-in-chief who believed that any future conflicts would be won by manoeuvre and mobility. The Luftstreitkräfte had been crucial in this role during the First World War and von Seeckt was determined that a covert German air force would continue to exist. He published his thoughts on the matter in 1929, predicting the air battles of 1940 with startling accuracy:

> The war will begin with a simultaneous attack of the air fleets – the weapon which is the most prepared and fastest means of attacking the enemy. The enemy is, however, not the major cities or industrial power, but the enemy air force. Only after its suppression can the offensive arm be directed against other targets. If both sides have a roughly equal force, decision will not be reached quickly. Even if one side is pushed onto the defence, it will employ every means to destroy the attacker.[42]

Von Seeckt ensured that funds were allocated for a small, secret air force, but to train his pilots he would need to look to an old enemy – Russia. Despite their bitter opposition during the war years and the Russian Revolution, Germany embarked on a policy of quiet diplomacy with her former foe, resulting in the Rapallo Treaty of 1922. Within the treaty were a number of secret clauses, which allowed for the establishment of German flying schools and training centres within Russia. In addition, many former pilots were simply employed as civil servants in so-called 'Training Inspectorates', but in reality helping to draft new aerial doctrines.

Moreover, it seems that interest in aviation was rapidly becoming a national obsession. Sports aviation, permissible in the terms of the treaty, was actively encouraged but was seized upon with an eagerness that few had expected. By 1929 membership of state-

The early bombing raids of 1914–18 by both sides were a strong motivating factor for the creation of powerful national air forces in the post-war world. Here a First World War German poster shows RAF bombers attacking German factories with a caption titled in part 'What England Wants'. (IWM PST 6917)

sponsored light aeroplane and glider clubs – the Luftsportsverband – exceeded 50,000 and the numbers would continue to grow. As a result, throughout the 1920s Germany had succeeded in retaining a secret cadre of trained military pilots and a ready reserve of civilian airline and glider pilots, resulting in a secret, shadow Luftwaffe.

Douhet's *The Air War of 19–* had an impact in Germany too. In 1932 Dr Robert Knauss, a senior Lufthansa official, published a follow-up volume entitled *Air War 1936: The Destruction of Paris*.[43] The book, set during a fictional war between Britain and France, details a fictional two-week RAF bombing campaign that is impervious to French fighter attacks, destroys economic and industrial centres of the city, and breaks the will of the people. Significantly, such thoughts on the power of the bomber mirrored many of the developments then taking place in civilian aviation, with several of the passenger planes designed by Junkers and Heinkel ideally suited to conversion to a bomber fleet. Just a year after publication, sweeping changes were made to the German political order, which would make such conversions a reality.

Dr Robert Knauss (on the left) shown in front of a Lufthansa plane and alongside its pilot in Asia in 1926. His work for Lufthansa creating longer-haul trips helped crystallize his thinking regarding the potential of long-distance bombers. He would later achieve the rank of Generalleutnant in Hitler's Luftwaffe. (Bundesarchiv Bild 102-02982)

HITLER'S AIR FORCE: THE LUFTWAFFE IN THE 1930S

National Socialism trumpeted itself as the first truly modern political system and with aviation as the clearest symbol of this brave new world the two would become irrevocably linked. Aviation had played a central theme in all Nazi propaganda prior to 1933 and Hitler's new government was committed to a new, world-leading German air force, one that would throw off the shackles of the Treaty of Versailles and the sham of secret flying schools and 'Training Inspectorates'. Hermann Göring, a First World War fighter pilot and ardent supporter of Hitler since the first years of the National Socialist Party, was appointed Air Minister while Erhard Milch was appointed State Secretary for Aviation. Shortly afterwards, in January 1934, the first large-scale aircraft building programme was implemented. It was still early days, however, and of the 4,021 planes ordered, a large proportion were elementary trainers or types that would become rapidly outdated. Nonetheless it was a portent of things to come, as Milch redirected all his organizational genius, which had transformed Lufthansa into the world's greatest civilian airline, towards the Luftwaffe. Milch was undoubtedly influenced by Knauss, who had been his number two at Lufthansa and who argued forcibly for the creation of a strategic bombing arm. Lieutenant General Walter Wever was appointed the first Chief of Staff of the Luftwaffe and readily supported such a proposal. Wever put his ideas to the test in a war game in 1934 where a scenario was played out in which Germany attacked south-western France. Wever's first act was to heavily bomb the French airfields, forcing the French to pull back and allowing German control of the air space over the battle. Ground attacks and low-level bombing raids could then be conducted and support of the army operations ensured as his directive had intended. However, there was a major flaw, Wever's only strategic heavy bomber was the Junkers 52, a converted transport plane. The war game's umpires predicted the Germans would take losses of at least 80 per cent in the face of resistance from the French fighters. Significantly Wever, a commander of undoubted ability, refused to accept this ruling, and the Luftwaffe henceforth failed to realize the risk that a coordinated defence from fighters could truly pose to a fleet of bombers. For the moment, however, the focus would be on the development of those fighters and bombers, which would be the future arsenal of the Luftwaffe.

THE LUFTWAFFE BOMBERS

Just as battleships symbolized the power of a navy, a long-range heavy bomber came to encapsulate the potential power of a nation's air force, and many countries began to experiment with the idea of developing such an aircraft. As early as 1934 the US Army Air Corps began work on what would later become the B-17 prototype, and Wever was undoubtedly committed to the idea of a four-engined heavy bomber. German manufacturers, who would prove to be excellent at delivering medium bombers as well as fighters, entirely failed at the task of developing a heavy bomber. German-designed

Walter Wever, the German air strategist and first Chief of Staff of the Luftwaffe, who was killed in a flying accident in June 1936. Many believe that had he not been killed the Luftwaffe would have pursued the development of heavy bombers as opposed to the medium and dive-bombers, which became the mainstay of the German bomber fleets and suffered heavy losses during the Battle of Britain. However, just as significantly, Wever failed to realize the potential danger fighter aircraft posed to bombers. (Bundesarchiv Bild 141-1941)

engines were at the time incapable of delivering the necessary power to transport such a heavy plane together with its bomb load at sufficient speeds. In 1936 Wever supported the decision to suspend the work by Junkers and Dornier on the unsatisfactory models and wait until the technology had effectively caught up with the thinking. Wever's death later that year in a flying accident together with an international situation that quickly spiralled into war ensured that the heavy-bomber programme was never resurrected. Instead, the Luftwaffe would have to rely on their force of medium bombers and dive-bombers to fulfil the strategic bombing role already envisaged as well as the tactical support of the armed forces on the ground. Both would prove to be easier targets for defending fighters than better-armed heavy bombers.

As such when the Battle of Britain began, one of the oldest types still in active service was the Dornier 17. Often referred to as the 'flying pencil' it was originally designed to have a small payload but the ability to outrun enemy fighters. Although some in 1940 were equipped with the DB 601 engine, the most powerful German engine at the time, the Do 17 (and its slightly improved sister plane the Do 215), had little chance of outrunning either a Spitfire or Hurricane. The Do 17 would be phased out of service in early 1941 due to its dismal record, while the Do 215 was used as a night fighter.

Opposite:
A 1931 Lufthansa poster with a Junkers Ju 52 passenger aircraft in the background. Just three years later another Lufthansa poster shows a Ju 52 flying over astonished onlookers whose 18th-century-style dress is designed to contrast with modern aviation. This Ju 52 is emblazoned with the swastika, as Lufthansa was nationalized once the Nazis assumed power. (akg images)

Right:
Erhard Milch (left) had served as an aerial observer in the Luftstreitkräfte before pursuing a career in civil aviation and became a devoted servant of the Third Reich, eventually promoted Air Inspector General with the rank of Field Marshal. In a bizarre twist, Milch's 'father' was Jewish but when this threatened to derail his fledgling career with the Nazi party it was revealed that he and his siblings had in fact been fathered by his mother's uncle, a non-Jew. He is shown here in 1934 alongside Theo Osterkamp (right), the First World War fighter ace, who later commanded Jagdgeschwader 51 during the Battle of Britain. (Bundesarchiv Bild 183-2008-1016-507)

One of the iconic planes of the early war period was undoubtedly the Stuka dive-bomber and its development can be traced back to the early days of the Luftwaffe. In September 1933 Colonel Ernst Udet witnessed a flying demonstration of Curtiss F8C biplanes. Udet was a former First World War ace who had been a colleague of both the Red Baron and Göring in Jagdgeschwader I. Post-war he had made a name for himself as an international stunt pilot and when he witnessed a flying demonstration of the F8C while on a trip to America he liked what he saw. Known as 'Helldivers' by the Curtiss company, who gave the same name to all their other designs of a similar nature, they were regarded as somewhat obsolete at this stage and so no objection was raised when Udet purchased two of these machines. Milch in turn recognized that with this early Helldiver there was the possibility to provide perfect close-support for the armed forces. The two aircraft were shipped back to Germany after which Junkers and other companies were asked to develop their own prototype. The end result was the famous Junkers Ju 87, commonly known as the Stuka. This was not the only dive-bomber developed by German manufacturers; Henschel and Heinkel also created models, but with the Stuka the Luftwaffe had created an aircraft that was supposedly capable of putting a 500-kilogram bomb within 100 metres of a given target. Later the Luftwaffe would introduce a siren that screamed a blood-curdling wail as it approached the target, following Douhet's directive to strike terror into the hearts and minds of the enemy population. Werner Roll was a Luftwaffe pilot who flew Stukas during the Norwegian campaign and the Battle of Britain:

The Stuka was the sharpshooter amongst the bombers. Whereas the horizontal bombers dropped an enormous number of bombs on an area, the Stuka had a small target and with a small number of bombs it could erase a target of importance. They had to be sturdy because they came out of a dive sharply. And the pilot had to be accustomed to that. It was

A Junkers Ju 88 under construction in a German factory in 1939 and another airborne in 1940. (Bundesarchiv Bild 1011-772-0472-42, Bild 10111-409-0885-30A)

easy to black out when you redressed the plane because the blood went out of your head. You could hear in the earphones when you were down to 1,000 metres and then you started redressing the plane and you levelled off about 700 metres above the ground. The Stukas had sirens in front of the wings, one on each side. When the speed was increasing during the dive, the sirens started making a terrific noise... There were also cardboard whistles on the tail rudders of the bombs so that when the bombs were released, the bomb itself started whistling.[44]

As the Stuka dropped its bomb load, the pilot would then begin to climb back up allowing the rear gunner to spray the ground with machine-gun fire and to protect the Stuka from attack. This was crucial because the Stuka, for all its ability to induce terror, was a particularly vulnerable attack plane. With a top speed of just 230mph it was surprisingly slow and could be easy prey for enemy fighters, who would only have the one rear gunner to contend with. The development of the Ju 87 began in 1933; two years later it was ready for testing, with the first Stukas rolling off the production line in 1936.

The same year saw the Heinkel III enter production. This was a medium bomber manned by a crew of five: the pilot, the bomber and navigator, the radio operator, the technician and a gunner. It was capable of a top speed of 217mph and could cover a range of over 900 miles while carrying a full bomb load of 3,300lb. The aircraft had developed out of a desire to create the fastest possible passenger plane. However with the Nazi government funding the Heinkel, the manufacturers quickly altered the design to create the fastest possible bomber. At the time it was indeed remarkably fast, and was therefore lightly armed in the mistaken belief that it would be able to outrun enemy fighters. The Heinkel III would see extensive service throughout the early years of the war and even after it became increasingly obsolete, as there was little opportunity to develop a better medium bomber when production was already overstretched. During the course of the Battle of Britain and throughout the war

A classic wartime photo of a Junkers Ju-87 Stuka 'in action'. (IWM GER 18)

With the knowledge that the Do 17 was obsolescent prior even to the outbreak of the war, Junkers had focused on creating a replacement fast bomber that would work perfectly in the role of tactical support of the army. This was the Ju 88. Unable to carry as much as the Heinkel III, it was considerably faster, capable of speeds of 290mph. It first flew in 1936 but did not see active service until after the outbreak of war due to extensive testing and modifications. Following the success of the Stuka during the Spanish Civil War, the Ju 88 was modified so that it could also serve as a heavy dive-bomber. Its combat debut was over the North Sea when a German flying boat stumbled upon the British aircraft carrier *Ark Royal*. With this prize target in range, four Ju 88s were scrambled. One Ju 88 piloted by Gefreiter (Aircraftman First Class) Carl Francke made a successful dive-bombing run against the carrier. The crew of the *Ark Royal* had seen the approach of the bomber and, timing it to perfection, the captain had successfully turned the ship out of the path of the falling 1,000lb bomb. However, the massive explosion alongside it together with the fire from the vessel's own anti-aircraft guns created the impression that she had in fact been hit. Later reconnaissance flights could not find her and the propaganda machine swung into overtime as Göring gleefully celebrated the fact that one of his planes had sunk the pride of the Royal Navy. Of course, it was not to be. In what could be seen as a portent of things to come, the Ju 88 had failed in its first operational mission.[46]

Although Ju 88s would see extensive service throughout the Battle of Britain it was not always as intended, Ju 88 crews frequently having to use the aircraft's diving capabilities to escape from attacking Spitfires or Hurricanes. The Ju 88 was formidably armed with two machine guns in the rear fuselage, another underneath and one more in the cockpit. In addition, there was a fifth machine gun, which could be operated by the pilot. However, the first four were all operated by the flight engineer, meaning one crew member had to constantly move between the guns, a flaw that was remarkably never resolved considering that the Ju 88 would see extensive service in a variety of roles until the very end of the war.

Two Dornier 17 bomber aircraft photographed from another German aircraft on 7 September 1940. West Ham, London is shown below. (IWM C 5423)

years Heinkel pilots quickly found that there was little chance of outrunning the faster, highly manoeuvrable fighters, so their only chance of protection was to fly in tight formation. It was not a pleasant experience, as Ernest Wedding, a Heinkel III pilot during 1940, later recalled:

> I flew my Heinkel III bomber in formation and I had to keep to my station. Even when the British fighters started attacking me, I couldn't do any intricate manoeuvres within the formation or else I would crash into the other bombers. It was a tedious job. All I was doing was watching the aircraft in front and on the left and right and hoping the chap behind was doing the same so that he wouldn't take my tail off. A bomber pilot had to be as steady as a bus driver.[45]

THE LUFTWAFFE FIGHTERS

Just as civilian transport aircraft had paved the way for the German medium bomber, throughout the dark days of the Versailles restrictions Germany's most gifted engineers honed their skills for creating fast fighters by designing touring and sports aircraft. One such man was Willy Messerschmitt. The great Messerschmitt was of course the designer of the Me 109, the Spitfire's famous rival during the Battle of Britain and beyond. He nearly didn't get to design it. In 1931 two Messerschmitt-designed aircraft crashed, killing all the passengers on board including a great friend of Erhard Milch. Milch never forgave Messerschmitt and ensured that when the rearmament programme began Messerschmitt's company would not share in the spoils. However, Milch could hardly ignore Messerschmitt's talents when it became clear exactly what kind of fighter was required. The Jagdwaffe, the Luftwaffe's fighter arm, was initially supplied with obsolete biplanes but in July 1933 the German Air Ministry issued the Tactical Requirements for Fighter Aircraft (Land) document. This called for a truly modern single-seat fighter capable of speeds of at least 250mph at 19,500ft and armed with two machine guns or one fixed cannon. It was to be highly manoeuvrable, adept at diving and turning in a dogfight without difficulty, and able to fly in virtually all weather conditions. With Milch's support and previous experience of building fighters, Heinkel and Focke-Wulf were considered the rank favourites to win the government contract. But Messerschmitt alone of the contenders had previously built truly fast aircraft, developing and constructing planes to compete in speed contests throughout Europe, just as Mitchell had done for the Schneider Trophy. When the German Air Ministry released their requirements for a fighter, Messerschmitt was already in the process of designing another prototype for the 1934 European Flying Contest. This was the Me 108 Taifun, a lightweight four-seater 'tourer'. It had a flush-riveted, stressed-skin construction and cantilevered monoplane wings with 'slots' along the leading edges, which meant that it handled equally well at fast and slow speeds. It was a truly advanced machine for the era and many of its features would be incorporated into the Me 109 prototype. In addition the prototype included trailing edge

flaps, which combined with the wing's small surface area gave it its much admired flexibility. Messerschmitt now simply needed to fit the required armament and therefore inverted the V-shaped 12-cylinder Jumo 210 engine designed by Junkers, creating the necessary room to include two machine guns along the top of the cowling. There was also room to include a 20mm cannon within the engine itself. The prototype was complete.

It first took to the skies in May 1935 and thereafter became part of the official trials programme with ten pre-production aircraft ordered from Messerschmitt and Heinkel for a series of exacting tests planned for the following autumn. Udet, Göring's old 'Flying Circus' compatriot, had been promoted within the Luftwaffe to the Inspector of Fighters and Dive-Bombers and then to Director of the Technical Department. This was largely a result of in-fighting within the Air Ministry. Throughout the early years Göring had

Professor Wilhelm 'Willy' Messerschmitt (on the far right) photographed alongside Albert Speer, Minister for Armament and Production (left), and General Field Marshal Erhard Milch (centre), in 1944. Variants of the Me 109 would continue to see service until the end of the war and Messerschmitt's firm was also responsible for the creation of the world's first jet-powered fighter, the Me 262. (Bundesarchiv Bild 183-H28426)

been content with his flashy uniform and position of power without any of the responsibilities. However, in 1936 Hitler had made Milch a general in the Luftwaffe, and Göring came to see his deputy as a real threat to his power. Following Wever's death in an air accident, Göring began to interfere directly with the expansion plans and running of the Luftwaffe. The promotion of Udet was a classic move by Göring, who sought to surround himself with familiar faces from his own flying days and effective 'yes' men who would not question his judgement. Udet was a brilliant pilot and therefore probably ideally suited to testing any of the new planes destined for the Jagdwaffe. But he had no qualifications to run the Technical Department, for which Milch was eminently better suited to manage without interference. Nonetheless, in this one instance Göring was proved right. Milch may well have allowed his personal animosity towards Messerschmitt to influence his decision. However, it was no longer his decision to make, and Udet, no technical genius but a highly competent pilot, could recognize a fantastic fighter. That is not to say that he was sold at first sight, however, declaring to Messerschmitt that this ultra-modern beast with its enclosed cockpit could never be a fighter plane because 'the pilot needs an open cockpit. He needs to feel the air to know the speed of the aeroplane.'[47] Messerschmitt later recalled that Udet looked nervous as he was sealed within the tiny cockpit of the Me 109 prototype, but once airborne the decision was made. In formal air tests the Me 109 was the obvious winner. It was faster than the rival Heinkel 112 design, and it could also easily out-dive and out-turn it. Later it was fitted with the more powerful DB 601A engine,

Top:
A photograph of the Messerschmitt Me 109 prototype, which first flew on 28 May 1935. At the time the plane was powered by a Rolls-Royce engine although this would later be replaced with the German-manufactured DB 601A engine. The Luftwaffe would begin officially flying the Me 109 from early 1937 onwards. (Eddie Nielinger)

Botom:
An Me 110 from Zerstörergeschwader 76 shown in May 1940, a unit that later served during the Battle of Britain. (Bundesarchiv Bild 101I-382-0211-011)

which gave it a further 400hp, but more significantly was fuel-injected. This meant that the Me 109 was capable of negative G flight so whereas in a steep dive the fuel supply in a carburettor engine would stop because of the excessive upward force, the Me 109's would not. This would allow many a German Me 109 pilot to escape an attacker. Further refinements were also made to the models that would eventually see action during the Battle of Britain. With the news that the Spitfire would have eight machine guns fitted to it, and the realization that the engine-mounted cannon wasn't viable, a new wing was designed with a 20mm cannon, giving the Me 109 undeniably effective armament. Indeed, the cannon packed a more powerful punch than the Spitfire's machine guns as Hans-Ekkehard Bob would find to his advantage over the skies of Britain in 1940:

> In a fraction of a second, I could bring down a Spitfire. If I could hit it twice, I could destroy it. The English had to score a great many hits with their machine guns to bring a plane down, but they didn't need to shoot as accurately.[48]

It is difficult to say whether the Me 109 was a better aircraft than the Spitfire. It certainly couldn't turn as tightly, due to its heavier wingload, but it had other advantages, as did the Spitfire. The real test was who sat in the cockpit. Indeed, the Me 109 was undoubtedly a far superior plane to the Hurricane and yet there were several instances of Hurricane pilots shooting down Me 109s. Pilot skill, and no small measure of luck, were more often than not the determining factors. Prior to the collapse of France, however, it was never envisaged that these rival fighters would ever meet in combat over British skies. The Me 109 simply did not have the range to operate so far from its air bases.

(Top) A posed photograph taken in 1937 showing a group of infantrymen alongside a 'B' variant of the Me 109. The majority of Me 109s which fought during the Battle of Britain were the 'E' or 'Emil' variant, shown here (bottom right), which utilized the fuel-injected DB 601A engine. (Eddie Nielinger)

¿QUE HACES TU PARA

EVITAR ESTO?

AYUDA A MADRID

One other fighter would serve alongside the Me 109, and this was the strange hybrid creature the Messerschmitt 110, which was also capable of carrying a significant bomb load. The Luftwaffe hoped to counter the increasingly obvious vulnerability of bomber fleets with the creation of long-range fighter escorts. The 110 was a twin-engined aircraft powered by the excellent DB 601A. It was capable of speeds of 340mph at 32,000ft, faster even than the Hurricane. It was armed with four forward-firing machine guns and two 20mm cannon, and with a strengthened undercarriage it was capable of carrying 2,200lb of bombs. However, the twin-engined design, with its large wingspan, meant that it was never particularly manoeuvrable. And although tasked with protecting the bomber fleet, it would only ever be able to do this if it could surprise enemy fighters by 'bouncing' them from a great height, otherwise it stood little chance. Their real successes in the Battle of Britain would be when they would act as a fast bomber force of their own, delivering a larger bomb load more accurately than a Stuka and capable of a quicker getaway. This was never fully exploited by the Luftwaffe and instead they would first and foremost serve as bomber escorts known as Zerstörer (destroyer) wings.

THE LUFTWAFFE AT WAR

While Europe looked on with horror, Spain descended into a terrible civil war. As Republicans lined up against Nationalists, this particular conflict would provide a unique opportunity for Hitler's fledgling Luftwaffe. Germany realized that Spain could prove a perfect testing ground for some of her latest aircraft and it would also be in Germany's favour if an eventual ally found itself in power in the region. Of course, at the time Germany was still in the midst of her rearmament programme so her efforts would have to be kept relatively small. The result was the Condor Legion, a 5,000-strong

The bombing raids of the Condor Legion during the Spanish Civil War and the resulting loss of civilian lives horrified the governments and populations of the rest of Europe. The actions of the Condor Legion became a rallying cry for the Republican forces as this poster illustrates. (akg images, 272712)

force armed with modern equipment and aircraft under the command of Major General Hugo Sperrle. Germany's most modern medium bombers, including the Do 17 and Heinkel III, were included among the first deployment, and in early 1937 the first production models of the Me 109 began to make their way to the frontline. It proved to be a far superior fighter to any of the Russian aircraft which were supporting the Republican forces, and the Luftwaffe pilots quickly honed their dogfighting skills. The Stuka joined the Condor Legion in 1938, where it showed that it was far more accurate than the other bombers, and as a result Stukas were often flying up to four sorties a day. Between 1936 and 1939, when the war was concluded, over 19,000 Luftwaffe personnel served in Spain. Their rotation back to their original units ensured that their knowledge of combat operations was carefully disseminated throughout the air force. Moreover, they had been used in a variety of campaigns from support of armoured and motorized formations to strategic bombing so that by the time the Condor Legion departed, the Luftwaffe could arguably claim to be one of the most experienced, combat-ready air force in the world.

Most infamously, of course, the Condor Legion was also responsible for the bombing of Guernica. The world was scandalized by the destruction of this ancient Basque town and viewed it as a blatant attempt to wipe out an opposing city and her people. The Luftwaffe claimed it had attacked the town not because of its significance to the Basque people who supported the Republican cause, but because of its critical location on the frontline. Nonetheless, the governments of Western Europe were horrified. They assumed that Germany was now pursuing a city-bombing strategy and feared the worst. In London the British government and RAF assumed the same and doubled their focus on defence to ensure that Germany would not succeed. Moreover, the German lessons drawn from the Spanish Civil War were not entirely accurate. Barring some opposition from Soviet-built fighters, there was no real match for Germany's modern aircraft, and as such Stukas and other bombers could do their worst. In the face of a coordinated defence it could potentially be a very different story. In 1936 General Wever had

Heinkel bombers of the Condor Legion on a Spanish airfield. Two Heinkels were used in the bombing of Guernica alongside a Dornier 17 and several Ju 52s. (akg images, 124061)

suspended the programme to develop a long-range strategic bomber. In 1937 Göring officially ordered a final stop to all developments. He had calculated that the German aircraft industry could produce more than two twin-engined bombers for just one potential four-engined aircraft, so quantity had won over quality. The events of the Spanish Civil War had seemingly vindicated his decision. He could not have been more wrong.

Following the 'Anschluss' (Union) between Germany and Austria in March 1938, Hitler set his sights on the German-speaking Sudetenland area of Czechoslovakia. During the resultant Munich crisis the powers of Europe gave in, largely due to fear of the Luftwaffe. Surprised by British protests over the situation in Czechoslovakia, Hitler ordered the Second Air Fleet, stationed in north-west Germany and therefore closest to Britain, to prepare for possible war. In a series of war games conducted throughout 1938 and 1939 the weaknesses of the Luftwaffe were increasingly revealed. In less than a year, they would be at war for real.

REICHSMARSCHALL HERMANN GÖRING

With his penchant for overindulgence, whether it was painkillers or excessively elaborate uniforms, Hermann Göring became an almost comic character in the later years of the war. It is easy to forget how significant a part he had played in the early development of the Nazi party or indeed his meritorious service during the First World War. Born in 1893 he was the son of a senior civil servant, but grew up in a castle near Nuremberg, the home of his wealthy godfather Hermann Epenstein, who was of Jewish descent and also his mother's lover. The young Göring attended boarding school, paid for by his wealthy benefactor, where it was recommended that he attend a military academy. When war broke out in 1914 he was a promising infantry officer and saw extensive service on the frontline but was hospitalized with arthritis. Unable to return to the trenches, he was eventually accepted as an aviator. Göring never looked back. He finished the war with 22 official victories to his credit, within the top 50 German fighter aces of the war, and commanded the famous 'Flying Circus', Jagdgeschwader I, the former squadron of the Red Baron, Manfred von Richthofen. After the signing of the Armistice, Göring was ordered to hand over his squadron's planes to the Allies, a humiliation that the charismatic and competent officer found difficult to accept. He and his squadron reportedly deliberately damaged their aircraft before their handover. Although Göring remained as part of the official, now greatly reduced, post-war German military, he became increasingly attracted to politics and was one of Hitler's earliest and most devoted lieutenants. He joined the Nazi party in 1922 and quickly took over its paramilitary wing, the Sturmabteiling (SA), more commonly known as the 'Brownshirts'. He was with Hitler in November 1923 at the abortive Munich Putsch when the then relatively small National Socialist Party attempted to seize control of the Weimar Republic. Göring was shot in the groin during the fiasco and was secretly evacuated to Austria to avoid arrest and to receive treatment. The following five years were marked by a severe morphine addiction as a result of the use of the drug to treat his injuries, and a nomadic existence around Europe. In 1927 he was finally able to return to Germany after an amnesty was declared for those who had participated in the failed putsch. Göring quickly resumed his political career as the Nazi party reinvented itself as a legitimate force within Germany and he was elected to the Reichstag just a year later. In the coalition government that was formed with Hitler in 1933, Göring was the only other Nazi in the Cabinet. His position as Prussia's Minister of the Interior was seemingly innocuous but ensured that he would have control over the largest police body in the country, a part of which was gradually converted into the Gestapo, the Secret Police.

Göring's rise to power, on the coat-tails of Hitler, ensured him a lifestyle more suited to a medieval lord than a political heavyweight and military commander. Grand estates, hunting lodges and art collections rapidly became Göring's personal property, part of a vast private fortune that he acquired through accepting bribes and confiscating Jewish property. Göring even later acquired a personal train, which included a cinema and separate sleeping coaches for him and his wife. Hans-Ekkehard Bob, a Messerschmitt 109 pilot, later recalled meeting Göring alongside a fellow pilot when receiving his Knight's Cross, which he had won at the height of the Battle of Britain:

> We reported in at Göring's office but he wasn't there. He was on his way back from Paris but then he showed up wearing a raw-silk shirt with puffed sleeves, a silk cravat with a great big emerald on the throat, light-grey riding breeches and red boots. Even by today's standards it was a pretty daring get-up. He received us with the words, 'What is your business here?' We both thought, 'What's going on?' but suddenly he dived into his pocket, pulled out the Knight's Cross and said, 'This is for you!'[49]

Göring photographed in April 1918 in the cockpit of a Fokker DR I. (Bundesarchiv Bild 183-R52897)

An Ultra signal even once picked up an order from Göring specifying that all pilots due to receive a decoration from him should be thoroughly deloused before making their appearance.[50] Hitler tolerated Göring's excesses because he was also a consummate politician, a skilful schemer and undoubtedly committed to the Nazi cause. He helped to plan the Night of the Long Knives (1934), whereby challengers to Hitler's authority within the SA were assassinated. He was not, however, an unquestioning supporter of Hitler's military policies and was initially opposed to the invasion of Poland and the possibility of war, knowing that conflict with the British Empire would come at a high price.

As head of the Luftwaffe Göring was also in command of the parachute and glider troops – the legendary Fallschirmjäger. Their successful assault on the Belgian fortress of Eben Emael in May 1940 and the huge successes the Luftwaffe achieved in the early stages of the war saw Göring promoted to Reichsmarschall, a special rank created by Hitler for him alone, thereby making him senior to all other military commanders. His first notable failure was his inability to gain control over the skies of Britain in 1940 but the continued Blitz campaign secured his position while Hitler was distracted by the East. With the launch of Operation Barbarossa, Göring became increasingly disinterested in the day-to-day running of the Luftwaffe. However, he continued to make promises he

could not keep and this contributed to the lack of sensible planning that characterized the early stages of the campaign. With a German army trapped in Stalingrad in 1942, Göring assured Hitler that he could deliver the necessary resources to the beleaguered defenders. Of course he could not, nor could he stop the RAF and USAAF bombings, and from this point their relationship faltered. As a result, Göring all but withdrew from public life and operational decisions.

As the Third Reich crumbled in 1945, Göring fled the chaos of Berlin with trainloads of Nazi treasure. He eventually surrendered and was tried at Nuremberg. Göring reportedly offered to accept the court's decision for the death penalty if he could choose a soldier's death by firing squad. This was refused and the night before he was due to hang he committed suicide with a cyanide pill.

A photograph taken in 1932 showing Göring shortly before his official appointment to government after Hitler took power in 1933. Göring's early loyalty to Hitler was richly rewarded. Despite failing to secure victory in the Battle of Britain his position with Hitler did not drastically deteriorate until the Luftwaffe's inability to sufficiently re-supply German troops during the Battle of Stalingrad. (Bundesarchiv Bild 102-13805)

THE PILOTS

RECRUITMENT AND MOTIVATION

Hans-Ekkehard Bob, a 109 pilot during the Battle of Britain, later recalled with pleasure the first time he was introduced to flying. Like his erstwhile foe, Archibald Winskell, who first flew with Cobham's 'Flying Circus', Bob's initial experience was also with a First World War veteran who took him up for a spin. It was an unforgettable experience:

When I was ten years old, my older sister got to know a First World War pilot, who in 1927 was performing advertising flights in a biplane. This pilot liked my sister and invited her to come flying with him and she asked him if her little brother could come along too. This was a very big thing, of course, because in 1927 hardly any planes at all were to be seen in the sky. My mother told me that afterwards I told her I was going to learn to be a pilot too, that I would steer the plane with my right hand while catching eagles with my left one.[51]

It was the start of a lifelong love affair. Bob joined the Luftwaffe in 1936 and served throughout the war as one of Germany's leading aces. At the age of 93 he still flies at the time of writing, one of the world's oldest qualified pilots. Just as young British recruits to Fighter Command were enamoured with the possibilities of flight, it was no different for prospective recruits to the Luftwaffe. Before the age of

regular civilian travel by air, and when aeroplanes were still a relatively uncommon sight, to fly was something akin to magic:

> The appeal of flying is you are free from the earth. Your horizon is unlimited. On a clear day you can see a hundred miles... And it was a terrific feeling to be free of everything.[52]

Moreover, pilots of the First World War had been, again like their RFC opponents, lauded as national heroes. Despite the Red Baron's death and Germany's eventual defeat in the war, the cult of the hero pilot continued, seemingly untainted by the disastrous end to 1918. Years later Wolfgang Falck, a participant at the secret German flying schools in Russia and later an Me 110 pilot, declared, 'We all wanted to be Baron von Richthofen.'[53]

Both sides had nurtured an ideal of a 'knight of the air' amidst the carnage of war. In reality, the concept of chivalry and honourably duelling pilots had little place in that war after the first couple of months of conflict, but the myth continued to flourish and would inspire another generation of pilots during the Second World War. In early 1940 Hans-Ekkehard Bob would try to emulate the heroes of his youth and act honourably when he found himself engaged in combat for the first time in 1940 during the Battle of France:

> On May 25th I had a heavy air fight with a Curtis P-36. It was a dog-fight, well-known from World War I. We banked for 20 minutes starting at a height of 4000 metres down to nearly the ground. While my plane was the quicker one, the Curtis was more manoeuvrable. For that reason I turned eastwards in low-level flight pretending to fly home. After a short while I turned and pursued the Curtis which was at a height of approximately 100 meters with course West. I was able to surprise it from behind at low-level-flight and shot it down. The P-36 made a belly

The great First World War hero Manfred von Richthofen, in the cockpit of his Albatros fighter. His successes helped create the cult of the fighter pilot despite Germany's eventual defeat in the war. One of the pilots in his squadron, Geschwader I, was a young Hermann Göring. (IWM Q 55465)

landing on a meadow. I landed beside it and could provide first aid for the wounded pilot, a French sergeant. The sergeant gave me his home address and I informed his family about the events.[54]

There would be little room for such actions in the coming months. Pilots would have to learn quickly that a new code of conduct, a determined ruthlessness, was required to ensure victory.

One of the major differences between Luftwaffe and RAF recruits was the politicization of the German air service. As soon as the Nazis came to power in 1933, flying fell under the total control of the state. It began at early age. German boys aged between ten and 14 could join the Deutsche Jungvolk, a Nazi childrens' organization. Here they were first introduced to the concept of serving their country through participation in the armed forces. From the Deutsche Jungvolk they would progress to the more explicitly political Hitler Jugend (Hitler Youth), which in 1936 became compulsory for all boys between the ages of 14 and 17. Membership of the Hitler Youth ensured exposure to a range of exciting opportunities but the most popular was flying, with the opportunity to qualify as pilots through a Hitler Youth Glider School, crucial for anyone considering joining the newly formed Luftwaffe service. It is difficult to determine the level of politicization among young recruits to the Luftwaffe. Undoubtedly many of those who learnt to fly throughout the forbidden years prior to 1935 were motivated by a desire to do something that they loved. It is harder to assess with regard to pilots who would have experienced the indoctrination of the Deutsche Jungvolk and Hitler Jugend. Like all members of the armed forces German airmen were required to take an oath of 'unconditional obedience to the Führer of the German Reich and Volk, Adolf Hitler'. It is impossible to ascertain now how many Luftwaffe pilots were motivated by a desire to simply learn to fly or whether political motivations played a part, large or small. Certainly some recruits would have been motivated by the future Hitler envisaged for the Third Reich, while even more would have been all too pleased to overturn the humiliations of the Treaty of Versailles, which had embittered virtually an entire generation.

A young Hitler Youth member receives instructions on the finer points of gliding from his trainer in the NSFK. (Bundesarchiv Bild 146-2004-0059)

Wolfgang Falck, a Messerschmitt Bf 110 pilot, later identified why it was so easy to be swept up by Nazism simply because it promised a brighter future for Germany, and it was all too easy to ignore the darker underside. Falck, who had been part of the secret training programme in Russia, recognized the dangerous similarities between the Soviet dictatorship of Russia and Nazism, and his post-war recollections reveal the impact of Nazi propaganda:

I remember when Hitler came to power. A little while before, we had marched through an area of Silesia that was known as being Communist. People threw pots at us. But after Hitler came to power, we came back to the area and all the people welcomed us like heroes, crying, 'Heil! Heil!' There were new flags with the swastika everywhere. These people had switched in a short time. It is very difficult for young Germans and

Glider training was an excellent way to introduce future pilots to the art of flying and in April 1937 all civilian clubs were amalgamated under the party-run Nationalsozialistische Fliegerkorps to prepare young gliders for service in the Luftwaffe. (Bob Stedman)

He marched into the Rhineland and made it all German property. There were no crimes any more. Everything was safe. All these things were brand new and they impressed the people very much. Many people had a much better condition of life than before. Everyone had the feeling that now was a new time and we are safe. Nobody knew what would happen in the future.

But we had seen the May Parade when we'd been in Russia and we had been impressed. The army, the girls, the boys were marching in uniform with guns and flowers and flags. Then we came back to Germany and we saw the parades under Hitler and we saw the youth, the workers, the SA and the SS and we said, 'We saw exactly the same last year in Russia. The only difference was there they had the hammer and sickles and here we have swastikas.'[55]

German Me 109 pilots flew in loose pairs, *rötte*, with two pairs forming a *schwarm*, and three pairs a *staffel*. This tactic had first been devised by the German ace Werner Mölders during the Spanish Civil War and it was far more effective than the British Fighting Area Attack formations. Flying in widely spaced pairs required little effort to remain in formation and ensured that pilots were able to scan the skies looking for enemy fighters. One aircraft acted as the lead of the pair with the second acting as a wingman to protect the leader's tail. This meant that most enemy 'kills' were scored by the lead aircraft.

foreigners to understand why. After the First World War, Germany was in a very poor condition. The Rhineland was occupied by the French, industry had gone, there were no aircraft and an army of 100,000. There were at least ten political parties, everyone fighting against the others. It was like a civil war. The Communists were trying to make revolution. Millions of people were jobless with nothing to eat. It was really catastrophic. Now, all of a sudden, came a man. He promised the Germans – 'You are somebody. You are Germans. You should be proud to be Germans. I will take care that you get enough food. I will take care that you get a job. No jobless any more. No hunger any more.' And the first things he did were like that. He started building the autobahns.

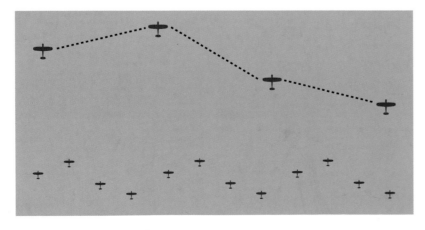

Once war broke out, however, as with all nations the real ties of loyalty were to those you fought with on an daily basis, as politics and ideology were superseded by a desire to simply live to fight another day. As the 'new' service in comparison with the navy or armed forces, the Luftwaffe was able to foster a generally egalitarian *esprit de corps*. Despite the fact that a number of the pre-war officers were drawn from the usual middle to upper classes, many were on first-name terms with their crewmen, and, as with the RAF, a greater importance was placed on a man's abilities than his background. However there was a clear, individualistic streak amongst the Jagdwaffe. Like their First World War forebears, German fighter pilots became part of an official attempt to recognize and promote heroes of the Reich through a series of awards. Although British pilots would receive gallantry awards for their flying service, and many were quickly granted in the early months of the war, they became increasingly few and far between. The Victoria Cross, Britain's highest award for courage in the face of enemy fire, was awarded only once during the course of the Battle of Britain, despite a number of undoubtedly heroic acts.

The German system could not have been more different. All the German armed forces operated on an accumulated-points system as the basis for awards. So, for example, in the Luftwaffe the destruction of a single-engined aircraft equated to one point, destruction of

a twin-engined aircraft garnered two points. Fighter pilots initially qualified for the Iron Cross 2nd Class for aerial victories equalling one point.[55] Three aerial victories, or a conspicuous act of gallantry by either a flight- or ground-crew member, resulted in an Iron Cross 1st Class. Ten aerial victories would be recognized by a silver goblet, engraved with the pilot's name, unit and date of the award. Forty points resulted in the Knight's Cross of the Iron Cross – the highest possible award at the time of the Battle of Britain. Some pilots viewed these awards with ironic humour – even referring to the silver honour goblet as the *Parteiabzeichen für Kurzsichtige* – 'the party badge for the short-sighted' – thanks to its large engraved swastika. Nonetheless, leading pilots would quickly begin to collect such awards from the Spanish Civil War onwards and there was fierce competition to see who would be Germany's leading ace. Adolf Galland, the top-scoring Me 109 ace during the Battle of Britain, was reportedly furious when Göring invited him to attend a

weekend shooting party as an opportunity for a rest and the chance to discuss tactics. A weekend away from the frontline would mean that Galland's rivals for the top position would have the chance to close in on him if they achieved enough aerial victories.

The German tactic of fighters operating in pairs, *rötte*, created a pair leader, responsible for making the kill, and a wingman, who protected the leader's tail. Although tactically very effective, this system undoubtedly favoured the accumulation of awards for the pair leader and often caused some resentment on the part of the wingman, who could not share in the associated fame and glory. There is also a question mark over whether this pursuit of 'confirmed kills' led to German pilots overinflating claims, and therefore a false impression of how well Luftwaffe units were really performing during the Battle of Britain. But before any claims could be made and awards received, pilots would have to undergo several years of training to create a war-winning air force.

TRAINING

Prior to 1935 training was on a somewhat ad hoc basis. Pilots were trained either as civilian pilots or as part of the secret air training programmes in Russia. This was excellent, thorough training, often conducted throughout the 1920s by seasoned combat veterans of the First World War. However there was an acute shortage of suitable aircraft for the nascent air force to fly. Often cunning and subterfuge were required to acquire aircraft and it was a strange existence for the trainee pilots alongside their Russian 'comrades', as Wolfgang Falck explains:

> Our bosses were officers but everything was done in civilian clothing... We flew the Fokker D13, a Dutch aircraft. All the writing on the plane was in Spanish because the aircraft had been ordered by a South American state and they had been transported on a big ship from Amsterdam. However the ship's captain must have been a very poor navigator because they didn't arrive in South America – they arrived in Leningrad.
>
> All the flight mechanics were Russian soldiers but the supervisor was German. We were kept separate to the Russians. We had our own barracks where we lived, our own officer club and our own hangar. The Russians were very friendly to us. We had civilian friends and girlfriends too but they were not supposed to have contact with us because we were bad capitalists.[57]

Once Germany was under the control of the Nazi party, however, the training programme was formalized. All potential recruits endured an initial six-month basic training where they were drilled in all the rudimentary military skills including foot drill, rifle drill, PT, basic map reading and some elementary wireless procedure. Once they had successfully completed this induction period the candidates would be tested in basic flight theory. Only then would successful candidates be put forward to a flight school – Flugzeugführerschule A/B – to achieve their pilot's licence. The flight-school training itself was broken into four parts and only after an average of ten to 13 months would a pilot be granted his licence. Fighter pilots would have an incredible 250 hours of flying time under their belts, including 15 hours of aerobatic training and attendance at an air war school where they would learn the principles of tactics, Luftwaffe law and military discipline prior to deployment to an operational unit. Training for multi-engined aircraft was no less thorough. Indeed, at this stage the bomber arm of the Luftwaffe was considered the premier service and often the best candidates were hand-selected. Potential Stuka pilots

The He 51 biplane had proved to be obsolete during its service in Spain with the Condor Legion. However, it did make an effective training plane for future fighter Battle of Britain pilots before they progressed to Erganzungsgruppen (Operational Training Schools) for tactical training on modern fighters such as the Me 109. (John Weal)

Originally captioned 'So sties ich auf die Engländer herunter' ('So that is how I discovered the English hunter'), the German ace Hauptmann Helmut Wick describes to his colleagues how he succeeded in yet another duel with English pilots, c. September 1940. The German tactics of operating in pairs, ensured success against many RAF pilots who were too inexperienced to know better than to stick to the rigid Flying Attack formations. (Bundesarchiv Bild 146-1986-013-04, Bild 146-1968-015-19)

YEAR 1940		AIRCRAFT		PILOT, OR 1ST PILOT	2ND PILOT, PUPIL OR PASSENGER	DUTY (INCLUDING RESULTS AND REMARKS)	SINGLE-ENGINE AIRCRAFT				MULTI-ENGINE AIRCRAFT						PASS-ENGER	INSTR/CLOUD FLYING [Incl. in cols. (1) to (10)]	
							DAY		NIGHT		DAY			NIGHT					
MONTH	DATE	Type	No.				DUAL	PILOT	DUAL	PILOT	DUAL	1ST PILOT	2ND PILOT	DUAL	1ST PILOT	2ND PILOT		DUAL	PILOT
							(1)	(2)	(3)	(4)	(5)	(6)	(7)	(8)	(9)	(10)	(11)	(12)	(13)
—	—	—	—	—	—	— TOTALS BROUGHT FORWARD	44.25	185.00		1.50	6.20	40.05		2.15	1.20		26.00		
Aug.	21.	SPITFIRE.	2239.	SELF.	—	SCRAMBLE.		.40											
"	24	"	9494.	"				.40											
		"	"					1.10											
"	25	"	"					.40											
		"	"					1.30											
		"	"					.20											
"	26	"	"			CRASH LANDING. SHELL IN S'BD OUTBOARD GUNS. SIMONE 1ST EXIT.		.40											
		"	"					.50											
"	27	MAGISTER.	N3858			TO ST EVAL.		1.40											
"	28	"	"			TO MIDDLE WALLOP.		1.35											
"	29.	SPITFIRE F				TARGET.		.55											
"	30	" F				PATROL BASE.		.40											
"	31	" F				PATROL BROOKLANDS.		1.10											
"	—	MAGISTER	N3858	"	SGT HORNPIPE	TO ST EVAL		1.30											
				SUMMARY FOR	"B"													
				AUGUST.	FLIGHT SPITFIRE.			28.10		.50									
				1940.	234. SQDN. MAGISTER.			5.45		1.00									
				SIGNED. K.L Benkmel. O.C. "B" FLIGHT.														
				SIGNED. M.V. Blaby O.C. 234 SQDN.														
				GRAND TOTAL [Cols. (1) to (10)] 351 Hrs 15 Mins.		TOTALS CARRIED FORWARD	44.25	199.00		1.50	6.20	40.05		2.15	1.20		26.00		

— Brockbank —

—"Now you let off the black smoke in both engines and let down the undercart while I dive into this cloud hopelessly out of control."

Above:

Pages from the log book of Sergeant Michael Boddington who flew Spitfires with No. 234 Squadron. His log book records not only hours flown, on which aircraft and from which base, but also notable engagements with the enemy, commenting at one point, 'Good interception at 25,000! Beam and front quarter attacks. Blue 1 in the half-crown seats. Rocketed seawards with Hun – just pulled out! Bust seat and very worried.' On a more poignant note he also listed his colleagues killed, wounded or posted as missing during the course of the Battle. But his log book for 1940 ends on an optimistic note nonetheless: 'Termination to an indecisive although fairly active year. With Wishes to see many more Huns in 1941 and none at all by 1942.' His wish was only partly granted. Sergeant Boddington did indeed tackle more than his fair share of 'Huns' with active service in the Middle East and eventual promotion to Squadron Leader, but it would be over four long years before the conclusion of the war. (IWM Documents 7078 77/85/1)

Opposite:

A flying school was established in Lipezk south-east of Moscow where many of the leading lights of the Luftwaffe were first trained. (Bundesarchiv Bild 02292-072)

would have to endure 15 physically demanding, and probably quite terrifying, test dives before they were judged suitable for further training. Those who did not possess the required nerve were transferred. Pilots of multi-engined aircraft spent several further flying hours receiving advanced training in instrument and astronomical navigation as well as the use of radio equipment. Once they had a total of 300 hours' flying time they were then trained in either bomber, reconnaissance or heavy-fighter aircraft before being sent to regular units who operated such aircraft.

The training of the air crew for Germany's bombers was equally specialized. Many were failed pilots who had a thorough understanding of how an aircraft worked but whose interest in aviation was better suited to the role of observer, wireless operator or air gunner. Specialist 'trade' schools were established, similar to those set up for the pilots, which air crew attended to hone their particular skill. There was, however, a significant element of cross-training within each curriculum to ensure that a crew would still be able to function in the event of casualties.

The Luftwaffe approached the training of its pilots with typical thoroughness. They were tested unrelentingly for months on end, and those who did not meet the exacting standards were quickly transferred. Undoubtedly, the Luftwaffe produced some of the world's finest pilots. Experience in combat would ensure that they would rank amongst the world's finest fighters. It was during the Spanish Civil War that Werner Mölders had first introduced the *rötte* system, which was then implemented throughout the Jadgwaffe. Two *rötte* flying together made up a *schwarm*, flying some 300 yards apart, and three pairs made up a *staffel* formation. The leading pair typically flew to one side and slightly ahead, with a staggered formation across the *staffel*. This ensured that, unlike the RAF's vics, German pilots had a clear view of the sky ahead of them. This tactic would give them a distinct advantage in the early months of the Battle of Britain.

Almost 20,000 Luftwaffe personnel had served during the Spanish Civil War, serving nine- to 12-month tours of duty, resulting in an experienced air force prior to the outbreak of the Second

World War. The Luftwaffe hierarchy ensured that once they returned to their units the knowledge they had gained was imparted to their colleagues. The greatest losses, incurred by the Condor Legion, had been as a result of flying in poor weather conditions or night flying. Therefore General Sperrle ordered extensive training to combat this, the only air force to have highly trained pilots in this regard at the outbreak of the Second World War. Since 1935 the Luftwaffe had been indoctrinating their pilots with the belief that they were the best in the world; that during the Spanish Civil War they had been unbeatable, and that now they could approach any future conflict with confidence.

BLITZKRIEG: GERMANY'S LIGHTNING STRIKE

" *… the bulk of that hideous apparatus of aggression which gashed Holland into ruin and slavery in a few days, will be turned upon us. I am sure I speak for all when I say we are ready to face it; to endure it; and to retaliate against it.* "

Winston Churchill, 19 May 1940

BATTLE OF FRANCE

As the British Expeditionary Force was mobilized and deployed to France, so too were four fighter squadrons. They were to serve as an escort to a small bomber fleet, optimistically known as the 'Advanced Air Striking Force'. In reality, from that first deployment in September 1939 until the following spring, events on the frontline were relatively quiet for the RAF. This was to Dowding's heartfelt relief. He had opposed even sending this pitiful force to France, with Britain's own position still unsecured. It would be the start of an uphill battle for Dowding to husband his forces for home defence. He was determined that when the eventual battle for Britain's survival came her fighter defenders should not have already been squandered in the French campaign. Dowding had, of course, already experienced one war on the frontline in France and recognized first-hand how resources could easily drain away for little or no gain. What is more, Dowding had a very prosaic view of the defence that France would be able to mount. In 1939 he had paid a visit to the French air defence system and had been distinctly unimpressed, as his personal assistant later recalled:

The object of the visit was to observe the French air defence system. We landed on this airfield near Lille where the grass was at least knee-high and lined up along the side were a lot of incredibly old aeroplanes with skis in between the wheels, which I didn't think still existed – even in France. We taxied up to the hangar, and lined up there were about a dozen beribboned French generals... Then we got into various motor cars and all went off to a large restaurant for a fabulous lunch, which went on for a good two hours, with an awful lot of wine, which of course 'Stuffy' didn't touch... I could see he was getting extremely uptight but worse was to come, because after lunch all these jolly generals packed into cars again, and we were driven to a cellar where we sat on some hard chairs. In one corner of this cellar was a phone box

Opposite:
The Luftwaffe triumphant: Me 110s fly over Paris. (akg images)

with another hard chair and a French airman sitting on it. Just opposite him was a blackboard covered in squares. We sat there for some considerable time and then the phone rang. The airman answered it and there were lots of 'Oui, oui, oui!' and then the airman put a red arrow on the blackboard. And this went on for an hour or so until the blackboard was covered in arrows of different colours. I don't think anybody knew what the hell it was all about. On the flight back, Stuffy never said a word. He was absolutely silent. I think that's where he got his utter distrust of the French.[58]

Dowding was right in his suspicions. Despite the fact that Britain had revealed the closely guarded secret of radar to the French, they had done little to create an effective early warning system. Although the French air service, the Armée de l'Air, had a paper strength of almost 1,200 combat aircraft, in reality it consisted of largely obsolete fighters that would be no match for a 109. There would be very little that four RAF fighter squadrons and one small bomber fleet could hope to achieve against the might of the Luftwaffe that Göring was amassing on Germany's western borders in late April and early May 1940. It totalled 3,500 modern aircraft, including two air fleets of twin-engined bombers, Stukas for ground attacks, almost 1,000 Me 109s and over 200 Me 110s. It formed up alongside the great massed force of 136 divisions, a grand total of some two million men. This force was divided into three large armies, one of which was meant to persuade the Allied forces that Germany was following the same route she had taken in 1914, with thirty divisions striking into Holland and Belgium. It was hoped that the best British and French troops were to be rushed into Belgium to prevent their progress. Simultaneously, in the south a second army group of 19 divisions would feint towards the Maginot Line, France's best means of defence. But the main attack would in fact come in the centre, where it was

A period of relative inactivity followed the British declaration of war and the deployment of forces to France. Here pilots from No. 87 Squadron practise a scramble to their Hurricane fighters during November 1939 while other RAF airmen settle into their billets for a long winter. (IWM C 465, IWM C 87)

least expected, with 45 divisions together with the Panzer forces breaking through Luxembourg and the supposedly impenetrable mountains and forests of the Ardennes, thereby using mobile armed forces to strike deep into enemy territory.

The Blitzkrieg officially began on 10 May 1940. The Allied governments were in turmoil and in no fit state to launch a coordinated defence in response to it. On the previous day the French premier and his Commander-in-Chief had both temporarily resigned in a fit of pique as they sought to apportion blame for the fiasco in Norway and the lack of preparations to meet the expected German assault. Less than 24 hours later France would be facing the largest army ever assembled against her. The situation was no better in London and as the battle commenced the Chiefs of Staff meeting in Downing Street struggled to absorb the intelligence reports that quickly mounted up. The most momentous decision of the day was in fact being made in Bournemouth. Here representatives from the Labour party met to decide whether to serve in a coalition government that would include representatives from all political parties. Labour agreed but would only do so under a new prime minister. Chamberlain, signatory of the Munich agreement, would have to go. Lord Halifax, the Foreign Secretary, Chamberlain's preferred choice for his replacement, had declined to be considered for the post. This left just one real contender, Winston Churchill.

In the early evening of 10 May, as the British Army moved up towards the Dyle river and as more German paratroopers proceeded to land in advance of them, Churchill was summoned to see the king. Here he agreed to form a national government with just a small War Cabinet to conduct operations. His return journey was made in almost complete silence as the enormity of the task ahead of him sank in. Then he turned to his bodyguard and said, 'You know why I have been to Buckingham Palace, Thompson?' The former Scotland Yard inspector said he did and congratulated him, remarking, 'I only wish the position had come your way in better times, for you have an enormous task.' At this point Churchill's eyes filled with tears as he replied, 'God alone knows how great it is. I hope that it is not too late. I am very much afraid that it is. We can only do our best.'[59]

As the Germany Army proved itself an unstoppable force, the French government unsurprisingly begged for further fighters to help stem the tide. By 13 May there were six Hurricane squadrons in France but that same day Lord Gort himself, the commander of the BEF, pleaded for more just as Churchill promised the British people that the road ahead would be full of 'blood, sweat and tears'. This was followed by a telegram from the French Premier Paul Reynaud requesting a further ten squadrons. Sir Archibald Sinclair, the Secretary of State for Air, and Sir Cyril Newall, Chief of the Air Staff, both vigorously briefed by Dowding, warned against sending any further squadrons. But the matter did not rest there. Reynaud called Churchill personally to plead his case and the Prime Minister summoned Dowding to hear from the man himself as to why the fighters could not be spared. Dowding stressed the dangers Britain would face if her homeland defences were committed to the Battle for France. Fifty-two squadrons had been set as the required number for the effective defence of the British Isles. With every squadron sent to France, and with every pilot lost, Britain's own chance for

An RAF Commanding Officer briefs the men of his squadron in a makeshift operations room somewhere in France, early 1940. The contrast with the highly organized defence system In the United Kingdom could not have been more marked. Operating without the benefits of an early warning system and with poor facilities, the Hurricane squadrons posted to France in support of the BEF suffered a number of casualties. (IWM C 403)

survival diminished. This was not mere melodrama. The losses in France experienced by Fighter Command had already been excessive. The very next day 27 Hurricanes were shot down, 15 pilots killed, and a further two later died from their injuries. This had been part of a concerted, combined Allied attempt to prevent the Germans crossing the River Meuse but it had been a dismal failure.

The pilots themselves were exhausted, frequently forced to fly four or five sorties a day. Denis Wissler was a 19-year-old Pilot Officer with No. 85 Squadron who had been in the RAF less than a year before being posted to France at the beginning of the month. His diary at the beginning of his deployment is full of youthful jubilation at finally being 'in the thick of it' and he remarks on 5 May that he hopes the war will 'warm up soon'.[60] He got his wish. Less than a week later his airfield had been bombed, two of his

fellow pilots had failed to return from a sortie and Denis himself was battling exhaustion. In one instance having had only six hours' sleep in 48 hours, he commented in his diary on Sunday 12 May, 'My God am I tired?' His wartime diary accurately conveys the confusion and general disorganization that British pilots had to contend with. Operating over unfamiliar foreign territory, sometimes even without maps, often at the extremity of their range and with little or no coordination of their actions, it was an impossible task. Frequently pilots were simply responding to sightings of enemy bombers called in by the French equivalent of the Observer Corps and there was little effective communication once they were airborne because of the short range and poor quality of their R/T. Speaking after the war, Peter Brothers later recalled with dissatisfaction the chaotic situation:

Pilots from No. 73 Squadron enjoy the benefits of a snug underground duty office at an airfield in Burgundy, France. The Sergeant Pilot to the right is shown speaking over the field telephone. The reality for many fighter pilots was poor communication links. (IWM C 748)

... communications were appalling; we couldn't get any instructions from anybody. We were trying to make contact with the Air Headquarters to find out what they wanted us to do, and we couldn't get through to them or get any kind of sense. We were having to refuel our own aircraft from jerrycans and start them ourselves. We were starting these Hurricanes on handles, which meant that I'd get into my aircraft and two of the chaps would wind the handles and start it and then we'd leave it idling until we'd got all 12 going. There was no food. One of our chaps spoke fluent French and begged food from a local farm... It was a sense of general chaos.[61]

On 16 May, in light of the rapidly worsening situation in France, further pleas from the French, and comments that Air Marshal Barratt, commander of the British Air Force in France, had made to Newall regarding pilot exhaustion, the decision regarding the squadrons was reviewed. Churchill suggested sending a further six squadrons, but Newall, conscious of the opposition he would face from Dowding, decided that four would have to suffice, with a further two squadrons held in readiness. The Prime Minister then left for France where he was bombarded by French pleas for assistance. Churchill, aware of the growing catastrophe that would

await if France succumbed, decided that, possibly because of a romantic desire to assist an old ally, France's request could not be denied. He telegraphed the War Cabinet that evening stating that the additional six squadrons would now be sent, along with the four that had been decided upon that morning. Due to the primitive conditions of most French airfields, which were increasingly vulnerable to bomb attack, three of the squadrons would in fact continue to be based in England, flying out to France in the morning and returning in the evening.

Nonetheless, Dowding was horrified by the decision and composed a ten-point memorandum for the Air Ministry, which was subsequently circulated to the Air Council, the Chiefs of Staff and finally the War Cabinet. Formally addressed to the Under-Secretary of State for Air, Harold Balfour, this simple two-page document is rightly considered to be one of the key documents in RAF history. Dowding reminded his superiors and the politicians guiding the war effort that his home defence strength had already been whittled down to a mere 36 squadrons, well below the figure of 52 that the Air Ministry itself had set as the standard requirement. For a man well known for his prickly nature and inability to work with politicians, it is a remarkably persuasive document, carefully calculated to hammer home his point without too much criticism of the current war effort and going far beyond his remit as Commander-in-Chief of Fighter Command. The document concludes with the following statement:

I believe that if an adequate fighter force is kept in this country, and if the Fleet remains in being, and the home forces are suitably organised to resist invasion, we should be able to carry on the war single-handedly for some time, if not indefinitely. But if the home defence force is drained away in desperate attempts to remedy the situation in France, defeat in France will involve the final, complete and irremediable defeat of this country.[62]

It had the desired effect. Although the Air Ministry would take over a week to reply to Dowding, and they did not grant him a direct response to his query but simply asked him to draw together preparations to cover the evacuation of the squadrons still in France, the end result was still the same. Churchill would vacillate over the issue throughout the final days of May but no further squadrons were deployed to France. The French continued to plead their case to Churchill but despite the enormous pressure he did not waver, especially once Dowding had personally presented a graph to the Chiefs of Staff illustrating the fighter wastage in France on 3 June. The figures did not lie. Of the total of 452 fighters ultimately deployed to France, only 65 returned home when the force withdrew. Thankfully only 56 pilots were actually killed between 10 and 21 May, 36 were wounded and 18 were taken prisoner. The discrepancy between the number of planes and pilots lost can be explained by the fact that over 100 aircraft suffering minor damage had to be destroyed during the chaotic retreat. Denis Wissler's diary notes the general confusion that characterized the fighting withdrawal in the face of the relentless German advance, and describes his squadron's eventual redeployment to British airfields:

Friday 17 May
...There is a dreadful flap on at the moment. The Germans are pushing on all fronts. We have all instructions ready for an immediate leave, and for the disposal of stores etc.

Sunday 19 May
We left Seclin aerodrome in a great flap, and moved about 40 miles to Merville. I flew in a lot of patrols, one an offensive patrol...

The aerodrome was bombed after a low-flying attack by Me 109s. Once again I was about 20 yards from the bombs, sitting in my aircraft trying to start the engine. Incendiary bombs were also dropped. On landing at Merville in avoiding a DH 89 which taxied across my path I went up on my nose and smashed the prop.

Monday 20 May
All the troops but 20 were packed up in transport vans and sent to Boulogne, plus some of the pilots. The 20 remained behind to service the a/c and one pilot for each machine also stayed. It was death or glory for us today but I missed both by going to lunch. The transport a/c arrived at 6.15 and at 9.30 I landed in England at North Holt, without any of my kit which was all left behind. We lost a further three pilots today ...[63]

These early losses were hard felt. The Venerable Guy Mayfield joined the RAF as a chaplain in 1939, spending the next four years serving at RAF Duxford, and noting in his diary the bitter blow of losing each young pilot:

But by June who will be left? Please God all of them but almost certainly not. And we shall be weeping for our children because they are not. Unlike real children, these young men are mature enough to know what they will miss, as it seems to them, if they go down. Of course, as a Christian, I should say, 'This doesn't matter; the real life starts when this one ends.' I know that is true and I believe it but if the physical joys are pagan, then one is still fond of them. How dreadful to die before finding out how much better life is at thirty than it was even at twenty-two, or how happy marriage can be.[64]

The only advantage to be drawn out of the entire fiasco was the experience it gave to the raw pilots of Fighter Command. They were up against hardened professionals who had often already experienced combat in either Spain or Poland, and if not, had battle-honed tactics to their advantage. As early as March some RAF pilots were recommending changes to both tactics and their aircraft to ensure that they could fight and fly to the best of their ability. Squadron

Leader Patrick 'Bull' Halahan, commander of No. 1 Squadron, had ensured that his Hurricanes would be fitted with steel plates behind the pilot seat to afford extra protection, a move so successful that they were then fitted as standard equipment to all fighters. He was also among the first to realize that British guns were incorrectly harmonized at 400 yards. The first pilots trying to engage enemy planes soon found that it was virtually impossible to do any damage with a .303 round at a distance greater than 250 yards. Getting in close, however terrifying, was crucial. Later this too would be adopted as standard by all squadrons. France also exposed many pilots to the horrors of war and hardened them to the task at hand. Nearly all witnessed the results of strafing runs on fleeing columns, many of which contained defenceless civilians. Seemingly, there were no 'knights of the air' present on these occasions.

The final French pleas for fighters were presented to Churchill on 6 and 11 June, just as the remaining British squadrons prepared to leave. By now defeat was inevitable and six days after the final request France asked Germany for an armistice. Most British pilots were quite relieved to be free of their erstwhile allies. Peter Brothers was one, recalling one particularly galling occasion when the Armée de l'Air had demonstrated its lack of stomach for a fight:

> To our horror, one of the days we were in France we'd landed and were refuelling, and a German bomber, a Dornier 17, flew over the airfield at about 2,000 feet. Fortunately he didn't take any notice of us – he was bound for somewhere else presumably. But there was a French aircraft, a fighter, doing aerobatics over the airfield, and we shouted furiously at

Once the Blitzkrieg was launched the Hurricane pilots deployed to France gained vital experience in the art of aerial combat. 'Cobber' Kain of No. 73 Squadron, top, shown in the cockpit of his Hurricane, was the first Allied 'ace' of the war with five or more confirmed kills. Other pilots such as Squadron Leader 'Bull' Halahan of No. 1 Squadron quickly proved themselves exemplary leaders. Here is he is shown (sixth from the left) with the fellow members of his squadron outside their mess at Neuville-sur-Ornain. Dowding's refusal to commit large-scale resources to the Battle of France ensured that Fighter Command was sufficiently manned to fight the subsequent Battle of Britain effectively. (IWM C 188, IWM C 1293)

the French squadron commander to get on the radio and to tell him about this Dornier 17. To our surprise the French squadron commander said that this pilot was only authorized for aerobatics this morning and not for combat, which didn't impress us very much.[65]

It was a comment not so much directed against the courage of individual French men and women, of which there are many recorded instances, but rather the uncoordinated, confused but still overly bureaucratic way the French government and military High Command chose to conduct their defence.

Churchill meanwhile had tried to prepare the British public for the defeat and the lonely road that lay ahead as early as the 19 May, declaring to the House of Commons:

> Our task is not only to win the battle – but to win the War. After this battle in France abates its force, there will come the battle for our island – for all that Britain is, and all that Britain means. That will be the struggle.[66]

The oil-covered body of a British soldier lies on the beach at Dunkirk at low tide after being washed ashore hours after the evacuation. (IWM COL 291)

Dowding, for one, was heartily relieved. On hearing the news of the capitulation of France he reportedly turned to Neville Chamberlain and commented, 'Thank God we're alone now.'

DUNKIRK

As the British and French governments haggled over the number of Hurricanes to deploy on the frontline to halt the Blitzkrieg, another crisis was developing. The BEF had managed to stage a fighting retreat and converge on the small fishing port of Dunkirk. Trapped on the French beaches, they would be rescued by what today is often regarded as a miracle. A flotilla of craft of all shapes and sizes sailed out of British harbours to carry home Britain's beleaguered army. In reality, although the so-called 'little ships' captured the imagination of the time and successfully portrayed a mood of defiance, this was a carefully planned and perfectly executed Royal Navy operation. Over the course of eight days, between 27 May and the early hours of the 4 June, 198,229 British soldiers and 139,997 French troops were evacuated from the beaches. This could not have been achieved without the contribution of the RAF. Fighter Command had been tasked with the responsibility of protecting the evacuating troops and this role had fallen to No. 11 Group, the Group command closest to the evacuation beaches.

In the eyes of many of the evacuated soldiers, strafed and bombed almost constantly by the Luftwaffe, their supposed defenders were nowhere to be seen:

> The RAF did a very poor job of defending us. The Germans were working close cooperation with their aircraft. When they wanted support, they called in their dive-bombers and their fighters, who strafed and bombed us to clear the way. And what support did we have? We had no damn thing at all. Not a bloody thing. We were just left to God and good neighbours.[67]

Indeed, Fighter Command was incapable of staging continuous patrols over the evacuation area to protect all of the soldiers all of the

The 'miracle of the little ships' as depicted by the artist Charles Chundall and now part of the Imperial War Museum collection. The evacuation of the BEF across the English Channel against the odds became a powerful rallying point for the British people and a story of defiance, which endures to this day.

The contribution of the 'little ships' was crucial due to the fact that the much larger Royal Navy vessels could not get close enough to the beaches to dock. (IWM ART LD 305)

time. There simply weren't enough aircraft. Air Vice-Marshal Keith Park had only 200 fighters to draw on against Luftwaffe forces of 300 bombers and 550 fighters. That is not to say that a valiant effort was not staged. The British fighter pilots endured an exhausting number of patrols throughout the evacuation period in the face of far superior numbers. Moreover, due to the weather conditions at the time, RAF fighter patrols had to operate above the thick cloud that engulfed most of the area in an attempt to avoid being bounced by any Me 109s. This undoubtedly meant that some Luftwaffe bombers could get through, below cloud level, to attack the beaches beneath them. Patrols were also sent north of the beaches to try to intercept the bomber fleets before they could make their attack. But both attempts would be hampered by the limited time that patrols could spend on the wrong side of the Channel. It was 20 minutes' flying time from Biggin Hill, a key No. 11 Group airfield, to Dunkirk, and this in theory should have allowed each fighter enough fuel for a further 30 minutes over the French coast. However dogfighting, with its ducking and diving, twists and turns, uses up a far greater amount of fuel than a standard patrol and the pilots would often have to turn for home far sooner than intended once their fuel ran low. No surprise then that the evacuees only ever seemed to see their attackers. As George Unwin, a pilot with No. 19 Squadron later recalled:

> They were on the beaches or damned near the beaches. Now very little fighting took place over the beaches. What we tried to do was to stop these people, catch these people before they reached the beaches. There was no point in stopping them when they were over the beaches and so what fighting did go on, most of it would be inland...
>
> Once you had got rid of your ammunition you simply went home ... for more ammunition and to refuel... When you arrived there would be Germans there, always, because they had such a very short distance to come and they had far more aircraft than we had. So the target was there when we arrived so we probably went over, not fighting for more than five minutes, and then off we went... I can understand the army thinking that but they were quite wrong, quite wrong. In fact if we hadn't been there I don't think many of them would have got out.[68]

In common with his fellow Spitfire pilots, this was Unwin's first experience in combat. Most of the Hurricane squadrons, which had been based in France, had been posted to northern England, out of No. 11 Group, for a chance to rest and recuperate. So for the vast majority of British fighter pilots operating over Dunkirk, this was their baptism of fire. They flew, as they had been taught to, in their tight formations of vics, as Unwin later remarked, 'better suited for a Hendon air display'. It was all too often a costly mistake:

> You went in, in formation, in threes, in line astern threes, and you picked off your target, which was supposed to be only a bomber, never supposed to be anything but a bomber, that was the foreseen enemy... So you went in formation attacking a formation of bombers, which flew straight and level, and didn't try to evade you. This was the plan and of course the first lot we saw were a load of 87s... We went in Fighter Command Attack No. 1 in threes and of course we were going about twice as fast as they were and rapidly overhauled them, throttling back trying to get a sight of them, forgetting all about the fact there might be escorts, and their escorts came down and clobbered us. The front three, the CO and his two wingmen, were shot down. One was killed; the CO spent the rest of the war in a prison camp.[69]

Those who wished to survive the war learnt quickly, and eight pilots achieved 'ace' status, with five confirmed enemy kills to their name, during the retreat from France. In total, the number of RAF planes lost during the Dunkirk evacuation was reckoned to be 106. Fifty-six Fighter Command pilots were killed, while eight were taken prisoner and 11 were wounded. For this grim total Fighter Command claimed 390 enemy aircraft. Unfortunately this was a gross overestimation, which occurred all too frequently during the confusion of aerial combat. German documents discovered after the war show that they estimated their losses to be 132 aircraft.

Most importantly, the army was off the beaches, and it had been a real test of the two nations' air forces. On 24 May, on the banks of the River Meuse, Hitler had reined in his Panzers of General Heinz

Guderian's XIXth Armoured Corps. Concerned that already overextended supply lines could be broken, and on the advice of General von Rundstedt, Hitler decided to allow the Panzer force a chance to rearm and resupply. This is what granted the BEF the breathing space it required to make its dash for the sea. In subsequent years this has occasionally been portrayed as Hitler's reluctance to crush the British Empire, an institution for which he had so much respect. This was certainly not the case, and the pause in operations was granted only because it was thought to be an advantage to the German military. Moreover, Göring assured Hitler that the Luftwaffe alone could destroy the retreating British forces, which it conclusively failed to do.

The Luftwaffe did indeed score some notable successes over Dunkirk. The destroyer *Grenade* was sunk on 29 May by air attack, and a further three British destroyers and one French destroyer were also lost thanks to the efforts of German pilots. But the flotilla of small ships was much harder to hit, and this, together with the actions of the Hurricane and Spitfire pilots, prevented wholesale slaughter of the evacuating soldiers. The British pilots may well have been frequently flying outmoded tactics but the German bombers in particular proved to be easy targets, especially when caught without their fighter escorts.

As on the French frontline the British pilots were operating without the benefit of radar, at the limit of their range and with the added worry of running out of fuel and being forced to ditch in the treacherous Channel. With these factors taken into consideration the successes these novice pilots achieved were quite remarkable. Hugh Dundas, a 19-year-old Spitfire pilot with 616 (South Yorkshire) Squadron later recounted the difficulties of operating over Dunkirk:

RAF pilots shot down during the fighting over Dunkirk would often require ingenuity and luck to make it back to England. The original wartime caption for this image states that this Fighter Command pilot was shot down over the Belgian border and had to disguise himself as a local peasant while on the run before finally making it home 12 days later. (IWM CH 361)

There was this enormous great pall of smoke, which was rising up from, I think, some oil tanks that had been set on fire – a huge black pillar of smoke that came up and spread out and then levelled off and went down the Channel for a distance of 75 to 100 miles. Underneath that there was a lot of haze and general mayhem. It was altogether a very confusing scene: cloud, smoke. I think that's one of the reasons why perhaps the army had the impression that the Royal Air Force wasn't there half the time, because there was no control. We were outside the range of our own radar. We just had to go in there. All the time one was playing a game of blind man's bluff. Very often one wasn't at the right height. Of course, the Germans were operating from fields that were comparatively close. They could come in and out very quickly. There was an awful lot of luck as to whether one was in the right place at the right time. Somebody looking back at it from an historical perspective who was there imagines the coast of France, and Dunkirk, and a clear summer sky and lots of things on the beach and the sea and perhaps a little cloud here and there. It wasn't like that at all.[70]

To achieve the dramatic escape from Dunkirk the army was forced to abandon all its heavy equipment and hundreds of vehicles. Soldiers escaped often literally with just the uniforms on their backs and the rifles in their arms, and not even either of those in some cases. Almost 500 tanks had been lost; 38,000 other vehicles, 1,000 heavy guns and countless rounds of ammunition had all been abandoned. Thanks to the evacuation the professional core of the British Army had been preserved and many would successfully avenge their humiliating defeat in France four years later with their return as part of the Normandy invasion. But for the moment the British Army was in no fit state to fight any further battles until it had re-equipped and rearmed. The frontline defenders would now be Fighter Command. Roland Beamont had flown a Hurricane with No. 87 Squadron in France and he bore no illusions regarding the coming task:

After the boat bringing them home from France had been bombed and sunk these RAF airmen were picked up by a destroyer and given the quaintly assorted costumes in the pictures. (IWM CH 385, IWM CH 390)

We who'd been in the French battle came home convinced that there was only one thing that was going to stop the enemy crossing the Channel and that would be us. We could see that coming all the way through the summer. By July and August it was building up to a fury. We knew absolutely that there was just one frontline holding. It had to be us that did it.[71]

He, like many of his compatriots in the air force, was just 19. It would be a heavy burden on such young shoulders throughout the long, hot summer months.

Spitfire Summer: The Air Battle for Britain

> 66 *May it not also be that the cause of civilization itself will be defended by the skill and devotion of a few thousand airmen.* 99
>
> Winston Churchill, June 1940

Preparing for Battle

In one of the most famous photos of the war, taken shortly after the successful Blitzkrieg through France, Göring stands with his High Command at Cap Blanc Nez staring out towards the chalky cliffs of Dover. It was a dream photograph for the German propaganda machine and the allusion was clear – Britain was the next target, and she could be beaten thanks to Germany's unstoppable air force. The Luftwaffe spent most of the latter half of June and early July preparing for the coming battle with the British, following the French surrender. This was their opportunity to organize their forces across their newly conquered territories. Prior to the war, Germany had been divided into four areas, each with its own air fleet capable of acting independently, with both bomber and fighter components under its own command structure, together with communications and administrative systems. The air fleets were perfectly suited to their role of tactical support during the Blitzkrieg, and had accompanied the invading armies so that each had established itself in a new zone of operations stretching from the Norwegian fjords to the heart of Poland and the western coast of France by early summer of 1940.

In light of the expanded responsibilities a fifth air fleet, Luftflotte 5, had been formed in April and posted to Oslo. The territory of Luftflotte 2 stretched from northern Germany, through Belgium and Holland as far south as Le Havre in occupied France. To the west of this stretched Luftflotte 3 in south-western France, and it would be these two latter air fleets that would act as the main striking forces against Britain. The air fleets themselves were divided into Geschwader, or Groups, consisting either of fighters or bombers – Kampfgeschwader (bomber units), Jagdgeschwader (fighter units), Stukageschwader (dive-bomber units) and Zerstorergeschwader (heavy fighter units). Typically a Geschwader had three Gruppen (wings), which were in turn composed of three Staffeln (squadrons). The Gruppe would act as the key operational unit, based generally

Opposite:
Squadron Leader Douglas Bader DSO (front centre) with some of the Canadian pilots of the 242 (Canadian) Squadron at their home station of Duxford. Bader was a champion of the 'Big Wing' tactic during the Battle of Britain for which he was criticized by some after the war. However, George Unwin had a far more favourable impression of his colleague at No. 12 Group decades after the Battle: 'He was an absolute out and out military type Bader was and he had no time for the Hun... He was the finest we ever flew with and the troops, the ground troops worshipped him.
He was a great character, a very forceful character and a very, very good pilot.' (IWM Sound 11544) (IWM CH 1413)

at one airfield and fighting together as a whole under the directions of each air fleet's commander.

At the start of the Battle of Britain, Luftflotte 2 and 3 were commanded by Kesselring and Sperrle respectively, both reporting directly to Göring himself. Kesselring had a genius for organizing and was a gifted, thoroughly capable commander. As a young major in 1929, he had written a report recommending the reorganization of the fledgling German air services prior to the Nazi programme of rearmament. Later in the war he would revert to his earlier career as an army officer and conduct the stubborn German defence of Italy, which won him the grudging admiration of his Allied opponents. He had previously been commander of Luftflotte 1 during the successful invasion of Poland, and was later appointed as commander of Luftflotte 2, responsible for supporting Army Group 'B' during the Blitzkrieg in the West. The one blemish on his thus far impeccable record had been his failure to prevent the escape of the British Army from Dunkirk. Hugo Sperrle, as the former commander of the Condor Legion and leader of Luftflotte 3 during the invasion of France, was another particularly competent addition to the senior Luftwaffe command. Both were promoted to the rank of Field Marshal on 19 July 1940. Their primary role during the last weeks of June was to ensure that their fighter and bomber units had sufficient time to re-equip and rearm. Aerodromes were built and runways improved. For most German pilots, these early days of the summer were an opportunity to take stock, enjoy the fruits of their victories and have a well-deserved rest.

It was also a period of reflection for the German High Command. Flush with their success, there was little doubt that Britain could not be subdued but Hitler preferred the idea of a peace settlement. Unfortunately there was no such talk of peace in Downing Street.

Göring, (sixth from the right) stands amid a group of German officers looking out across the English Channel towards the white cliffs of Dover on 1 July 1940. (IWM HU 1185)

On 18 June, one day after France had requested an armistice, Churchill addressed the House of Commons with probably his most famous of speeches, in which he declared, 'We shall fight on the beaches, we shall fight on the landing grounds, we shall fight in the fields and in the streets, we shall fight in the hills; we shall never surrender'. Although most of the British public, even today, might be able to quote some lines from this legendary piece of oratory, the speech itself was more than just one passage. Churchill spoke for just over 20 minutes, carefully outlining the forces Britain still had at her disposal, as much to reassure the British public as it was to convince the listening American government that there were no plans for capitulation on this side of the Atlantic.

He detailed the strength of the Royal Navy and even the Local Defence Volunteers, but, most significantly, summed up his opinion of the Royal Air Force in comparison to the Luftwaffe and reviewed his opinion of the threat of invasion:

This brings me, naturally, to the great question of invasion from the air, and of the impending struggle between the British and German Air Forces. It seems quite clear that no invasion on a scale beyond the capacity of our land forces to crush speedily is likely to take place from the air until our Air Force has been definitely overpowered. In the meantime, there may be raids by parachute troops and attempted descents of airborne soldiers. We should be able to give those gentry a warm reception, both in the air and on the ground, if they reach it in any condition to continue the dispute. But the great question is: Can we break Hitler's air weapon? Now, of course, it is a very great pity that we have not got an Air Force at least equal to that of the most powerful enemy within striking distance of these shores. But we have a very powerful Air Force which has proved itself far superior in quality, both in men and in many types of machine, to what we have met so far in the numerous and fierce air battles which have been fought with the Germans. In France, where we were at a considerable disadvantage and lost many machines on the ground when they were standing around the aerodromes, we were accustomed to inflict in the air losses of as much as two to two-and-a-half to one. In the fighting over Dunkirk, which was

WAAF plotters at work in the Operations Room of No. 11 Group, Uxbridge. (IWM CH 7698)

a sort of no-man's-land, we undoubtedly beat the German Air Force, and gained the mastery of the local air, inflicting here a loss of three or four to one day after day. Anyone who looks at the photographs which were published a week or so ago of the re-embarkation, showing the masses of troops assembled on the beach and forming an ideal target for hours at a time, must realize that this re-embarkation would not have been possible unless the enemy had resigned all hope of recovering air superiority at that time and at that place.

In the defence of this island the advantages to the defenders will be much greater than they were in the fighting around Dunkirk. We hope to improve on the rate of three or four to one which was realized at Dunkirk; and in addition all our injured machines and their crews which get down safe – and surprisingly, a great many injured machines and

GROUND CREWS

The successes enjoyed by Fighter Command could not have been made without the sustained efforts of their ground crew, who worked tirelessly throughout the summer and are the unsung heroes of the Battle. The significant proportion of photographs of ground crews at work during the Battle were undoubtedly posed, showing as many as six men working on rearming just one plane. In reality, a flight within a squadron, or six aircraft, would have just six men, and they would have to work against the clock to ready the planes for their next sortie. One chief technician later recalled how these posed photographs could create an entirely inaccurate impression and didn't do justice to the care with which they would have to handle the planes and even the ammunition rounds:

One photograph shows an armourer with a belt of ammunition draped around his neck. He would have been shot. Ammunition belts were made up by Station Armoury personnel in the ammunition dump. Cartridges were linked together by spring steel links. Each link had two circular clips on one side and a single clip on the other side. The single clip fitted between the two clips and the inserted cartridge held the links together. As the cartridges were withdrawn the loose links were ejected, together with the empty cartridge cases. Belts were made up generally with two ball cartridges, two armour piercing cartridges and two 'De Wilde' cartridges. The De Wilde cartridges had a hollow bullet filled with an explosive/incendiary mixture. They were very effective in setting target aircraft on fire. Belts were made up on an assembly jig, and then passed through a belt positioning machine. This machine positioned each cartridge in the belt very precisely. Every armourer knew that one cartridge in a belt that was as little as one sixteenth of an inch out of place would ALWAYS cause a gun stoppage so belts were handled with great care and never thrown about.[72]

Ground crew and armourers refill ammunition belts with .303 bullets beside Hawker Hurricane Mark Is of No. 85 Squadron RAF at Lille-Seclin. (IWM C 1519)

An armourer re-arms a Spitfire at RAF Fowlmere, while the pilot speaks with the mechanic. (IWM CH 1458)

men do get down safely in modern air fighting – all of these will fall, in an attack upon these islands, on friendly soil and live to fight another day; whereas all the injured enemy machines and their complements will be total losses as far as the war is concerned.

... I am happy to inform the House that our fighter strength is stronger at the present time relatively to the Germans, who have suffered terrible losses, than it has ever been; and consequently we believe ourselves possessed of the capacity to continue in the war under better conditions than we have experienced before. I look forward confidently to the exploits of our fighter pilots – these splendid men, this brilliant youth – who will have the glory of saving their native land, their island home, and all they love, from the most deadly of attacks.[73]

The pilots themselves largely shared Churchill's unshaken confidence. That is not to say that some pilots weren't feeling the strain of their first experiences in combat and the exhaustion of continuous patrols. Paul Richey, a pilot with No. 19 Squadron, had already claimed ten victories before the end of May but, after being forced to bail out, noted that he frequently felt 'a bit teary'. Guy Mayfield, the RAF chaplain at Duxford, had begun a close friendship with a young pilot officer called Peter Watson, and noticed with alarm the careless attitude he had towards his own life and the dangerous flying practices he had picked up since his combat debut:

I talked to him about low flying; what I've experienced with him is mild compared to what he does in a Spit. I told him plainly and, at the risk of wounding his esteem, that other pilots who like him thought he is doing things in the air [for] which he isn't good enough yet, and, even if he is good enough, are damned silly anyway. I talked about the girl at Norwich, the gist of what I said being that he isn't old enough to be stable yet, and this piece, even from his own account, didn't sound extra hot. He accepted it all and replied in a very depressed way: 'What does it matter? I shall be killed anyway; if not killed, I shall be maimed; there won't be much left to live with, and no job to go to after the end of the war. What kind of experience is this for taking a job and settling down?'

ALBERT KESSELRING

Kesselring was a career army officer who had served during the First World War and did not learn to fly until the age of 48, when he was reassigned to help with the secret development of the Luftwaffe. He was appointed its Head of Administration in 1933 and performed this role so successfully that in 1936 he was appointed Chief of Staff following the death of General Walter Wever in an air accident. However, following Kesselring's disagreements with Erhard Milch he asked to be relieved of his role and placed in an operational capacity instead, becoming head of Luftflotte 1 shortly before the outbreak of war. After a successful campaign in Poland he was appointed head of Luftflotte 2 to spearhead the Blitzkrieg. He continued in this role throughout the Battle of Britain and Operation *Barbarossa*. Transferred to Italy in November 1941, he later became the Commander-in-Chief South, from where he would conduct a stubborn defence of the region for three years. In March 1945 he became supreme commander of the German Army in the West in an attempt to resist the Allied drive towards the Reich. Kesselring, the Luftwaffe Field Marshal, eventually surrendered to Allied troops on 6 May 1945 as Commander-in-Chief of Southern Germany. (IWM HU 51040)

He said the RAF would contract when the war was over; there would be no future for him there. So why not grasp some experience of something, anything, while there is a short time left? We talked and talked for a long time, very frankly about many things with a directness that I never wanted to talk to any young man about. It clouded over the impression of wonderful weather at Old Catton, the spring and the distant hopes. Hanging over everything is the threat of the ominous and immediate future. We both of us smelled death. So he feels the hurry to do things while there is still time, and before they go or he goes. Love and life are flying away ...[74]

A veteran of the First World War Luftstreitkrafte, Hugo Sperrle (1885–1953) served as the commander of the Condor Legion during the Spanish Civil War and led Luftflotte 3 during the Blitzkrieg and the Battle of Britain. Luftflotte 3 was redeployed to North Africa in 1941 where his forces acted in support of Rommel and he eventually became head of the Luftwaffe in the West shortly before the D-Day landings. He was dismissed from this position in August 1944 for so-called failings; however in reality the limited number of available aircraft restricted the Luftwaffe's chances of success. (IWM MH 6096)

There was no tendency towards a feeling of inferiority in personnel or equipment. I think we had a respect for the Messerschmitt 109. We thought it was probably a very capable aeroplane but we didn't think there was any reason why it should be more capable than our Hurricanes.[75]

But many European and American observers did not share this confidence. Joseph Kennedy, the American Ambassador to London, had already evacuated his children back to the United States unconvinced by Britain's ability to resist. General Weygand, the defeated French Commander-in-Chief, dismissively commented, 'In three weeks, England will have her neck wrung like a chicken.'[76] In an effort to disprove such defeatist attitudes, and convince the United States that Britain would be worth supporting in her war effort, Fighter Command was ordered to take the attack to the German forces gathering along the French coast through a series of offensive patrols. Once again operating without the benefits of their highly effective defence system, and with all the disadvantages that had characterized their operations over Dunkirk, they were not particularly successful. Peter Brothers later recalled the dissatisfaction with which the pilots viewed these missions:

We were doing offensive patrols at around 15,000 feet, penetrating into France and coming back up the coast, and the snag was that the Germans took no notice of you on the way in – they waited until you were on the way home and they knew you were getting short of fuel. The sun was behind you, so they could then take off and climb up and attack you from behind when you were on the way home and these ... we decided were a terrible waste of time, because all we did was suffer casualties without very much success. And finally, fortunately, Stuffy Dowding himself came down to Manston where we were ... and we complained bitterly to him. He grunted and said nothing, and the next day the whole series was cancelled ...[77]

Peter's premonition of his early death was not incorrect. Tragically he was shot down on 26 May near the coast of Calais and was last seen swimming strongly towards the shore. But for the most part Fighter Command pilots, as recalled by Roland Beamont of No. 87 Squadron, retained a buoyant confidence despite their exhaustion or the prospect of taking on a numerically superior enemy, and never even entertained the thought that they could lose to their foes:

What is remarkable about this account is the fact that Brothers, a lowly flight lieutenant, was able to express his concerns to Dowding himself and, what is more, that Dowding was willing to amend tactics or even alter strategy as a result. This would later be in marked contrast to the Luftwaffe, where many pilots on the frontline felt that they were not being used to the best of their abilities throughout the course of the war and suffered severe losses as a result.

The Luftwaffe would also be handicapped by a general state of confusion about how to conduct any campaign against Britain. Hitler clearly hoped for a peace settlement, even issuing a temporary ban on the Luftwaffe flying into British air space following the French formal surrender on 22 June, and there was little early agreement about how best to proceed at the highest levels. Eight days later, on 30 June, Göring issued his first Directive, stating that the task of the Luftwaffe was to destroy the RAF and to cut off Britain's overseas supplies. However only weakly defended targets should be selected and attacks carried out only under perfect weather conditions. Presumably Göring was hoping that a limited assault together with

Churchill's inspiring oratory rallied the British people to their nation's defence during their 'finest hour' and he became the living embodiment of the national spirit of defiance. (IWM MH 26392, IWM PST 14971)

an economic siege would be enough to force the British to the negotiating table.

However, with the British failing to make any formal peace overtures, Hitler allowed the Supreme Command of the Armed Forces (Oberkommando der Wehrmacht – OKW) to begin making formal plans for a proposed invasion. As a result, on 2 July the OKW issued a request for planning documents for an invasion, stating that the Führer would be willing to consider sanctioning this if air superiority could be achieved. The Luftwaffe was thus called upon to specify when German air superiority over British skies could be

Winston Churchill inspects a Thompson sub-machine gun during a tour of invasion defences near Hartlepool, 31 July 1940. (IWM H 2646)

guaranteed. This was followed by an order issued on 11 July by Göring's Chief of Staff, Hans Jeschonnek, which indicated that the armament industry was also to be considered a target, and that it should take just two to four weeks to achieve the defeat of the RAF.

That same day Admiral Raeder visited Hitler at his mountaintop retreat near Berchtesgaden in Bavaria. Raeder was adamant that an invasion should not be attempted, fearful of the damage that a still powerful British navy could achieve, particularly against his much smaller force. Raeder's main aim was to convince Hitler that a blockade would be a more effective way to secure peace rather than attempting an amphibious assault. Raeder envisaged concentrated air attacks on the British mainland, combined with air and U-boat attacks on shipping attempting to bring in much-needed supplies. Hitler agreed that invasion should only be considered as a last resort. Nonetheless, the Führer allowed the plans for a purported invasion to continue apace. Over 12 and 13 July detailed scenarios were prepared, involving an assault by 39 German divisions, or half a million men. Entitled Operation *Löwe* (Lion), the plans involved what the Chief of Operations Staff General Alfred Jodl optimistically referred to as a 'river crossing', which of course bore little reality to the dangers that would involve crossing the heavily defended, often stormy Channel.

On 16 July Hitler issued Directive No. 16, formally stating his intention to invade the British Isles if it became necessary and granting the operation a new name – *Seelöwe* (Sealion):

As England, despite the hopelessness of her military situation, has so far shown herself unwilling to come to any compromise, I have therefore decided to begin preparations for, and if necessary to carry out, an invasion of England.

The aim of this operation is to eliminate Great Britain as a base from which the war against Germany can be fought, and, if necessary, the island will be completely occupied.[78]

Three days later Hitler made what he referred to as his 'Last Appeal to Reason' to the British government and the British people.

Dowding, as head of Fighter Command, reported to the Chief of the Air Staff, who in turn reported to the Air Ministry, or more specifically the Air Council, which ran the Ministry. The Air Council was chaired by the Secretary of State for Air, who was himself directly responsible to the War Cabinet. Here we see the members of the Air Council meeting in July 1940. Sixth from the left is the Rt. Hon. Sir Archibald Sinclair, Secretary of State for Air and to his right is Air Chief Marshal Sir Cyril Newall, Chief of the Air Staff. (IWM CH 966)

Addressing an electrified Reichstag Hitler declared, 'A great Empire will be destroyed, an Empire which it was never my intention to destroy or even to harm... I consider myself in a position to make this appeal since I am not the vanquished begging favours but the victor speaking in the name of reason.' Remarkably, the BBC decided to issue its own response to this appeal before the government formally rejected the offer. A *Daily Express* journalist called Sefton Delmer announced the repudiation in rather colourful language that same

evening, stating: 'Let me tell you what we here in Britain think of this appeal of yours to what you [are] pleased to call our reason and common sense. Herr Führer and Reichkanzler, we hurl it right back at you, right in your evil smelling teeth ...'[79]

The Luftwaffe largely ignored the Directive's plans for the proposed invasion, as they were too busy compiling their own strategy for an independent air assault. Moreover, Göring was convinced that *Sealion* would not be necessary once the full might

Next page:
Hitler addresses the Reichstag at the Kroll Opera House in Berlin on 19 July 1940 with his self-titled 'Last Appeal to Reason' speech. (akg images, ullstein bild)

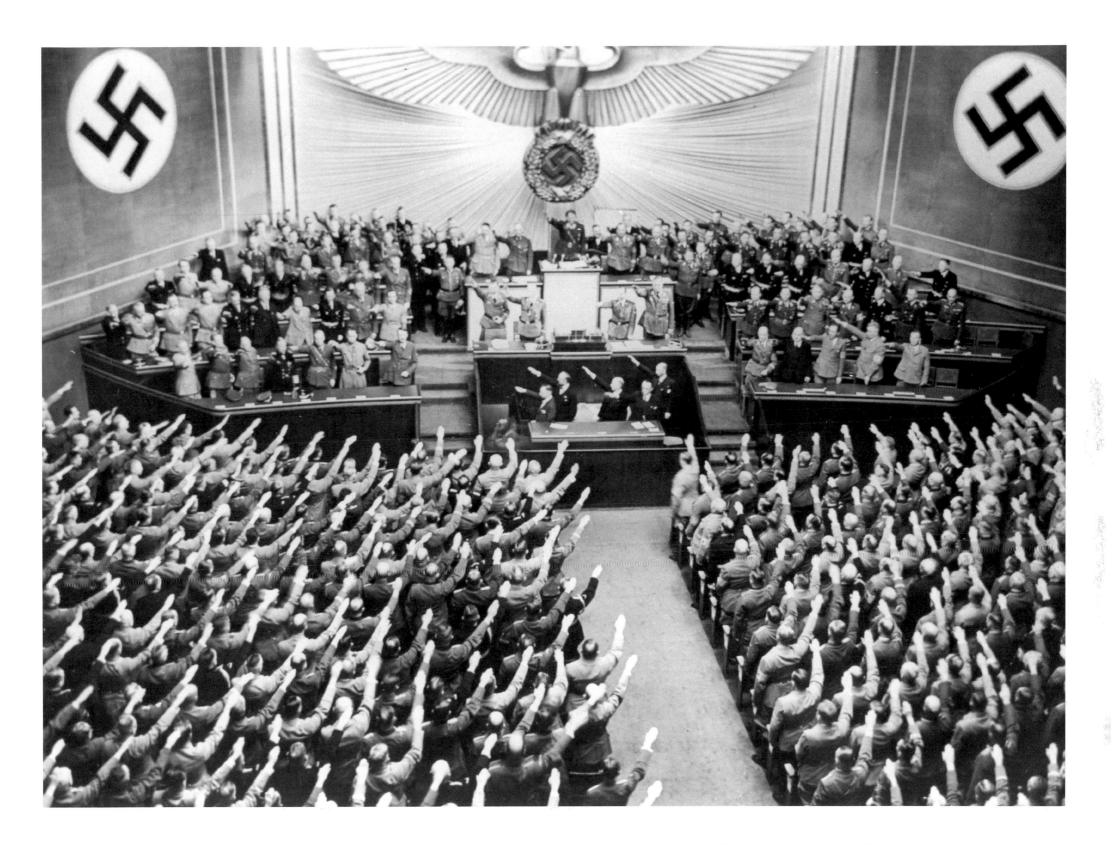

LORD BEAVERBROOK AND THE 'SPITFIRE FUNDS'

The production of Britain's fighter defence had begun slowly. The first Spitfires and Hurricanes did not roll off the production line as quickly as anticipated by the Air Ministry. Throughout the mid- to late 1930s production began in fits and starts. It was hampered by the difficulty of producing an aircraft as highly engineered as the Spitfire, and new production facilities were required to mass-produce fighter planes properly as Britain slowly began her rearmament process. It took an astonishing 13,000 hours to build a Spitfire, roughly three times longer than either an Me 109 or a Hurricane. Not surprising then that aircraft production was at the forefront of Churchill's mind. His solution was an abrasive Canadian who knew nothing about aircraft but everything about steamrolling people so that he got his way. Max Aitken, Lord Beaverbrook, was a self-made millionaire who had begun his career in finance but had reinvented himself as the baron of Fleet Street, acquiring a controlling share of the *Evening Standard*, the *Daily Express* and the *Sunday Express* among others. He had previously served as Minister of Information during the First World War but it was in this second world conflict that Beaverbrook would come into his own. Churchill, a long-time personal friend, decided to appoint him as Minister for Aircraft Production, a post reporting directly to the War Cabinet, on 11 May 1940. His contribution to the actual production of aircraft has been widely debated ever since. In many ways his appointment came after the foundation for effective production had been laid by others. But his energy and ruthlessness, along with his direct access to Churchill, ensured that he was capable of smoothing any kinks in the system throughout the summer months, cutting through the red tape of bureaucracy that had existed when the Air Ministry had been responsible for production.

Throughout the pre-war years British rearmament had been dwarfed by Germany's. Critically, however, this did not matter as much as it might be presumed. Most pre-war production was based around outdated models. From 1939 the production of fighter aircraft was a primary focus of rearmament and by the following year Britain, in a display of typical thoroughness, actually out-produced Germany by an astonishing 47 per cent. Hitler had crucially failed to place the German economy on a war footing, reluctant to impose the privations on his civilian population that would invariably result. The British government had no such qualms and mobilized her people on an unparalleled level. Herein lay Beaverbrook's most remarkable contribution to the Battle of Britain. With the instincts of a true tabloid genius, Beaverbrook realized that a battle fought by a few hundred men needed to become a struggle that all could share in. On 10 July he produced an appeal in all the national newspapers declaring: 'We want aluminium and we want it now. New and old, of every type and description, all of it.

The funding of fighter aircraft captured people's imaginations throughout Britain and the Commonwealth. It began during the height of the Battle of Britain but continued throughout the war. Here the Leeward Islands are thanked for their donation of funds to purchase new Spitfires. (IWM PST 8261)

We will turn your pots and pans into Spitfires and Hurricanes, Blenheims and Wellingtons.' It was the start of something extraordinary. From the royal family to those of the humblest origins, families throughout the country stripped their kitchens bare to make their small contribution to the coming defence. In reality, of course, very little of this aluminium was used in the production of fighters but it was a brilliant campaign that made the public feel that they 'were doing their bit'.

Of a far greater material advantage were the so-called Spitfire Funds. The idea had first originated in Jamaica when a newspaper there had cabled Beaverbrook to ask how much it would cost to buy a bomber. The figure of £20,000 was quoted and the readers subsequently raised the amount in just a couple of weeks. The popularity of this idea quickly grew and Beaverbrook used all his organizational skill to turn it into a national campaign. A figure was set of £5,000 for fighter aircraft (although the real cost of production was closer to £12,000) and villages, towns, societies and clubs throughout the country and the Commonwealth contributed to the appeal, the Spitfire in particular capturing the heart of the population and inspiring the greatest number of donations. By the middle of August, at the height of the Battle of Britain, over three million pounds had been raised. Before the Blitz had even begun and the British public were truly on the frontline of war, Beaverbrook had harnessed a mood of defiance and fired ordinary people's imaginations. What is more, a further 1,500 Spitfires would be airborne directly as a result of these appeals, each proudly bearing the name of their contributing fund on their fuselage.

The response to the 'Saucepans for Spitfires' campaign was huge, although many families came to regret the loss of certain essential items, particularly as the war went on and these items became harder to replace. How many were actually melted down to turn into planes is a debatable point although it was a fantastic morale boost to the civilian population to feel that they were contributing to the war effort. (Topfoto)

of German air power had been directed against Britain. Picked up by secret German radio message and decrypted at Bletchley Park, the British were well aware of Göring's boasts of bringing Britain to her knees.[80] This would be Göring's victory, without any assistance from the rival services of the army or navy.

The one significant problem with the battle-winning scenario that Göring envisaged was his fatal miscalculation of the strength of Fighter Command. As plans were made for the Kanalkampf – Battle over the Channel – Göring remained in blissful ignorance of the true strength of forces he had at his disposal. Campaigns in Norway,

Operation *Sealion* was the proposed invasion of Britain by the German forces. How successful such an invasion would have been is open to debate. Without control of the skies the invasion could not be launched. However even if this had been achieved, the Royal Navy would have posed huge difficulties for the Kriegsmarine and the Kriegsmarine was reluctant to commit to such a hazardous scheme when the Royal Navy was much larger and more powerful. But for the British people and the British government it seemed a very real possibility throughout the summer of 1940, especially when invasion barges were massing in French ports, clearly visible in this aerial photograph of the harbour of Boulogne in July 1940. (IWM MH 6657)

the Low Countries and France had taken their brutal toll, and at the start of the Battle of Britain the Luftwaffe could muster only 1,380 bombers and 428 dive-bombers (see Appendix 6), nowhere near the 5,000 Göring frequently referred to in his propaganda. Later in the summer, he would react with astonishment when he calculated the actual resources he had at his disposal, lamenting, 'Is this my Luftwaffe?' In addition to available bombers, he had a further 1,100 frontline fighters. With these forces combined, he still enjoyed an overwhelming superiority against the British, outnumbering their fighter defenders of 754 by almost five to one. But, seen from the German pilots' perspective, there was actually only a small advantage in terms of fighter aircraft. The bombers were simply potential 'kills' for the British fighters, as they would be incapable of tackling a Spitfire or Hurricane themselves. If the British fighters were deployed correctly, and without the dated tactics that had characterized the Battle of France, then the dice would not be so heavily stacked against them as was commonly believed.

Of course, the number of British fighters had also been severely curtailed by the RAF's efforts in France and over Dunkirk. However, since the outbreak of war strenuous efforts had been made to revolutionize the production process, with a streamlining of procedures, the creation of new factories and a newly appointed Minister for Aircraft Production – Lord Beaverbrook. Britain could therefore be confident of an increased output of Spitfires and Hurricanes throughout the summer months. As Churchill had pointed out, damaged fighters could also be patched back together and redeployed to fight again, thanks largely to the efforts of the Civilian Repair Organization (CRO), which in a remarkable act of foresight had been created a full year before the outbreak of war. In contrast, any Luftwaffe planes that were forced to crash-land on British soil were immediately lost to the German war effort and, somewhat ironically, could even end up being scrapped for use in British war industries.

But now the real danger lay in surviving the fighting over the Channel, reviled by British and German pilots alike, and whose icy waters claimed the lives of all too many young men that fateful July in 1940.

Hitler meets with some of his planning staff in 1940, including (l to r) Field Marshal Walther von Brauchitsch, General Alfred Jodl, Field Marshal Wilhelm Keitel and two unidentified Kriegsmarine staff officers. The photograph was taken at Berghof, Hitler's mountain retreat from where he made many of his major strategic decisions during the war. On 17 July he met with his military chiefs to discuss Operation *Sealion* and again on 31 July to discuss tentative plans regarding the proposed invasion of Russia. (IWM HU 75542)

THE CHANNEL BATTLES

The Kanalkampf was the first phase of the Battle of Britain. In reality, Kesselring and Sperrle had already begun unauthorized attacks on convoys in the Channel in late June, as Göring and the OKW muddled towards a decision on how to tackle the problem of the British. Now this policy was officially endorsed with specific and sustained attacks on the coastal convoys as well as transatlantic shipping bringing in much-needed supplies to the beleaguered island. Raids were also planned on Britain's ports and harbours.

The aim of these attacks were two-fold – the destruction of the shipping would significantly dent Britain's war effort and the fighters that would be invariably drawn up to defend them would be engaged in a battle of attrition. Moreover, the destruction of port or harbour defences would also make for easier landings, if an invasion should prove to be necessary. In particular, it was believed that slow-moving coastal convoys would make for easy pickings now they were in reach of Stuka units based at the new German bases Luftflotte 2 and 3 had created throughout Belgium, Holland and France.

ENGAGING THE ENEMY

The best way to tackle an enemy plane was to dive from a greater height out of the sun, hence the old Royal Flying Corps adage, 'Beware the Hun in the sun', which still rang true during the Battle of Britain. The aim was to get in a short-fire burst and pull away, in a classic fighting manoeuvre known as the 'bounce'. However, if sufficient height could not be gained in time then the only solution was to dogfight, or to try and get on your opponent's tail through a better use of speed or manoeuvrability. If a pilot could turn his aircraft tightly then he had a better chance of getting behind his opponent and into a firing position. The Me 109 could outdive a Spitfire, but the Spitfire had a smaller turning radius and this saved many RAF pilots' lives. George Unwin later recalled getting tangled up with some Messerschmitts when the turning ability of the Spitfire was his saving grace:

> ... in the distance I saw some ack-ack, and I went, I was at about 25,000 feet, and I went towards it and suddenly saw these waves of German bombers coming in. It was a fascinating sight and I was watching these things and I wondered whether anyone was going to attack them. There seemed to be hundreds of them pouring in and I forgot all about the fact that they may have an escort... Damn fool, I was lucky again! Anyway, I went into a tight turn and stayed in it and shot at several of them as they went through my sights and I actually shot two of them down... That was what probably saved me; you kept on turning and turning because the Messerschmitt couldn't turn like a Spitfire and I got away with it.[81]

Firing too soon was an easy mistake for novice pilots and wasted precious machine-gun or cannon rounds, especially once you consider that fighter planes carried only between 12 and 15 seconds' worth of ammunition. An ability to judge distance was essential and the optimum range was 250 yards. But as George Unwin later recalled it was all too easy to miscalculate:

> ... it was just sheer estimation, sheer estimation. I mean, you see an aeroplane and it is astonishing how close you think he is and you are not within 400 yards of your estimation. Two hundred and fifty yards, which was the optimum range against an aeroplane, most people estimate as 600 yards in the air against an airborne target.[82]

It was a finely honed skill not only to judge the distance but also to estimate where to aim, especially at enemy fighters travelling at 300mph. If the target was not flying on the same course as the attacker then the pilot would have to line up a deflection shot, which meant allowing for the speed, direction and distance of the target and placing a stream of bullets in its intended path. It should come as no surprise that many of the most successful aces on both sides were either seasoned hunters or useful with a shotgun prior to the outbreak of war. The South African ace Sailor Malan had grown up on a farm, while Adolf Galland had been taken on his first hunting trip when he was just five.

Few pilots allowed themselves to think of the man in the opposing plane during the heat of battle. As Pete Brothers later recalled:

> ... you don't think much of the individual, because you don't think you've hit him and you hope that he will bail out or something; it's the aeroplane you've hit ... normally it was more of a game if you like, you were outwitting and shooting down another aircraft, you were simply hitting metal.[83]

The 'kill' of a German Me 110 as recorded by a gun camera on board a British fighter. In the first frame the Me 110 is shown trying to escape through an increase in speed; the engines are at full throttle with twin trails of exhaust smoke. Tracer ammunition streaming through the air can be seen in the second and third frames with an eventual hit on the port engine and the Me 110 finally bursts into flames. (IWM C 2344)

As a result, Oberst Johannes Fink, commander of the bomber unit Kampfgeschwader (KG) 2, was appointed as Kanalkampfführer, with executive control over two Stukagruppen and a Jagdgeschwader of fighters, the latter designed to 'bounce' the RAF fighters as they attempted to engage the Stukas. Fink was a First World War veteran and an ardent believer in the power of the dive-bomber, having seen its potential from Guernica through to France. He had a force of at least 60 to draw upon, as well as 75 twin-engined bombers and at least 200 fighters from nearby Jagdgeschwaders.

This battle-hardened veteran was not one to stand on ceremony, and set up his command centre in an old bus at Cap Blanc Nez, with a clear view of the English coast ahead of him. One of the first actions Fink authorized was the establishment of a mobile radar station. The Kriegsmarine had developed these 'Freya' units, supposedly named after the Norse goddess of war, in 1937. Unlike the British radar stations, which were immobile radio masts, Freya could be transported and set up at any location. Fink would now use it to track and locate convoys, supplemented by reports from reconnaissance planes. The British would also make use of radar during the ensuing battle, but it was not as effective as they'd hoped. Although the British could vector in on enemy formations, there was not enough time to identify whether the approaching target were Stukas, which Fighter Command would want to engage, or Messerschmitts, which Dowding had ordered them to avoid. The greatest difficulty, however, was attempting to get fighters airborne in time. It took less than ten minutes to cross the Channel but 15 minutes for Hurricanes and Spitfires to gain the necessary height to safely engage the enemy.

The first major attack occurred on 4 July when 33 Stukas appeared above Portland in Dorset and dived on the assembled convoys as well as naval installations in the harbour. No British fighters could be scrambled in time to counter the attack. One solution would have been to mount standing patrols but Fighter Command still did not have sufficient aircraft to offer that kind of continuous defence. Nor did Dowding want to allow the battle of attrition that Göring was so keen to initiate. Here the Ultra

recordings that Frederick Winterbotham was forwarding to Dowding from Bletchley Park played a key role in confirming Dowding's desire to closely husband his precious resources:

> We had a signal from Göring establishing his strategy with his commanders. He told them that they were to fly over Britain and bring the whole of the Royal Air Force to battle because only that way could it be destroyed in the time that they had... It became evident that Hitler and his generals wouldn't contemplate an invasion unless they had absolute control of the air over the Channel.[84]

The attack was not entirely unexpected, as German reconnaissance planes had passed overhead the day before. Nonetheless, it was a devastating strike at the British home defences, directed in particular at HMS *Foylebank*, an anti-aircraft ship anchored just off the south-east breakwater within Portland harbour. As part of Portland's key

Richard Eurich's painting of an air fight over Portland, Dorset 1940. The first attack on the naval installation here, an important destination for convoy shipping, took place on 4 July 1940. (IWM Art LD 769)

defences she would fly a yellow flag if enemy planes were reported and a red flag if the raiders were seen approaching. She had reportedly been flying the yellow flag for several days when the Stukas suddenly dived out of the sun, taking the crew by surprise. Manning one of the 2-pounder (40mm) rapid-fire pom-pom guns was 23-year-old Leading Seaman Jack Mantle. Despite his young age he was already a seasoned veteran, having joined the navy at 16, and had already claimed one enemy raider during coastal convoy duties, for which he had been Mentioned In Dispatches. He never left his post, despite being wounded in a bomb blast by the attack of one of the first Stukas, and managed to destroy another as its machine-gun fire raked across his gun position. His extreme gallantry under fire was witnessed by *Foylebank's* captain, who subsequently recommended him for the Victoria Cross, Britain's highest award for gallantry. His brief yet poignant citation was later published in the *London Gazette* on 3 September:

> Leading Seaman Jack Mantle was in charge of the Starboard pom-pom gun when HMS *Foylebank* was attacked by enemy aircraft on the 4th of July 1940. Early in the action his left leg was shattered by a bomb, but he stood fast at his gun and went on firing with hand-gear only: for the ship's electric power had failed. Almost at once he was wounded again in many places. Between his bursts of fire he had time to reflect on the grievous injuries of which he was soon to die but his great courage bore him up till the end of the fight, when he fell by the gun he had so valiantly served.

If the Fighter Command pilots had the good fortune either to be vectored correctly or to stumble upon a formation of unescorted Stukas then they were easy targets for the increasingly experienced British pilots, particularly as they made their dash across the Channel for home. As former Flying Officer Geoffrey Page later recounted:

> Don't forget, after the Stukas pulled out of their dive at sea level, they had to fly back to France, at about ten feet above the waves. In our Hurricanes, by throttling back the engines, we could sit behind the Stuka and there was the poor rear gunner with just one pop gun to

defend his aeroplane while we were sitting there with eight machine guns. They were a pretty easy target and I'm not proud of the fact that one just knocked them off like skittles.[85]

To reduce the risk for the increasingly vulnerable Stukas, the German fighters would have to operate almost exclusively as a defensive screen for the German bombers. The German fighters had been practising a policy of 'frie Jadg' – 'free hunting' fighter sweeps. This had allowed them to act in conjunction with bombing raids but relatively independently, swooping down to bounce the RAF fighters as they strove to protect the precious convoys. Now they would be forced to be tied more closely to the vulnerable bombers. Theo Osterkamp was the colourful Kommodore of Jagdgeschwader 51, one of the fighter units that fell under Fink's operational control. Osterkamp was old-school, a veteran of the First World War, where he had been a leading ace and a friend of the Red Baron; he was already 48 years old by the time of the Channel battles. Osterkamp wanted to emulate his successes of the First World War, where he had scored 32 confirmed victories, and engage enemy fighters. He was horrified by the thought of being forced to protect the bomber fleets. As a result, Fink and Osterkamp reached a gentleman's agreement whereby the twin-engined fighters, the Me 110s, would perform escort duty instead of the Me 109s.

The raids therefore began to take on a predictable quality. In the early morning, meteorological units from Luftflotten 2 and 3, and occasionally even Luftflotte 5, would sortie to report back on the projected weather conditions for the rest of the day, which would help determine the kind of attacks to be made. Throughout the day, reconnaissance planes would be deployed to photograph likely targets and to report on the damage created by previous attacks. These land-based targets were usually attacked at dusk but if Freya reports pinpointed the movements of large convoys then these could be attacked at any point during the day.

In reality, both the British and German fighter pilots were operating with significant drawbacks and the losses quickly began to mount for both sides. On 7 July, just four days after the first major raid on Portland, six British fighters were shot down and four pilots killed. Besides the obvious dangers of being bounced while trying to protect the vital convoys, there were also the more mundane risks of extreme tiredness and boredom associated with such patrols, which made the pilots even more vulnerable to surprise attack, as Denis Wissler noted in his diary:

> We escorted convoys all day long and I did four-and-a-half hours flying…We didn't see a single thing again today, soon I feel we shall run into a packet. I felt very tired going round and round the convoys and only just managed to stop myself dozing off.[86]

The following evening, 8 July, a further three British pilots were killed and No. 79 Squadron, which had been in continuous action since the Battle of France, was posted north to regroup, rest and recuperate. Leutnant Albert Striberny was a German fighter pilot who was shot down that same evening as he attempted to protect a Dornier 17:

> Having reached an altitude of 4,500m over the Channel we found ourselves in sunshine but saw that there were a lot of cumulus clouds over the English coast and Dover. The Do 17, contrary to our agreement, dived into the clouds and us three Bf 109s had to move together and follow him. At about 1,700m, the clouds ended and together we flew over Dover. Besides photographing, the Dornier threw out some small bombs and then climbed back into cloud and we again joined up and followed. When the clouds ended, I quickly noticed the Do 17 near us but then, much higher, saw the sun shining on many aircraft – Spitfires!

Theo Osterkamp shown inspecting the Mc 108 'Taifun' ('Typhoon') in 1938. Osterkamp served during the First World War with 32 victories to his name. With the outbreak of the Second World War he commanded Jagdgeschwader 51 during the Battle of France and later commanded all fighter aircraft in Luftflotte 2. He was eventually dismissed from the Luftwaffe in 1944 following a series of disagreements with High Command. (Bundesarchiv Bild 183-H16409)

ADOLF 'SAILOR' MALAN

Malan was born in Wellington, a small town in the wine region of the Western Cape, South Africa. An early career in the South African Merchant Navy earned him his nickname 'Sailor', a name that stuck even once he decided to join the RAF. He learnt to fly in 1936 and after receiving his wings was posted to No. 74 Squadron. It was to be his home for the next ten years and he duly became a Pilot Officer shortly before the outbreak of war. Early on Malan had been earmarked as a leader of outstanding ability, a solid pilot and a crackshot. It was unfortunate then that his first foray into operational duties had tragic consequences. In the early hours of the morning of 6 September 1939, just three days after war had been declared, Malan's 'Red' Section of 'A' Flight was scrambled to intercept a flight of German bombers. But instead of German bombers they were in fact mistakenly hunting down a group of Hurricanes from No. 56 Squadron, who were also attempting to track the phantom enemy raid. Two of Malan's flight opened fire and one Hurricane pilot was killed. The tragic incident brought home the vital necessity of refining the communication links between the various branches of Dowding's complex defensive system. A court martial was held and Malan was exonerated of all responsibility. The incident became known as 'The Battle of Barking Creek', in reference to a popular music-hall joke at the time, and some pilots simply referred to the location as 'Shit Creek' for several years afterwards. It was a sober lesson that even the best could get caught up in the fog of war, and Malan, unquestionably, was one of the best pilots throughout the whole of Fighter Command. He quickly achieved ace status, with five enemy kills during the fighting over Dunkirk and was later promoted to command of No. 74 Squadron at the height of the Battle of Britain on 8 August 1940. He concluded his official flying career in 1941 with 27 confirmed kills, but even as a Group Captain and Station Commander of Biggin Hill he could not resist the occasional foray, leading a fighter wing over the beaches on D-Day. Despite his much higher commands later on in the war, he is best remembered today for his tactical developments during the Battle of Britain and the instinctive skills of the hunter, which he tried to impart to the men under his command. Malan had been motivated to join the RAF partly for political reasons and was staunchly anti-Nazi prior even to the outbreak of war. He continued his political activism after his return to South Africa in 1946, joining a number of anti-Fascist ex-servicemen's organizations and protesting strongly against the implementation of apartheid, which he saw as a violation of the Allied wartime ideals. Throughout the 1950s Malan led rallies against the South African government, ironically headed for a time by another Malan (Prime Minister D. F. Malan, 1948–54), as it sought to institute its racial policies. Sailor Malan died in 1963 at the age of just 53 after battling against Parkinson's disease. Sadly today his illustrious wartime record and his valiant anti-apartheid campaigns are not celebrated or even well known in the land of his birth.

A formal portrait of Sailor Malan. (IWM CH 12661)

Our situation was bad – low speed due to climbing through the cloud and so many aircraft coming down on us with the advantage of speed. I think now of the clear silhouette of our three aircraft against the white clouds.

In spite of our efforts to try and gain more speed, in no time they were on us and the battle was short. Whilst I was behind a Spitfire, another was behind me. I heard the sound as if one throws peas against a metal sheet and my cabin was full of dark smoke. I felt splashes of fuel on my face so I switched off the electrical system, dived back into the cloud and threw off the cabin roof. The smoke disappeared and I could

breathe freely and noticed that from the wings there came white streams of glycol. Whilst diving, I tried several times to start the engine, switching on the electrical system, but in vain. When I came out of cloud, I decided to bale out and undid the clasp of my seat belt and was about to climb onto the seat and jump when I thought of the high speed of the aircraft and I was afraid to be thrown against the tailplane

Left: An oil painting of Jack Mantle, who was awarded a posthumous Victoria Cross (VC), Britain's highest award for bravery, for manning his AA gun despite mortal wounds on 4 July 1940 during an attack on Portland by 33 Stukas. (Royal Naval Museum, Portsmouth)

Below: Only one VC was awarded to a fighter pilot during the course of the war. On 16 August 1940 Flight Lieutenant Nicholson of No. 249 Squadron engaged an Me 109 during an air battle over Southampton. His aircraft was hit by four cannon shell, wounding him in the neck and legs, and setting his petrol tank on fire. Engulfed in flames he began to exit the plane when he sighted another Me 109. He strapped himself in again and succeeded in shooting down his adversary before finally baling out. He officially received his VC in November 1940. Many similar acts took place during the course of the Battle of Britain for which gallantry medals were not awarded. Nicholson himself returned to active service and rose to the rank of Wing Commander. A modest man, he often referred to the achievements of others as being far worthier of a VC. He was tragically killed on 2 May 1945 during an air accident. (IWM CH 1700)

so I pulled back the stick and slowed the aircraft down. This took a matter of seconds; I did a half roll and fell out.[87]

Striberny made a safe landing and spent the rest of war as a prisoner of the British. Throughout the weeks of July the Luftwaffe would continue to lose young, inexperienced pilots. To use Jagdgeschwader 51 as an example, of the ten pilots who were lost during July, half of them had never achieved a single victory and the other five had only five between them. In contrast 'Onkel' Theo, as he was affectionately known, achieved a further two victories to add to his original First World War tally. If a novice fighter pilot could survive his first couple of encounters then generally his chances of survival improved dramatically, if only for the duration of the Battle of Britain. Pilot losses were also a severe concern for Fighter Command. Production figures of Spitfires and Hurricanes had been consistently improving over the last couple of months but pilot shortages was a problem that could not be remedied quickly for either side.

The tenth of July heralds the official start of the Battle of Britain, although in reality this date does not signify a change in German policy but rather a reaction on the part of the British to the fact that the frequency and intensity of Luftwaffe raids was undoubtedly increasing. The day itself saw the largest dogfight yet fought over the Channel. It began with eight convoys at sea in bad weather. Spotted by a German reconnaissance plane mid-morning, one large convoy code-named 'Bread' steaming towards the Dover Straits was too enticing a target for Fink to ignore. A large force was put together, including Dorniers escorted by Me 110s, loosely supported by some Me 109s flying at a higher altitude and hoping for happy hunting amongst the RAF defenders that were bound to be deployed.

The defenders themselves were scrambled from No. 32 Squadron, a Hurricane unit based at Biggin Hill in No. 11 Group. Air Vice-Marshal Keith Park was commander of No. 11 Group and, like Dowding, was determined to follow a cautious policy with regards to committing his limited resources to battle. As such, just a single flight, or six aircraft, was sent up to offer some measure of protection to the ships below. Shortly before 2pm British radar operators identified that an exceptionally large formation of enemy aircraft was seemingly heading towards Folkestone. The pilots from No. 32 Squadron spotted the menacing forms of at least 60 enemy aircraft and confirmed what was already suspected – the target was the convoy. The pilots requested reinforcements and were joined by pilots from Nos. 56, 111 and 74 Squadrons. Following Fighter Command policy, No. 111 Squadron ignored the fighters, formed into line abreast and headed straight for the formation of Dorniers. Flying Officer Tom Higgs went in for a particularly close attack and either intentionally rammed or accidentally clipped one of the Dorniers. The damaged bomber plunged to a watery grave and Higgs was forced to bale out of his stricken Hurricane; his body was recovered several weeks later.

This was not mere bravado on the part of F/O Higgs. No. 111 Squadron had already earned a reputation for their dangerous head-on attacks, which they had pioneered in France to great success. Peter Brothers was a fellow proponent of this risky tactic:

The urgent thing was to get at the bombers before they dropped their bombs, and if you were short of height you wanted to carry out a stern or beam attack, the best thing to do was to take them head-on and go straight through the formation. I always dived underneath the bombers short of impact because I always thought that the instinctive thing for pilots to do was to pull up rather than push down when faced with collision, and the last thing I wanted was to meet a Dornier or Heinkel at close quarters. This manoeuvre also produced additional speed, thus enabling me to pull the Hurricane around once clear of the bombers and turn back into them again for a more conventional stern attack.

Head on shots were the easiest of the lot to perform because there was no deflection needed whatsoever. I would press home the attack until I thought a collision was almost inevitable. In many respects this was the best form of attack, as most bombers had less protection from both guns and armour at the front.[88]

The formation broke up and a confusing mêlée ensued. Four British fighters were damaged but Higgs was the only RAF pilot lost, despite the fact that they were heavily outnumbered. Most significantly the Bf 110s utterly failed in their task of protecting the bombers. Instead three were shot down in addition to the three Dorniers also lost, while only one ship was successfully sunk. This was not all. One Me 109 from the experienced Jagdgeschwader 51 also fell victim to Fighter Command. Indeed, the British fighters had achieved an astonishing rate of success that they would not always be able to match during the course of the Battle. What is surprising is that it did not send major alarm bells ringing within the higher echelons of the Luftwaffe. Instead, the Luftwaffe was a victim of its own optimistic intelligence reports. Although this was the largest engagement of the day it was by no means the only, and by sundown the RAF had lost seven planes against the Luftwaffe's total of 13. The Luftwaffe, however, claimed to have hit an astonishing 35 British aircraft.

Monday 2

We took off at about 6.30 for Debden and arrived about 45 mins later. We did two patrols over Thames Haven, the first time we saw hundreds of huns but they were fleeing back home. Our A.A. guns fired at us, and came much too close. We had one more flip, but opps, had there fingers so far up that everything was mexed up and we never saw a thing.

Tuesday 3

We did two patrols, on the first we intersepted about 100 E/A (Do.215 + Me 110) F/Lt Bayne and I got on a Me 110's tail and firing together sent it down in flames. We then attacked a Do 215, P/O Many finishing the attack and the bomber crashing in a field just North of the River CROUCH. I collected a bullet in the radiator, and got covered with glycol, once landing at Castle camp. Collected a Hurricane of 111 sqd. flew back to Debden and got my own plane Pack. We did one more patrol over the Thames, Then in the night I was aerodrome control pilot.

SEPTEMBER, 1940.

Friday 6

I did two trips today but we did not meet anything, on the last patrol they bombed the oil wells at Thames Haven and set about half a dozen on fire. Each patrol was at 20,000 ft and were full of busters (full throttle) and we used up a lot of petrol, having arrived back at the aerodrome and just about to land opps. (dam and blast them) tried to make us go up to 20,000ft again. Oh!! opps as get my goat, they are so dim!!

SEPTEMBER, 1940.

Saturday 7

I did two trips again today, the one in the morning was uneventful, the second at 5.30, on which we used V.H.F. wireless for the first time. we saw four large enemy formations but we were only 6 and did not engage. We had one short scrap with Me 109's but I only had one short burst with no effect. These raids created a lot of damage in London, the provisional casualty list says 400 dead 1500 seriously injured. What complete swines these Jerries are.

Denis Wissler was just 19 when he was posted to France in May 1940 as part of No. 85 Squadron to counter the German Blitzkrieg. He would also fight in the Battle of Britain with this squadron and later with No. 17 Squadron. His diary from 1940 captures all his thoughts, hopes and fears from his initial training to his baptism of fire in aerial combat. It is a poignant, and ultimately tragic, insight into a young man growing up, falling in love, and striving to do his duty for his country. In early October he notes in his diary how he has met and fallen in love with a young WAAF called Edith Heap. By 18 October they are engaged but he remained keen to 'do his bit'. On 8 November he notes in his diary, 'Squadron had a party with Ju 87s, each one of the blokes got at least one. Total score 15 destroyed and some probably. Oh God, fancy missing a party like this with no casualties to ourselves.' It was his final entry. Just three days later he was killed in action and Edith was a widow before she could even be a bride. His diary now forms part of the IWM collection, gifted to the museum by his fiancée. (IWM Documents 786 91/41/1)

looking plane. It bore some relation to the Hurricane but was heavily armed, with a gun turret behind the pilot's cockpit. The Defiant had been born during an era when it was assumed that the RAF would simply have to tackle long-range, unescorted bombers. This more mobile but well-armed fighter could therefore manoeuvre either below or alongside a bomber to destroy it with a well-aimed burst of concentrated fire. But the heavy turret ensured that, despite being powered by the same engine as a Spitfire or Hurricane, it could never achieve similar speeds. This made them instantly susceptible to Me 109s, particularly as they were not armed with any forward-facing armament.

Initially Luftwaffe fighters often mistook Defiants for Hurricanes and so they had enjoyed a brief moment of success thanks to their devastating fire-power from the gun turret. But once the German pilots had cottoned on there was no stopping them, and they would stalk the slow-moving Defiants until in position for a head-on attack. As a result, the Defiants had already suffered heavy losses during the Battle of France. No. 264 Squadron, which had been posted to France, developed some limited counter-measures that involved Defiants flying together in defensive circles, therefore offering a wider arc of fire, and at lower heights so that the risk of attacks from below was at least limited. However on 19 July, the same day that Hitler was appealing to the British public's sense of reason, the as yet untested No. 141 Squadron was deployed. As always, Fighter Command had failed to implement successful squadron tactics across the board and six Defiants and their crews were lost in the space of just eight minutes. This horrific tally could even have been worse had it not been for the intervention of some Hurricane pilots from No. 111 Squadron.

Göring was not dismayed with how things were proceeding. Despite their own regrettable losses, his pilots were regularly reporting a high number of enemy kills; at this rate Fighter Command could not last long. Over-claiming naturally occurred on both sides throughout the summer months. The problem was that false Luftwaffe claims meant that they continued to believe that each day brought Germany closer to the destruction of Fighter

The RAF did suffer higher losses as soon as they deployed older, more obsolete aircraft to perform the duties of Spitfires or Hurricanes. On 19 July, following a series of minor raids, a force of Boulton Paul Defiants was sent up to protect yet another convoy. It is a measure of the pressure that Fighter Command found itself under that Defiants were used at all. The Defiant was a strange

Boulton Paul Defiants of No. 264 Squadron, 1940. The slow Defiant proved to be an easy target for marauding Me 109 pilots. (IWM CH 884)

Command. For the RAF, even if they got the total tally of enemy kills wrong, it didn't really matter. Dowding and Park would continue their more cautious approach of committing limited resources until the blue skies over southern and eastern England were no longer dotted with Luftwaffe aircraft.

On 21 July Göring called together his commanders for a review. While the Kanalkampf had been underway, Göring had been making plans for an all-out assault against Fighter Command on the British mainland. In preparation for this he appointed Theo Osterkamp to the newly created position of Jagdfliegerführer 2, responsible for coordinating all the fighters of Luftflotten 2, and an opposite number, Werner Junck, at Air Fleet 3. Werner Mölders, one of the great Luftwaffe aces of the war, took Osterkamp's role as commander of Jagdgeschwader 51. Mölders had not been in action since he had been shot down during the opening blows of the Blitzkrieg, spending more than two weeks as a prisoner of the French, and was eager to return to the frontline. Mölders was already something of a national hero. He had been the leading ace of the Condor Legion with 14 kills to his credit, and was expected to easily acquire a similar number of British victims. Osterkamp, as outgoing Kommodore,

gently warned Mölders that the British were a much tougher opponent than either the Republican Spaniards or the French but his warnings went largely unheeded. On 27 July, the day he officially assumed command, Mölders led a flight of Messerschmitts to intercept some Spitfires over the Dover Straits. He did succeed in shooting down one Spitfire but failed to realize that another was on his tail. Thanks to the actions of a fellow Luftwaffe pilot, Mölders survived the unexpected encounter with only minor injuries, but had to nurse his damaged plane back to base. This was not going to be some sudden Blitzkrieg. Here was an enemy that was going to stand and fight, and German pilots would need to keep all their wits about them in future engagements. Mölders had learnt his lesson. He would go on to claim a further nine kills during the course of the Battle of Britain before he was eventually killed while a passenger in a Heinkel III bomber during a non-operational flight within Germany.

For all pilots, however, fighting over the Channel posed a particular set of difficulties. Unlike their First World War forebears, both British and German pilots were equipped with parachutes, but pilots were unable to survive more than four hours in the treacherous and icy waters of the Channel. The Luftwaffe was better organized in this regard and had a fleet of seaplanes to search for downed pilots, who were also armed with flares and one-man dinghies. The British, in contrast, failed to make adequate provisions in the event of pilots ditching in the sea, and pilots only had their 'Mae West' lifejackets to help keep them afloat. British pilots were ordered to shoot down any German rescue aircraft that they came across, as they were suspected of being reconnaissance aircraft. Those who landed close to the British coast and were spotted therefore had a better chance of survival, even if downed German pilots were

Werner Mölders, shown here in November 1940, displaying his Knight's Cross with Oak Leaves. A veteran of the Spanish Civil War, where he had developed his 'finger four' flying tactic, Mölders was shot down on 29 July 1940 shortly after assuming command of JG 51. He survived and returned to combat a month later. He was eventually killed in an air accident when he was a passenger in a Heinkel 111 en route to the funeral of Ernst Udet. (Bundesarchiv Bild 146-1971-116-29)

AIR VICE-MARSHAL KEITH PARK

Born in 1892, Keith Park was a tough New Zealander whose valiant service throughout the summer of 1940 was intrinsically crucial for the survival of Britain. Born of Scottish parents, he had volunteered for service during the First World War and as a young NCO had survived the Gallipoli landings. His commitment to duty and obvious leadership qualities earned him a battlefield promotion. The young Second Lieutenant Park was then posted from the squalor of the trenches at Gallipoli to the mud of the Somme in 1916, just in time for the main Allied offensive that July. While serving with the Royal Field Artillery he was seriously wounded by a shell blast and was evacuated back to England. Declared unfit for active duty, Park decided to offer his services to the Royal Flying Corps (RFC). He had worked in close cooperation with the RFC during the Somme, using reconnaissance planes to help plot his artillery strikes. Now Park would be one of those pilots flying over the frontline rather than enduring the cruel life of the trenches. But the RFC, as Park was to find, required different, but no less tough, levels of endurance. Posted back to France in 1917 he was seconded to No. 48 Squadron near Arras. Flying the Bristol Fighter he quickly achieved his first successes against German pilots and would eventually receive both the Distinguished Flying Cross and the Military Cross and bar, as well as the French Croix de Guerre. He was promoted to squadron commander, proving himself to be a tough but fair, inspirational leader. By the time the war ended Park was beginning to feel the strains of so many years' service on the frontline. Nonetheless he decided to remain in the newly created RAF, holding down a number of diverse command and flying roles.

In 1938 Park was appointed Dowding's Chief of Staff. This allowed the two to build up a successful professional relationship and with Park Dowding had picked a deputy of first-rate ability. So much so that in April 1940 Dowding bypassed Trafford Leigh-Mallory, the more obvious choice, and appointed Park as Controller of No. 11 Group. This would place Park at the heart of the Battle of Britain as his fighters bore the brunt of all fighting. Park instantly grasped the benefits of the intricate defence system that Dowding had created, and devised tactics for his fighters that immediately played up to its strengths. Throughout the Battle Park would carefully deploy his fighters in small numbers to tackle the bombers, which could do the real damage, and gave his fighters strict instructions to ignore the more dangerous bait of Messerschmitts unless absolutely necessary. By doing this, Park was relying heavily on his fighters not buckling under the strain of perpetually tackling a numerically superior enemy. To counter this, Park made every effort to visit his pilots, to talk to them and to reassure them of the successes they were achieving. Park had endured Gallipoli, the Somme and aerial combat on the Western Front. He knew first-hand how important it was to keep up morale. To do this he used his own personal Hurricane, 'OK 1', to make literally 'flying' visits to the various airfields within his command and his pilots found him an inspirational leader.

His relationship with his fellow group commander Trafford Leigh-Mallory was less successful. Park was a vocal critic of Leigh-Mallory's attempts to commit the so-called 'big wing', or large formations of RAF fighters, to battle, preferring Dowding's tactics of a more cautious commitment of defenders. Following Dowding's unceremonious removal from Fighter Command, Park was also reassigned to Training Command. In many ways it was natural that Dowding's second-in-command would need to be replaced following a change at the top but it was a decision that many of his subordinates deeply regretted. Worn out by six months of intensive command, Park brought his immeasurable experience to Training Command. But he was to have a number of other operational postings throughout the course of the war. In 1941 he was posted to Egypt as Air Officer Commanding and was later sent to Malta. Here again, his skilfulness under intense pressure was clearly on display as once more he was defending an island under attack. Thanks to Malta's position in the heart of the Mediterranean it was a crucial staging post between Europe and North Africa. It was vital for Britain to hold on to the island, and for Germany to seize it, if either side was to claim victory in the North African campaign. In 1942, the year Park took control of the aerial defences, Malta was attacked repeatedly; in the first six months of the year there was only one day without a Luftwaffe bombing raid. However, Park staged a valiant defence that eventually crippled the German attempts to seize the island. Malta, the island Churchill had referred to as 'the largest aircraft carrier in the world', had been preserved thanks in no small part to Park's crucial leadership.

Later he would be posted to South-East Asia to command the air force spearheading the assault into Malaya, before eventually retiring at the end of the war. Park was perhaps one of the greatest tactical air commanders the world has ever seen but received remarkably little public accolade during his lifetime. He died peacefully at the age of 82 at home in New Zealand.

Park regularly made flying visits to his squadrons throughout the Battle of Britain using his personal Hurricane, 'OK 1'. He continued this practice during his skilful defence of the island of Malta in 1942 and here he is shown in his flying kit that year. (IWM CM 3513)

Pilots between sorties would grab a few precious minutes of relaxation when they could, as dogfighting was both mentally and physically draining. Here pilots of No. 601 Squadron are shown relaxing at RAF Hawkinge in July 1940 still wearing their 'Mae West' lifejackets. (IWM HU 1062)

On 1 August Hitler issued Directive No. 17, which called for the destruction of the RAF on the British mainland as part of the intensification of the still somewhat tentative invasion plans:

In order to establish the necessary conditions for the final conquest of England I intend to intensify air and sea warfare against the English homeland. I therefore order as follows:

1. The German Air Force is to overpower the English Air Force with all the forces at its command, in the shortest time possible. The attacks are to be directed primarily against flying units, their ground installations, and their supply organizations, but also against the aircraft industry, including that manufacturing anti-aircraft equipment.

2. After achieving temporary or local air superiority the air war is to be continued against ports, in particular against stores of food, and also against stores of provisions in the interior of the country. Attacks on the south coast ports will be made on the smallest possible scale, in view of our own forthcoming operations.

3. On the other hand, air attacks on enemy warships and merchant ships may be reduced except where some particularly favourable target happens to present itself, where such attacks would lend additional effectiveness to those mentioned in Paragraph 2, or where such attacks are necessary for the training of air crews for further operations.

4. The intensified air warfare will be carried out in such a way that the Air Force can at any time be called upon to give adequate support to naval operations against suitable targets. It must also be ready to take part in full force in Operation *Seelöwe*.

5. I reserve to myself the right to decide on terror attacks as measures of reprisal.

6. The intensification of the air war may begin on or after 5 August. The exact time is to be decided by the Air Force after completion of preparations and in the light of the weather. The Navy is authorized to begin the proposed intensified naval war at the same time.[89]

not exactly made to feel welcome by their rescuers. In just three weeks in July, 220 British pilots had been shot down over the sea. Dowding and Park recognized that they could not risk losing any more pilots by drowning. Thanks to Ultra reports, the British commanders knew that Göring was planning an all-out assault on the British mainland. Fully trained fighter pilots were already too few in number and would have to be protected to face the main assault. The RAF could no longer enforce protection for the vulnerable convoys. Moreover, the Admiralty had also come to the conclusion that daylight movement of merchant convoys through the Channel was simply becoming too costly. By 29 July all convoys were rerouted and coastal shipping severely curtailed.

As the Luftwaffe High Command met with Göring to finalize their plans, there was a couple of days' lull in German aerial activity over the Channel. As a result, the Admiralty allowed some merchant

Spitfires of No. 610 Squadron flying in 'vic' formation on 24 July 1940. Throughout the course of the Battle Fighter Command squadrons continued to practise such outmoded tactics, with dire consequences. After having borne the brunt of many German attacks throughout July and August No. 610 Squadron had to be posted away from the frontline for rest and recuperation. (IWM CH 740)

convoys to set sail on 7/8 August, although they travelled at night through the dangerous straits of Dover. Attacked by German E-boats, a number of ships had already been lost when the Luftwaffe launched their raid on the target. Of the 20 ships that had sailed, only four limped into their destination port of Swanage. Six were so badly damaged they had to take refuge in other ports and seven had been sunk outright. However, the cost for the attacking and defending airmen had also been particularly high. The Luftwaffe lost eight Me 109s, four Me 110s and ten Stukas. The British in turn had lost 13 Hurricanes and Spitfires. It was the last major Channel battle.

ADLERANGRIFF – EAGLE ATTACK

George Unwin, the son of a coal miner, had originally joined the RAF as an Administrative Apprentice but was eventually selected for pilot training. Unwin became one of the great Battle of Britain aces and was awarded the Distinguished Flying Medal in September 1940 for his 11 enemy kills. Here he is shown with No. 19 Squadron's mascot 'Flash'. (IWM CH 1343)

Despite the high losses during the Channel battles the mood among those in Fighter Command was upbeat as the pilots had made consistently high claims throughout the month of July and early August. Although some would have undoubtedly realized that these were not strictly accurate, Dowding was in no doubt about the losses he had sustained and what this meant for his defence of the British mainland. The deaths and severe injuries of the pilots concerned were, of course, regrettable, but for the moment it had not significantly weakened Fighter Command's ability to wage an effective campaign against the Luftwaffe. Between 29 June and 2 August, 322 new Hurricanes and 166 Spitfires had been produced. This more than adequately replaced the damaged or destroyed aircraft that had been lost in the previous fighting. Fighter Command also had more pilots to draw on now than during the Dunkirk evacuation, when it had been forced to reduce the required strength for each operational squadron. At the end of July, Dowding had an establishment strength of 1,456 pilots, nearly all of them operational. Nearing peak establishment, Dowding simply raised the bar, setting a new required figure of 1,588, (see Appendix 1). The quality of pilots was naturally a critical question. The loss of experienced pilots inevitably meant that new pilots, fresh out of training, would have to be posted to the frontline. There was also the issue of fatigue. His pilots and their ground crews had performed sterling work throughout the Channel battles. But tiredness could lead to careless mistakes, mistakes that pilots could ill afford to make when they were travelling at 300mph or with an unseen enemy on their tail. The pilots of No. 11 Group had borne the brunt of the fighting throughout July and would do so again in August. Dowding could have rotated more squadrons out of the frontline, but to do so risked a dilution of quality as less experienced pilots were deployed. His pilots may have been weary but those who had survived had learnt invaluable lessons in the art of aerial combat.

A pilot's first dogfight was a terrifying experience, as George Unwin, who was to become a highly decorated fighter pilot, later recalled in an interview several years after the war:

Despite the fact that I had a good four years – or more than that – flying experience and that was ... a lot of experience in those days, this is still what I regard as the most dangerous time in any fighter pilot's life. I mean, I have talked to many of them about ... the first time you are shot at, and most of them agree with me, you freeze. I did. We got mixed up. Turning around, twisting and turning and trying to attack and then I suddenly saw a Messerschmitt coming up inside me and I saw little sparks coming from the front end of him and I knew he was shooting at me and I did nothing, absolutely nothing. I just sat there in a turn; just sat there. Not petrified but, I don't know, frozen, for maybe ten seconds, fifteen seconds but never again did I do that.

After that, of course, you don't hesitate, you being ... I suppose, blooded. But despite all my experience I just sat there and watched him shoot at me. Ha ha, a stupid thing to do, I know but, as I say, fortunately he knocked a few little holes in the back of my aircraft but did no damage at all and didn't hit me luckily. From then on you realize what a mug you were and you'd never do it again. But I suppose one isn't used to being shot at in any walk of life and I suppose most people freeze anyway wondering what on earth is happening.[90]

Dowding and Park had also devised a clear strategy to tackle the forthcoming assault. They had decided that the Luftwaffe would eventually be forced to abandon the attack if it became clear that their efforts were in vain. High German losses would play a part in this, but their efforts to rule the skies over Britain would primarily have to be abandoned if they were still facing severe opposition by the end of the summer. Timing was everything. The British were well aware that a sea-borne invasion could not be attempted in the autumn as the weather turned. If Fighter Command could hold on, then it would be pointless for the Luftwaffe to continue their daylight assaults if the British were not going to concede defeat or if an invasion was not possible. Key to this policy was the small but consistent deployment of forces against far larger enemy raids.

But it was more than just a careful management of resources; it also made tactical sense. Deploying groups of fighters no larger than squadron-size ensured that a large enemy raid could be tackled time and time again by a number of different squadrons as it made its way inland. It also meant that Park would not run the risk of all of his fighters being on the ground refuelling at any one time. It was potentially demoralizing for German pilots to realize that there was a constant danger of British attacks, albeit from a small number of enemy aircraft. Besides, Heinkel and Stuka bomber crews would soon learn that just a few Hurricanes or Spitfires could cause a phenomenal amount of damage.

British and German pilots respectively relax between sorties in early August 1940. With the onset of *Adlerangriff* there would be fewer opportunities to do so. (IWM CH 868, akg images, ullstein bild)

Part of Portsmouth ablaze after the raid at approximately midday on 12 August. (IWM MH 156)

The Luftwaffe enjoyed a less coherent strategy thanks to their High Command. The plan seemed simple enough in principle – Fighter Command was to be destroyed in southern England through a series of systematic raids moving steadily inland until daylight attacks could take place anywhere over the British Isles without encountering opposition. But there was little clarity in terms of prioritizing targets. There was a multitude to choose from, including airfields and all their support buildings, anti-aircraft defences, aircraft factories and the defenders themselves. In addition, there were the ancillary targets of harbours and shipping that Hitler had included in his Directive. There was also the question of the British radar sites. During the course of the Channel battles, the Luftwaffe had become increasingly aware that British pilots were being efficiently guided via radio to intercept incoming raids by forces on the ground. The Head of the Luftwaffe Signals Service, Generalmajor Wolfgang Martini, therefore requested that prior to the start of *Eagle*, attacks should be made on the 'radio stations with special installations' clearly sited along the coast of southern England.[91]

The task fell to a special trials unit – Erprobungsgruppe 210. They had only been formed the previous month and were designed to fulfil the task of true fighter-bombers, capable of delivering a precision bomb attack from specially modified Me 109s and Me 110s, and afterwards being able to revert to their original role as fighters. Their targets were the four radar stations between Dover and Southampton. Setting out from Calais early on the morning of 12 August, the incoming raid of approximately 20 aircraft was picked up by British radar, as was to be expected. However, the plotters quickly realized that the raiders were travelling too fast to be a bombing party and, in line with Fighter Command's policy to ignore enemy fighters, no defenders were scrambled to intercept. In fact there was some confusion as to how to plot the raid and so it was given an 'X' designation to identify it as either of 'unknown origin' or a 'mistake'. The raiders split into four groups to launch separate attacks on the radar stations at Dover, Pevensey, Rye and Dunkirk close to Canterbury. Suddenly the plotters found that this unknown 'X' raid was directly overhead, attacking the radar stations with impunity.

The success of this small-scale raid was followed by the more standard large attacking force. It was first picked up just before midday as it seemed to move towards Brighton. This was Kampfgeschwader 51 virtually in its entirety, almost 100 Ju 88s, accompanied by 120 Me 110s. There was also an escort of 25 Me 109s from Jagdgeschwader 53. A radar station based at Poling, which had not been hit during the morning's attacks, picked up the raid. Now the WAAF plotters noticed how the enemy planes turned away from Brighton, heading towards Southampton and the Isle of Wight. What followed was a fierce attack on the city of Portsmouth and the radar station of Ventnor on the Isle of Wight. Hurricanes were scrambled to deal with the main bombing raid on Portsmouth but they were forced to steer clear of the city itself due to the intense anti-aircraft fire, which did succeed in claiming two enemy aircraft. As the German raiders turned for home, the Hurricanes, some of which were from No. 257 Squadron, bounced them. This squadron had only been operational since 1 July but gamely tore into the German bombers, despite their overwhelming numbers. One pilot, Flight Lieutenant Hugh Beresford, as part of 'A' Flight encountered the enemy seven miles east of Portsmouth as noted in his after-action report, and decided to engage the raiders on his own:

The Gosport area of Portsmouth suffered heavily during the raids on 12 August. For some British civilians the so-called 'Bore War' was at an end. (IWM MH 148, IWM MH 149)

I first saw e/a [enemy aircraft] when I was about seven miles east of Portsmouth. Flying behind green section at about 11,000 feet, I noticed a large number of Ju 88s circling at 14,000 feet. I then saw a large number (about 60) Me 110s in echelon of five, or six each above the bombers. I climbed to engage the fighters, but I could not catch them up as they climbed also. On the way up to the enemy fighters, I saw two Do 17s flying towards me and I gave one e/a a short burst head-on from 100 yards with no known result. After this encounter, I noticed about five Me 110s break away and go into sun, and then dive towards my tail. I turned quickly, came in behind the Me 110 and gave a five second burst from about 250 yards. It dived and started to turn from side to side. I followed it down and fired all the rest of my ammunition into it. A piece flew off the e/a which slowed up and then lurched heavily out to sea. My windscreen was covered with oil, probably from my own engine, and I had to break away. I claim a Me 110 probably destroyed.[92]

Flight Lieutenant Beresford's report gives some insight into the difficulty of accurately reporting on a confused dogfight. RAF claims could be verified if there was a crashed aircraft on British soil but it could just as easily be claimed by more than one pilot. Similarly, flying at such high speeds the pilots could often catch just a glimpse of an aircraft and mistakenly identify it, and there are known cases of claims being put in for aircraft that weren't even flown by the Luftwaffe during the course of the Battle. Or, as in the case of Beresford, a damaged aircraft could be seen heading out to sea with no way of knowing with certainty if it and its crew would survive to fight another day.

Meanwhile the splinter attack group succeeded in destroying the radar link on Ventnor, creating a potential gap in the accurate reporting of incoming raids. However, the enemy had already been clearly identified and its route confirmed by Observer Corps sightings. They too were bounced by British defenders, this time Spitfires of Nos. 609 and 152 Squadrons. Naturally the bombers had their high-flying Me 109 escorts to protect them. Or at least they thought they did. In fact the Messerschmitt pilots delayed their descent to protect the bombers because they did not believe that the small groups of British pilots

could be the main attack. Reluctant to relinquish their advantageous position at a higher altitude, the German fighter pilots failed to act until ten bombers had been shot out of the sky.

These were not the only attacks of the day. Now one of Fighter Command's own airfields was the target. Strafed initially by the fighter-bombers of Erprobungsgruppe 210, who were back in the fray just hours after their initial strike, Manston airfield was heavily bombed by the Dornier 17s of KG 2, led by no less a personage than Johannes Fink himself. In many respects, Manston was an easy target. Hugging the north-east Kent coastline, German attackers could turn for home after attacking the airfield before even encountering any defenders. It would be attacked several times during the course of the Battle until Fighter Command was eventually forced to withdraw to other better-protected airfields.

In many ways the attacks on 12 August were a stunning success. The experimental unit of fighter-bombers had sneaked through the British defences and attacked at will. British radar stations had been placed out of action and a number of British fighters claimed. Yet the successes were remarkably short-lived. Of the four radar stations hit during the course of the day, three were back on the air after only a couple of hours. Ventnor was the only station seriously damaged but the British continued to transmit signals from a nearby station to confuse the Luftwaffe Signals Staff, who assumed that all four remained operational. Moreover, the British defensive screen was more than just one tier, and the Observer Corps sighting had helped to confirm the routes of raiding parties even when the radar picture was unclear.

Worryingly for the Luftwaffe, they failed to recognize the potential of their own successes. They had not committed all their energies to strike at the radar stations, which could have caused the greatest potential damage, despite clear instructions to do so. Kesselring's own Chief of Staff, Oberst Paul Deichmann, had commented that he wanted the British listening stations to remain intact so that they would commit their defenders to a large dogfight. Instead the reverse occurred, and the Me 109s waited for vast wings of RAF fighters that never appeared. Manston itself had been chosen not because it was a Fighter Command airfield but because it was simply an airfield that was easy to attack, clearly visible on the flight path of the attacking raiders. More attacks on Manston and other fighter airfields would follow throughout August, placing considerable strain on Fighter Command, but the Luftwaffe were just as likely to attack ancillary airfields not in regular use or airfields not within No. 11 Group's command.

13 AUGUST – EAGLE DAY

Adlerangriff officially began on 13 August, dubbed Adlertag, 'Eagle Day'. It started rather unpromisingly. The Luftwaffe High Command awoke to grey skies and mist, and Göring was forced to issue a postponement order. Unfortunately, the order failed to reach all of the raiding parties for that day's missions. Dorniers, once again under the command of Oberst Fink, together with their Me 110 escorts departed at daybreak for the English coast. Whilst airborne, the Me 110s received the message to abort the mission due to the poor weather conditions. The Dorniers did not do so, nor, thanks to the mist, did they see their escort turn for home. Unfortunately for the lumbering Dorniers they flew straight into first No. 74 Squadron and then No. 111 Squadron as they followed the winding course of the Thames inland. The German bombers were badly mauled. Five Dorniers were lost and another five that limped back to their base in France were declared unfit for duty. Similarly a raid by Stukas and Me 110s that also failed to be aborted suffered heavily in the face of the strong British defence.

In the afternoon the weather cleared somewhat and the official go-ahead was granted. The main focus of the afternoon's activities was primarily Fighter Command airfields in addition to other military targets. But again there was little understanding of which airfields were actually operational fighter stations. A devastating attack was made on Detling airfield and 67 personnel were killed, but this was a Fleet Air Arm base and, despite the high loss of life, it would have little real impact on the outcome of the Battle. With poor weather in some parts of southern England, a number of

intended targets were ruled out and the raiding parties made opportunistic bomb drops on Portland and Southampton. Many of the German pilots must have felt buoyed by the success of their bombing raids and the obvious destruction that had been caused. A total of 87 RAF aircraft had been destroyed on the ground, but in reality only one of these was a Fighter Command aircraft. In fact only 13 British aircraft were lost during aerial combat, with just three British pilots killed. In contrast, the Luftwaffe had lost 87 personnel, either killed or captured. Moreover, Fighter Command could take heart from the performance of No. 10 Group. The large afternoon attack had been within their sectors, and as the raid approached the Dorset coast squadrons based at Warmwell, Exeter and Middle Wallop were scrambled. For many of these pilots this was the first time they had encountered a raid of such overwhelming numbers. The British pilots benefited from the fact that many of the

A German bomber squadron commander receiving a report from his crew after they returned home from an accomplished mission on Adlertag, 'Eagle Day'. (akg images, ullstein bild)

Therefore I let the motor, being in neutral gear, become cooler first. Then [when] the temperature had fallen to normal again, I switched the ignition on again, opened the throttle and went up as high as possible until the motor was overheated again; I repeated this for several times and barely reached the French coast where I made a forced landing on the sand beach. According to my experience report this method was later called 'to Bob' across the Channel.[93]

After nightfall the German attacks did not diminish. Bombing raids were conducted against a number of prominent cities throughout the British Isles and two lucky strikes were made against aircraft factories in Belfast and Castle Bromwich. There was little that Fighter Command could do against night attacks. Occasionally Spitfires and Hurricanes were deployed but it was almost impossible to find the enemy in the inky black sky and there was a high proportion of accidents due to the difficulties of taking off and landing in the dark. Not until mid-November would a squadron of Bristol Beaufighters fitted with airborne interception (AI) radar become available. Until then, the Luftwaffe would simply have to run the gauntlet of the anti-aircraft defences before attacking at will.

15 AUGUST – BLACK THURSDAY

In comparison to Adlertag, the subsequent day was relatively quiet. Manston was raided yet again and there was a large dogfight over Dover from which the Luftwaffe could claim few real gains. This relative lull allowed Dowding the opportunity to rotate No. 145 Squadron out of the frontline. It had been decimated after continual fighting in France, over Dunkirk and now the Battle of Britain. It was posted north to No. 13 Group to regroup and would not return until October. Not all squadrons that had suffered heavy losses were pulled out. Others that had been badly mauled, including Nos. 609 Squadron and 111 Squadron with five pilot losses each, were kept in to reduce the number of inexperienced pilots at the frontline of

Ground-crew members of a German air base sign a bomb with the inscription 'Hermann's Trademark Brand', 13 August 1940. Several German bombers were lost in the face of the stiff resistance put up by Fighter Command that day. (akg images, ullstein bild)

German fighter escorts were operating at the extent of their ranges. The Me 109s had only a limited amount of time to engage in combat before being forced to turn for home because of fuel shortages. This would be a constant worry for Luftwaffe fighter pilots throughout the course of the Battle. Hans-Ekkehard Bob was one pilot who managed to nurse his aircraft home across the Channel after running dangerously low on fuel, and his methods were later copied by a number of other pilots:

> The Me 109 had in case of motor failure a gliding angle of 1:13, for example of a height of 1km you could in the best possible way cover a distance of 13km. One day I was shot at over England, approximately 80km from the French coast, at a height of 4000m in such a way that the cooling system of the motor failed. Usually we had to put the air screw to gliding position and try to glide homeward. According to my consideration this was not normally possible from a height of 4000m.

ADOLF GALLAND

Unlike many of the high-scoring German aces of the Second World War, Adolf Galland (1912–96) scored his total of 104 victories entirely on the Western Front. A Condor Legion veteran, Galland immediately benefited from previous combat experience, claiming 25 Spitfires alone between 1940 and 1941. Galland had always loved to fly and used to fashion home-made gliders when he was still at school. He was one of the elite few selected for civilian pilot training but transferred to the still illegal Luftwaffe in 1933. He succeeded his colleague Werner Mölders to the position of General de Jagdflieger when Mölders was killed in an air accident in 1941. From late 1942 onwards he was removed from operational flying and instead helped develop tactics as well as test-fly prototypes such as the Messerschmitt Me 262, the first ever jet fighter, which he enthusiastically endorsed. Frustrated by Göring's inept leadership and the incessant squandering of resources he quarrelled frequently with High Command. In January 1945 he was eventually removed from his position and returned to the frontline, where he served alongside several other leading pilots, known as *Experten*, in Jagdverband 44. He was eventually captured by US forces in May 1945 and his fighting days were over. Post-war Galland continued his love of flying by acting as an independent aviation consultant. He also established some long-standing friendships with old adversaries such as Douglas Bader, their mutual passion for flying overriding their wartime hatreds, before passing away in 1996.

Above:
Adolf Galland, the great German pilot, pictured in a captured RAF Bomber Command sheepskin flying jacket. (IWM HU 4128)

Left:
A more formal portrait of Adolf Galland photographed in 1942 in his Lieutenant Colonel's uniform together with his Knight's Cross award. (Bundesarchiv Bild 146-2006-0123)

defence. The following day, however, would test the pilots of Fighter Command the length and breadth of the country.

The Luftwaffe's reliance on German pilots' claims to construct an image of how the battle was progressing ensured that it was assumed Fighter Command was now drastically short of both aircraft and men. They had little knowledge of the increased production output nor the regular supply of pilots. Instead they assumed that No. 11 Group was now relying on reinforcements from across the country. The fifteenth of August was therefore designed to test these weakened resources throughout the British Isles.

The early morning began with a number of low-level raids in the south to distract the defenders. Manston was once again targeted, as were Hawkinge and Lympne airfields. But the main bombing force was drawn from Luftflotte 5 and was heading not for Kent, but Yorkshire. Unfortunately for the German pilots, the squadrons of No. 13 Group were already on high alert as they were protecting a convoy due to sail out of Hull. They made easy work of the Dorniers as well as the Me 110s, particularly as they were operating without an Me 109 escort. Next it was the turn of No. 12 Group. Hugh Dundas was flying a Spitfire of No. 616 (South Yorkshire) Squadron, based at Leconfield on Humberside. Dundas had not been in action since Dunkirk, and unlike his No. 11 Group compatriots was not used to the urgent scramble call, which was suddenly sounded when a 40-plus-strong raid was spotted heading directly towards the Leconfield airfield:

We were sitting in the mess on that day, actually at 30 minutes' notice, when the tannoy went, telling us in rather urgent tones to come to readiness. I'm not even sure it didn't tell us to scramble, which we thought was an unorthodox message to receive while having lunch in the mess at half an hour's notice, but we put down our knives and forks, rushed out to get into the cars and pushed off down to the field as quickly as we could. When we got there the operations clerk was jumping up and down for us to take off as fast as we could individually, just to get airborne. Off we all went in ones and twos. We were told on the R/T that there was a large force of German bombers, indeed of Dornier 17s, which were aiming for Driffield. We had quite a field day that day and succeeded in shooting down quite a few of those wretched aeroplanes, which of course hadn't got any escort and were in broad daylight, without any loss to ourselves.[94]

The British fighters claimed 14 enemy aircraft for no losses themselves and although ten aircraft of Bomber Command were destroyed on the ground there was little other damage. A second raid launched by Luftflotte 5 was also heavily punished. After its dire performance, Luftflotte 5 ceased to play any further significant role in the Battle. The failure of the attacks to the north conclusively proved that Fighter Command had not drained its other substantial resources to protect the more vulnerable south-east and London in

A crashed Heinkel He III from Kampfgeschwader 27 lies on the side of the road in Charterhouse, Somerset. It had reportedly been shot down by Blue Section of No. 92 Squadron at 6pm on 14 August 1940. (IWM CH 1887)

Pilot and navigator in the cockpit of a German Heinkel He 111 bomber during a mission against England on 15 August 1940. The high losses they suffered on that day caused the Luftwaffe to informally refer to it as 'Black Thursday'. (akg images, ullstein bild)

particular. Moreover, without their Me 109 escorts, the bombers and even the twin-engined fighters were little match for the Hurricanes and Spitfires.

To the south the raids were somewhat more successful. Bombers managed to evade their attackers, assisted by the vigorous defence mounted by the large force of Me 109 escorts, and the aircraft factory producing the RAF's new heavy bomber was severely damaged. There were a number of smaller harassing raids throughout Kent during the course of the afternoon before another large raiding force was deployed at 4pm. Almost 50 Stukas, approximately

60 Me 109s and 40 Me 110s were deployed to attack Warmwell, the main fighter base in Dorset that protected Portland's naval base. Thanks to the strong British defence, the German planes were forced to divert instead towards Portland itself. Nos. 234, 213 and 87 Squadrons were scrambled to counter the threat, among whose number was Roland Beamont of No. 87 Squadron. He along with eight others from his squadron attacked the vast formation, although flying with so many aircraft crowding the skies required a certain amount of skill and no small measure of bravado:

... my squadron was scrambled at about 4 o'clock in the afternoon to intercept what was described by the controller as 'a 100-plus heading north from Cherbourg'. We were vectored to Portland. We climbed out to Portland as quickly as we could and as we started heading south over Weymouth at about 15,000 feet, the controller was saying, 'Your 100-plus is now 150-plus, 20 miles south of Portland Bill, heading north-east.' We thought, 'Right, they're just going to go up over Portland Bill and then turn left into a dive-bombing attack on Portland Harbour', which is exactly what they did. We continued on our course. We had about nine aeroplanes that day. We were pulling our harness straps tight and turning on the gun sight and getting all the anticipatory moves necessary. Then the controller said, 'Bandits now 20 miles ahead of you; you should see them directly ahead.' Almost immediately the clear sky ahead started to turn into a mass of little black dots. It could only really be described as a beehive – that's what we used to call them. Our CO continued to lead us straight towards it. I just had time to think, 'I wonder what sort of tactic he's going to employ – is he going to turn up sun and try and dive out of the sun at them or go round to the right and come in behind ... what's he going to do?' While I thought that, it was quite apparent he wasn't going to do anything. He bored straight on into the middle of this lot until we seemed to be going into the biggest formation of aeroplanes you ever saw. Then his voice came on the radio and he said, 'Target ahead. Come on, chaps, let's surround them.' Just nine of us.

We went right into the middle. By that time we were no longer as inexperienced as we had been in France. I suppose many of us were now getting quite overconfident. We thought we were fully trained fighter pilots so there was less apprehension, there was more concentration and picking out a target out of this great mass ahead you would have two things to do. First thing would be to watch your immediate leader and make sure you didn't run into him, and that you hadn't selected the same target as he had. In other words, if he was directly ahead of you it was no good trying to fire at his target because you might hit him. That wasn't regarded as a good thing to do.

You picked your own target; went in on a firing pass. Then with all this great mass of aeroplanes around, the next high priority was to avoid a collision because you would be diving into a mass formation. They, in turn, would start breaking formation under fire. The whole place would be a mass of aeroplanes going in all directions so you have to fire at a target and then to evade anything that's in your way.

I fired at a Ju 87 at point-blank range and I hit it. I don't know what happened to it. I could see my tracers going into it; I rolled away from him straight behind another of his mates, a 110. I fired a long burst at him and his port engine stopped and started to stream smoke and fire and pulled away from that.

There seemed to be a lot of activity immediately behind my tail at that time so I went into a very tight turn, a diving turn, dived out of it until I seemed to be free of all the other aeroplanes, levelled out, climbed back up, and – as happened in that sort of confused fight – there was no sign of any Hurricanes. I could see a formation of aeroplanes in the distance, which were probably the rest of the enemy heading off back across the Channel, and two or three streaks of smoke going down the sky where there were fires, burning aircraft. Then, immediately below – I was over Lyme Bay just south of Abbotsbury Swannery – I could see great boils in the water where either aircraft or bombs had gone in, I didn't know what they were. Then there was nothing else to do because I was out of touch with everything. I'd used most of my ammunition so I throttled back and opened the canopy, cooled down a bit, and flew off back home.[95]

Three Stukas were lost, as were, astonishingly, 13 Me 110s, the days of the latter surely numbered in the face of such crippling losses. The Luftwaffe's greatest successes of the day in fact came from some of its smallest actions. The large unwieldy bomber formations had reaped very little reward for their heavy losses. However, the experimental unit Erprobungsgruppe 210 had once again enjoyed some success. They had managed to breach the British defences without early detection thanks to a previous accidental strike on the power-supply lines connecting some of the Chain Home Low stations, and dive-bombed Martlesham Heath. This put the airfield out of action for a full 48 hours and destroyed some fighters of No. 17 Squadron on the runway as they prepared to take off. Free of their heavy bomb load and on their way home, they were also able to bounce a group of RAF pilots pursuing some Me 110s from a different raid.

But as the afternoon stretched into early evening, the unit decided to chance its luck once more. The target was Kenley airfield, and as this was within the range of the Me 109, a separate fighter escort was also provided from JG 52. This time, however, there were no gaps in the radar screen and British fighters were scrambled in good time to counter the threat. The Me 110s were forced into their usual defensive circle as they lost their Me 109 escorts in the failing light and the incoming mist. Furiously attacked by Hurricanes from Nos. 111 and 32 Squadrons, eventually the Me 110s decided to break for home but a number were picked off by the pursuing British fighters. Although the Luftwaffe pilots had managed to drop their bombs on the airfield before being forced to flee, they had failed to identify the correct airfield. Instead of targeting Kenley, they had bombed the satellite airfield of Croydon. What is more, amid the general chaos, some of the bombs had also fallen on outlying factory buildings. Göring's air force had effectively bombed London, despite Hitler's explicit orders forbidding such action.

What of Göring? On the day the Luftwaffe launched this massive attack to follow on from Adlertag, Göring and his commanders were nowhere near the German air bases in France. Göring had in fact summoned the commanders of Luftflotte 2, 3 and 5, together with some other senior officers to Karinhall, his sumptuous estate 40 miles outside of Berlin. The Luftwaffe's weather unit had predicted poor weather conditions for 15 August. On the basis of this, Göring assumed that the strikes against the British mainland would not go ahead and the presence of Kesselring and other key commanders would not be missed. However as the weather started to clear in the morning the German planes began to form up and commence their crossing of the Channel. At least one relatively senior officer realized the folly of launching such a huge operation without any of the commanding generals being present but Göring had issued strict orders that his Karinhall conference was not to be disturbed, so the planes flew on regardless. The commanders returned to dismal news. Most sources

Roland Beamont was just 19 when the Battle of Britain began. He survived and became a test pilot for Hawker before returning to operational flying during the D-Day invasions. Later he became one of the most successful pilots to tackle the V-1 rockets, accounting for 32 of the unmanned bombs that were wreaking havoc across southern England. Post-war he continued his test pilot career and was the first man to make a double Atlantic crossing in a jet in 1952. (Norman Franks)

agree that the Luftwaffe had lost 75 aircraft or just over 20 per cent of the attacking force during the course of the day. The RAF inaccurately claimed 182 enemy aircraft but the reality was sufficient for Luftwaffe personnel to quickly dub 15 August 'Black Thursday'.

The results of their conference with Göring should have been equally disturbing for Kesselring, Sperrle and Stumpff. Göring's primary concern had been the losses to his bomber fleets, in

to give up our speed and to fly alongside the bombers. In this situation, when the English arrived and were flying towards us from high altitudes and at a great speed, we didn't have the slightest chance ...[96]

Significantly, Göring also remained unconvinced about the success of the attacks on the radar stations, famously remarking that 'It is doubtful whether there is any point in continuing the attacks on radar sites, in view of the fact that not one of those attacked has been put out of action.' Post-war, this has been heralded as one of the single greatest errors of the war. In one respect Göring was right; the radar stations had suffered only short-term damage, despite concentrated bombing efforts. Although clearly visible to attacking bombers, as many of the Chain Home stations were more than 300 feet high, their open-frame steel girder construction ensured that the blast could be absorbed on impact, nullifying much of the potential damage. But Göring's decision was primarily based upon a lack of understanding regarding how radar worked and the impact it had on the British defensive screen. In this he was not alone, and none of the senior commanders recognized the true impact it could have on the Battle if the Luftwaffe concentrated exclusively on radar stations. Ironically, the very next day the radar station at Ventnor was attacked again, despite Göring's new orders. This time it was off air for a further seven days. A mobile radar unit was rushed to the site to plug the hole but its performance was quite poor. Again, however, it was enough to convince the Germans that their attack had failed, and immediate follow-up raids were not ordered.

A publicity photo showing a pilot of No. 64 Squadron preparing for duty on the morning of 15 August 1940. The plane in the background appears slightly damaged. (IWM HU 54420)

particularly the steady depletion of his Stukas. His solution was to provide greater fighter cover, with each Stuka wing protected by three fighter wings. In many ways this could be considered sound advice. It would offer a far greater degree of protection, with one fighter wing flying ahead of the Stuka fleet, another flying alongside it and yet another flying above it at a greater altitude to ensure that it was not bounced by enemy fighters. However, such advice bore no relation to how things actually stood on the ground. The Me 109 fighter pilots were already flying countless sorties a day and it would be virtually impossible to fulfil such an order. The pilots themselves hated close escort duty as it placed them in such a vulnerable position:

Göring ordered us to adapt to the bombers' speed and fly alongside them. This meant throwing away the fighters' advantage. The whole point of the fighter is the fact that it's fast. And now we were ordered

18 AUGUST – THE HARDEST DAY

Despite the high losses that the Luftwaffe was enduring, there remained a sense of optimism among the High Command thanks to their false impression of the ability of the RAF to continue mounting an effective defence. The attacks on 'Black Thursday' had been launched because the Luftwaffe believed that Fighter

Command's resources had been stripped to bolster the supposedly weakening defences in south-east England. The events of that day should have forced the Luftwaffe's intelligence service to re-evaluate all their previous assumptions. Instead, the Luftwaffe continued its reliance on inaccurate pilot claims, which could not be verified and explained away the persistent resistance of the British as mere last-ditch defences. As such, the Saturday after 'Black Thursday' the 5th Directive of the Luftwaffe High Command, the body responsible for intelligence gathering and reporting, released a document that stated that as a result of the sustained fighting there were just 300 serviceable aircraft available to Fighter Command throughout the British Isles. They had arrived at this figure by simply subtracting the 770 aircraft – assumed to have already been destroyed – from the total of 900 they believed to have existed on 1 July. Added to this total were 300 new fighters thought to have come off the production lines since this date. These figures bore no relation to the truth. In fact, Fighter Command had more than triple this number of operational aircraft, with over 400 Hurricanes and more than 200 Spitfires produced since the start of July.

With such welcome figures to hand, Kesselring and Sperrle decided to launch a series of ambitious assaults on key Fighter Command airfields. Luftflotte 2 was to focus on Kenley, Biggin Hill, Hornchurch and North Weald, each individually crucial to No. 11 Group as these were all both large airfields and sector stations. These four airfields had been chosen because German reconnaissance aircraft had identified them as being among the largest and most heavily used airfields in the south-east. They had no prior knowledge that each airfield housed a sector station, which was responsible for the deployment of fighters, acting as one of the many nerve centres within the complex defence system. Luftflotte 3, in contrast, was to focus on the area around Portsmouth, forcing the defenders to fight on two frontlines. However the intended targets for Luftflotte 3 were less promising. It included the radar station at Poling but also three airfields that were not used by Fighter Command.

Luftwaffe bomber crews shown being briefed prior to a mission. (IWM MH 5321)

The wreckage of a Dornier 17 near Biggin Hill on 18 August 1940. The base itself was attacked heavily that day. (IWM HU 3122)

Biggin Hill was to be attacked by 60 Heinkels from KG 1 and KG 76, while a combined force of Dorniers and Ju 88s from KG 76 was to attack Kenley. More than 100 fighters were to be drawn from a variety of Jadgeschwader to provide the necessary cover as prescribed by Göring. The mission was postponed when the dense haze failed to lift shortly after sunrise. The prayers of Alan Deere, a pilot with No. 54 Squadron, had been answered:

> The weather was ... we used to say 'rotten weather' because it was fine every day, almost every day. There were exceptions obviously but it was a very fine summer. We used to wake up – we were up [at] five in the morning – get down to the dispersal and say, 'God, another fine day', knowing that the Germans would come. We used to pray for cloud.[97]

It had been an unusually clear summer, but this morning the British fighter pilots would have breathed a sigh of relief as they happily spent the morning occasionally being scrambled to chase off the odd reconnaissance plane. This relative inactivity could not last and at 11am with the weather clearing the mass of German bombers began to warm their engines. Shortly before 1pm, the advance guard of Luftwaffe fighters crossed over Dover. Behind them, like gathering clouds, the vast swarm of German bombers droned on towards the British mainland. Such a vast concentration of enemy raiders could not fail to be spotted by the watching eyes of the British radar stations as the WAAF plotters frantically marked their progress inland. Soon No. 11 Group began readying its own fighters in response as the air-raid sirens sounded all over eastern Kent. A total of 97 Hurricanes and Spitfires raced into the air to counter the German raids. In addition, the Luftwaffe sent a small party of nine Dorniers to fly in low, beneath the radar screen, to support the attack on Kenley as a surprise addition. As they roared over Beachy Head their large ominous crosses were clearly visible to the stunned Observer Corps watchmen just a couple of hundred feet below. They too were added to the markers criss-crossing the WAAF plotters' maps of south-east England.

In the operations rooms at Kenley and Biggin Hill it became increasingly clear to the operations-room staff that they were the intended targets. All their aircraft were ordered airborne with a flight from No. 111 Squadron at Croydon hoping to gain sufficient height to deal with the low-flying attack. All non-essential ground staff were ordered into the bunkers but the men and women in the operations rooms remained at their posts, simply donning steel helmets as the markers continued to inch forward. As the Dornier pilots glimpsed the hangars at Kenley airfield, No. 111 Squadron were already on their tail and firing. Nor was Kenley itself undefended. It had four 40mm Bofors guns, which could lay down a punishing rate of fire of 120 rounds a minute. Supporting them were a couple of First World War-era guns, which were far less effective, and a couple of recently improvised anti-aircraft measures, including the deployment of parachutes to distract and even ensnare an unlucky bomber. As the Dorniers screamed into view, the gunners burst into action. The fire was so intense that the attacking Hurricanes were forced to pull back.

Several of the Dorniers were damaged but the bombs continued to rain down on Kenley.

Pilot Officer Ronald Brown was with No. 111 Squadron as they desperately tried to attack the German raiders. It was no easy task as the British fighters had to avoid both the anti-aircraft fire and the homes of local families:

When they did the big Dornier low-level raid on Kenley on August 18, they scrambled us to get us off the airfield. When we were airborne, we were vectored to intercept these Dorniers. We picked them up about 10 miles from Kenley. I had just got into firing range and I got a long-burst in at the leader of one of their sections when he broke formation and pulled up. I was damn certain that I must have hit him but just at that moment, as we were about to cross the airfield, the airfield defence system went into action. Rockets fired wires and parachutes into the air. I had heard of these things but I had never seen them before and I damn near hit them. I went up fast to avoid them. In the meantime bombs were bursting below us. I got over the other side of the airfield and picked up another Dornier, which was right down in the valley. I got in a good long burst on his starboard quarter and down he went. He burnt up in a field. I saw another one going over a housing estate. I was about to fire at him but at that moment I visualized a woman and kids in their kitchen cooking the Sunday lunch. So I sat behind this fellow for quite a long time while his rear gunner popped off at me. When he was clear of the estate I took a burst at him but that was my third attack and by now I was out of ammo. I don't know if he got home.[98]

Not all of them did. Within minutes of the attack two bombers were already burning wrecks in the fields surrounding Kenley, a testament to the ferocity of the defenders' attempts to protect their airfield both on the ground and in the air. A further two Dorniers would crash before reaching the safety of the French coastline, and those that successfully landed back in German territory did so with badly damaged aircraft and wounded crews on board.

But this had simply been the preliminary blows as the main raiding party of 27 Dorniers and some 20 Me 110s now swung into

action. No. 32 Squadron was ready for them, however, attacking head-on and forcing the bombers off course so that Kenley was spared the full force of their attack. The Luftwaffe bombers broke for home, with a desperate chase ensuing as the RAF pursued their prey through Surrey and Kent towards the coast.

Just as one group of German bombers was frantically fleeing, the 60 Heinkels of KG 1 were streaming towards their chosen target: Biggin Hill. Their attack was relatively unopposed. The anti-aircraft gunners held their fire, well aware that British fighters were in the area, and as a result the Luftwaffe pilots had an easy run of it. But they did not make the most of their opportunity, as a number of the bombs fell off target. They too turned for home as the British fighters began their relentless pursuit. As a haze started to settle over the skies again a confused series of dogfights took

WAAFs under fire. The ability of women to remain at their posts despite bomb attacks was a pleasant surprise for the upper echelons of the RAF. Here three members of the WAAF have been awarded the Military Medal (MM) for gallantry in remaining at their posts under heavy aerial bombardment. Picture shows left to right: Sergeant Joan Mortimer from Yorkshire, Corporal Elspeth Candlish-Henderson from Edinburgh and Sergeant Helen Turner, a Londoner. Bomb damage to the buildings of Biggin Hill is clearly visible behind them. (IWM CH 1550)

place throughout the German pilots' return leg. One further action occurred that lunchtime when a group of Ju 88s dissuaded from attacking either Kenley or Biggin Hill, due to the intense fighting in the area, chose instead to attack their secondary target of West Malling. This was fortuitous for Fighter Command as it was not one of the key sector airfields.

It was still only lunchtime when Luftflotte 3 bombers swung into action. They made successful runs against the radar station at Poling and the naval air station at Ford. However, as they approached Gosport the Messerschmitt fighter escorts were attacked by No. 234 Squadron and three were shot down. More than 150 Me 109s were in the air at the time, providing the three-wing cover to the 109 Ju 87 Stukas. This was the largest ever deployment of Stukas in one attack, and this large formation was visible for miles as it streamed towards its targets. But then the Stukas themselves became the target.

With some of their fighter escort still embroiled with No. 234 Squadron, and the Stukas already lining up for their dive-attack, they were relatively easy targets for the Hurricanes of Nos. 601 and 43 Squadrons. One pilot from the latter squadron was able to fly down a line of five Stukas raking each of them with his .303 machine guns and watched two go down in flames. The skies filled with the burning, falling wrecks of the one-time pride of the Luftwaffe as the British fighters drove home their attack. Spitfires of No. 602 Squadron and even some Bristol Blenheims of Coastal Command, whose airfield at Thorney Island the Stukas dived down to attack, joined them. But the high-flying Messerschmitt escort quickly descended to protect their charges and four Spitfires of 602 were hit in quick succession as the Stukas began their frantic retreat.

Behind them they left a trail of destruction. The naval base at Ford had been unprepared for the attack and inadequately protected. Mangled bodies were strewn across the base as black smoke from the burning aerodromes clouded the skies above. A total of 28 people were killed and a nearby village hall had to be converted into a temporary mortuary. Gosport and Thorney Island did not suffer any deaths but there was considerable destruction of aircraft hangars and planes on the ground. In all instances, none of the losses directly impacted on Fighter Command. Far more dangerous was the potential loss of radar coverage because of the attack on Poling. Here the bombs had destroyed one of the 240ft-high receiver towers but the operations room remained intact. The Chain Home early-warning radar was now off-line until repairs could be carried out, but the Chain Home Low radar, which reported on low-flying aircraft, was still running. Besides, thanks to the positioning of other radar stations along the coast, there was no real gap in the radar coverage for the Luftwaffe to exploit. Meanwhile, the Stuka fleets had suffered devastating losses of 17 aircraft. A further eight Messerschmitts were shot down during the attack by Luftflotte 3. In return, Fighter Command had lost five aircraft with two pilots killed.

The day was not yet over and in the early evening a wave of Dorniers and Heinkels streamed towards North Weald airbase, where they were met by forces from both Nos. 11 and 12 Groups. Faced

Alan Deere, shown on the right, alongside a Fighter Command colleague. New Zealand-born Deere concluded the war as a Wing Commander and a highly successful fighter pilot. (IWM CH 9455)

RECRUITING CENTRE OR DIRECT TO F.O.V.E., ADMIRALTY, LONDON

R.A.F. VERSUS 'LUFTWAFFE' TO-DAYS SCORE 14 & TO 20

A newspaper seller in the street with a RAF vs Luftwaffe score on a blackboard behind him. The media took great glee in reporting the inflated figures, which showed much heavier Luftwaffe losses in comparison to Fighter Command casualties. Fighter Command at least had the advantage of visible wrecks on the ground to counter accidental overclaiming by pilots. The Luftwaffe did not have such an advantage and erroneously believed that their attacks were decimating Fighter Command beyond all possible recovery. (IWM HU 810)

with such stiff opposition and in worsening weather conditions the bombers turned for home, jettisoning the payloads short of their real target. As the skies darkened with heavy cloud cover, the weary defenders could finally rest easy.

It had been a hard day. At face value there had been five German attackers for every British defender. In reality, however, there were generally only three Messerschmitts for every Hurricane or Spitfire,

as the bombers did not pose a direct threat to the defenders themselves. So, while still outnumbered, it was not quite the David and Goliath contest as is often assumed, especially considering that Park still held a number of fighters in reserve. Only during the Stuka attack by Luftflotte 3 had Fighter Command's resources been stretched, with 68 Hurricanes and Spitfires airborne. This was virtually all the defenders available in the area, as the fighters at the

COMBAT REPORT.

Sector Serial No. _____ (A) _____

Serial No. of Order detailing Flight or Squadron to
    Patrol _____ (B)   N.A.

Date _____ (C)   6/9/40

Flight, Squadron _____ (D) Flight :   A   Sqdn.: 303 Polish

Number of Enemy Aircraft _____ (E)   200   )   80 - 100)

Type of Enemy Aircraft _____ (F)   ME 109   )   Dornier?)

Time Attack was delivered _____ (G)   0900

Place Attack was delivered _____ (H)   Sevenoaks

Height of Enemy _____ (J)   20,000 ft.

Enemy Casualties _____ (K)   1 ME 109 Destroyed & 1 Probable.

Our Casualties _____ Aircraft _____ (L)   Nil

                    Personnel _____ (M)   Nil

GENERAL REPORT _____ (R)

    I was Red 3. We were flying South East. To port some Messerschmitts were
making zigzags of white smoke above us. We turned towards them, and then
turned South West and saw about 80-100 Bombers and 200 ME 109's. Two
ME's were attacking a Hurricane out of the sun. One broke away and I
banked round and gave 4 bursts at the ME which was firing at the Hurricane.
The Hurricane went down out of control, and the ME went down after it in
flames. I turned right, thinking the other ME was on my tail but I could
not see it. A ME then attacked me head on and we turned round each other.
After 1½ turns I was on its tail and gave him two long bursts and ran out
of ammunition. I hit the engine, and the ME broke off with thick black
smoke pouring from the engine. I circled round a British Pilot who had
baled out, and saw him land safely. Then I went home.

Signature

O.C.   { Section
           { Flight   Wunsche Sgt.
           { Squadron A   Squadron No.
                          303   Polish

airbases around London were still rearming following the attacks on Kenley and Biggin Hill. Indeed, for the Luftwaffe pilots and crews there would have seemed to be a disturbing number of British defenders for an air force that was reportedly on the brink of collapse. Each side had reaped its grim harvest. A total of 69 German aircraft were destroyed in comparison to Fighter Command's 29. It was the greatest losses for either side so far and still the Battle raged.

FINAL DAYS IN AUGUST – THE ATTACKS ON AIRFIELDS

The newspapers on both sides trumpeted the heavy toll inflicted on the opposing side on 18 August. But in reality it was just one day in an ongoing battle of attrition. In subsequent days the weather worsened and there were few opportunities for large-scale raids. Instead, this was an opportunity for each side to re-evaluate. Göring, faced with the slow destruction of his air force, decreed that the Stukas would have to be withdrawn until more favourable conditions existed. In addition, the majority of the fighters of Luftflotte 3 were to be transferred to Kesselring's command. The Battle was to resume with renewed vigour as soon as the weather cleared. Aircraft factories, Bomber Command airfields and other ancillary targets were to be ignored during day attacks. Fighter Command was to be the exclusive target, with the brunt of the fighting to be borne by Kesselring's strengthened Luftflotte 2. This meant that No. 11 Group would be spearheading the defence yet again.

Dowding used the lull in the fighting to realign his forces as well. Despite the losses of 18 August, Dowding was able to add four new squadrons to the frontline. Both 302 (Polish) and 310 (Czech) had become operational on the 18th and were joined by the first Royal

An example of a combat report. This was usually completed as soon as possible after returning from a sortie and it was not unknown for pilots to dictate their report from a hospital bed. (IWM Documents 4175 83/15/2 7/08)

Canadian Air Force Squadron the following day. Moreover, the Poles of No. 303 Squadron, although not quite operational yet, were granted permission to patrol over vulnerable airfields when necessary. Park called a conference of his Sector Commanders and Controllers on 19 August. Henceforth their primary defence must be the sector airfields and, in doing so, their squadrons' efforts should focus on the attacking bombers. Dogfights with German fighters were to be avoided as they were costly and did not yield any real results. Fighter-to-fighter combat was the stuff of legend, the real test of a pilot's flying skill and his killer instinct, and it was no easy task reining in the British fighters on this score. In addition, Park ordered that raiding parties should be intercepted as quickly as possible by the nearest available squadrons, continuing the piecemeal deployment of forces tactics that had served Fighter Command well thus far. This would later result in friction with Park's opposite number at No. 12 Group, Air Vice-Marshal Trafford Leigh-Mallory, who favoured the use of larger flight formations in the style of a 'big wing'.

The real test would be the supply of pilots to Fighter Command. Production of Spitfires and Hurricanes continued at a steady pace but to ensure that operational levels remained high the training schedules were severely curtailed. Prior to July a novice pilot would have spent six months with an Operational Training Unit (OTU) honing his skills. By early August this had been reduced to just two weeks. Moreover, many of these inexperienced pilots still flew the antiquated 'vic' formation and were badly mauled by the Luftwaffe as a result. Dowding was well aware that the fighting attack formations required serious refinement but was unable to implement any real changes when the Battle was at its height. Officially ordering a radical overhaul could have had dire consequences. It was left to Squadron commanders to ensure that new pilots were given a rudimentary lesson in the art of aerial combat. Others went further. Adolf 'Sailor' Malan, the South African commander of No. 74 Squadron, quickly realized that the traditional 'vic' flying was suicidal. During the Battle of Britain he started to experiment with 12-aircraft squadrons flying in three sections of four. Thus, if a section had to split up it converted into two pairs, the ideal fighting component as demonstrated by the

German *rötte*. In 1941 this tactic would be formally adopted by Fighter Command and Malan's *Ten Rules of Air Fighting* was widely distributed among operational squadrons:

1. Wait until you see the whites of his eyes. Fire short bursts of one or two seconds, and only when your sights are definitely 'ON'.
2. Whilst shooting, think of nothing else, brace the whole of your body, have both hands on the stick, concentrate on your ring sight.
3. Always keep a sharp lookout, 'Keep your finger out!'
4. Height gives You the initiative.
5. Always turn and face the attack.
6. Make your decisions promptly. It is better to act quickly even though your tactics are not the best.
7. Never fly straight and level for more than 30 seconds in the combat area.
8. When diving to attack the enemy, always leave a proportion of your formation above to act as top guard.
9. 'Initiative', 'Aggression', 'Air Discipline' and 'Teamwork' are all words that 'Mean' something in air fighting.
10. Go in quickly – Punch Hard – Get Out!

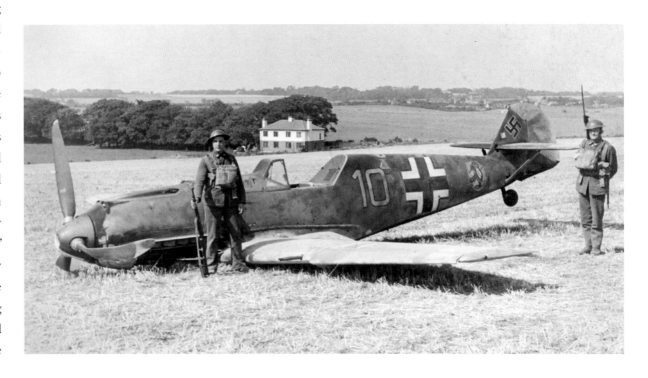

An incongruous scene of a crashed-landed Me 109 in the middle of the Kent countryside, 24 August 1940. This downed German aircraft is now on display at the Imperial War Museum, Duxford. (IWM HU 66615)

It is to Malan's credit that many of the pilots under his command received these instructions informally during the height of the Battle. Despite Dowding's concerns regarding inadequate training, little was formally initiated to give novice pilots real insight into the skills of aerial combat. It is difficult to level criticism at Dowding when he was attempting to conduct the defence of Britain. Nonetheless, it seems a missed opportunity on the part of other senior officers that good pilots who did not have the benefit of such teaching were being risked on an almost daily basis. It was one of the few mistakes made during Fighter Command's skilful conduct of the Battle.

With the weather clearing on 24 August the Battle began again in earnest. Raids were launched against Hornchurch, North Weald, and poor beleaguered Manston twice. The decision was finally taken to formally abandon the airfield and to use it for emergency landings only. Nigel Cameron was a 14-year-old schoolboy living in Herne Bay on the Kent coast. On this day he recorded in his diary witnessing a dogfight over the once sleepy coastal resort town that was his home:

> After lunch there was a great deal of activity over us and, while Peter and I were looking for planes, we suddenly saw a parachute floating down towards the sea. It went quite quickly, for we immediately got on our bikes and raced to the front. Already quite a crowd had gathered. There was nothing to be seen of the parachute or pilot for he had landed about five miles out to sea. Then some fishermen rowed out and got into a motorboat. By this time Mum & Dodie had turned up. We watched it disappear over the horizon (almost) and saw it through binoculars. After a quarter of an hour or so it turned round and started back. By this time the front was packed with people. Soon the motorboat was within a few hundred yards of the shore. The crowd increased (if that was possible) and the road was full of vehicles of every description, ambulances, trailers, even military lorries. Tin hats were to be seen in great abundance. All for one miserable pilot! The crowd surged towards the landing point. Police, ARP wardens, Home Guards and soldiers (all in tin hats), even a fireman, met him and made a gangway. Luckily I was very near and saw him well. He was a German. The whisper spread through the crowd – Jerry, German, etc. He had on a dingy blue-grey uniform, with wings sewn on and an iron cross (like every German airman appears to have). His hair was disheveled and his face streaked with yellow grease. He appeared quite unhurt but extremely sullen for he wouldn't take his eyes off the ground. He didn't speak a word.
>
> The crowd was silent except for a few remarks. The man next to me growled his disapproval and other remarks Mum, Dodie & Peter heard were 'Now he'll taste some butter' and a policeman said 'Treat him rough!'
>
> He was bundled into an ambulance and that was the last we saw of him.[99]

For the crowds who were watching the progress of the Battle throughout the July and August of 1940 this was a very personal war effort. It was their roofs that the pilots saw as they careered over Kentish towns, Sussex villages and Hampshire cities. All too frequently it was their homes that would be bombed by Luftwaffe raiders who missed their real targets or simply needed to jettison the weight of the bombs as they attempted to escape the marauding defenders. No surprise then that some members of the Herne Bay community angrily greeted the arrival of downed German pilots.

But the entire population eagerly followed the Battle, not just those living in the direct path of Luftwaffe raiders, and the fighter pilots were rapidly approaching heroic status in the eyes of the public. Churchill's famous speech on 20 August went a long way to glamorize the so-called 'fighter boys', who were the country's most effective, and best, means of defence against the Luftwaffe. Addressing a packed House of Commons almost a full year after the outbreak of war, Churchill uttered the immortal words that have since come to epitomize the contribution of the pilots of Fighter Command:

> The gratitude of every home in our Island, in our Empire, and indeed throughout the world, except in the abodes of the guilty, goes out to the British airmen who, undaunted by odds, unwearied in their constant challenge and mortal danger, are turning the tide of the war by their prowess and by their devotion. Never in the field of human conflict was

so much owed by so many to so few. All hearts go out to the fighter pilots, whose brilliant actions we see with our own eyes day after day ...[100]

On 25 and 26 August they were once again called upon to perform such brilliant actions on a large scale throughout the south-east of England. Denis Wissler, a Pilot Officer flying with No. 85 Squadron, recounted two days of difficult fighting in his personal diary:

Sunday 25 August

This was our hard day being at 15 mins and readiness the day long. At about half past seven we had a hell of a scrap over Portland, in which about 100 a/c were engaged. F/L Bayne made an attack below and astern quarter. The Me 110 whipped up in a stall turn and I gave him a long burst while he was in a stalled condition, it fell over and went down. I then went on my own and made a Me 110 break formation, I gave it another burst and it went towards the sea. F/L Bayne shot down but OK. S/L Williams lost. Wing shot off.

Monday 26 August

We had another crack today when we were bought to readiness from 30 minutes available and sent off. As we took off a He IIIK waffled across the aerodrome at about 15,000 ft. F/L Bayne put us in line astern and we went roaring after it however it was already being attacked by Spitfires and its undercart was down. We gave it a good burst each and it turned back for land crashing by Ford aerodrome... There was a terrific battle at 25,000 feet, three of 43 Sqn being forced to take to their parachutes.[101]

The incessant sorties, patrols and dogfights were beginning to take their toll on the British pilots in No. 11 Group, many of whom were bordering on mental and physical exhaustion, especially the veteran pilots who were also responsible for leading the more inexperienced additions to their squadron, as Alan Deere later recalled:

You were either at readiness or you were in the air. It was pretty tiring. I was bloody tired, I can tell you; very tired. My squadron, 54, I think

A Luftwaffe squadron commander bids farewell to his crew prior to their forthcoming mission, August 1940. (akg images, ullstein bild)

we were down to five of the original pilots so we were operating on a bit of a shoestring, all new pilots. Those who were left were obviously the two flight commanders, of which I was one, the squadron commander had already been taken off for a rest, and a couple of experienced pilots. We had to do all the flying. We had to do all the leading. There was nobody else...

You'd then go days, for example, without actually seeing the mess in daylight. We'd go off to dispersal. If we were operating from the forward base, Manston, which we generally were up till towards the end, we'd be off before first light so we'd be landing at first light at Manston. Similarly we'd come back in the evenings at last light. The rest of the time was spent either sitting at dispersal, which was way out the other side of the airfield with a tent or a telephone or in the air. We used to have meals brought out to us... Never saw the public, never got off the airfield.[102]

NIGHT RAID 1940.

Of course, the Luftwaffe pilots were battling similar signs of fatigue. German pilots began to report cases of 'Channel Sickness'. Originally believed to be simply instances of feigned illness to avoid flying duties, many pilots were genuinely ill, often with stomach ulcers or repeatedly vomiting because of the stress. Nor were pilots the only ones to suffer. British ground staff lived and worked with the ever-present dangers of an air raid. Courage, and in some cases ingenuity, was called upon to survive an air raid and get the airfield operational again as quickly as possible. The Station Commander of Biggin Hill, Richard Grice, even resorted to blowing up his own hangars so that Luftwaffe reconnaissance planes would report that the airfield was no longer in use due to heavy bombing.

The final days of August and early September are often highlighted as the most dangerous period for the British during the whole of the Battle. The attacks on airfields had begun again in earnest after the weather had forced a delay. What is more, they seemed to be more precise. Throughout the summer the Luftwaffe was essentially flying blind, with no clear understanding of which targets were the most valuable, as they made few attempts to find out which airfields were being used by Fighter Command. During the fighting in Poland and France, German bombers had been accustomed to finding neatly parked lines of aircraft, which they could attack with ease. This goes some way to explaining the initial reliance on reconnaissance flights to identify targets during the early stages of the fighting. However, this had often resulted in the bombing of airfields that were not in regular use by Fighter Command. In this later phase in the Battle, Kesselring increasingly relied on earlier Luftwaffe intelligence, which had correctly identified the location of each RAF squadron that was within reach of his fighter escorts.

With Luftflotte 2's attacks on the airfields of No. 11 Group, Kesselring was attempting to cause maximum damage on the ground as well as forcing the defenders to engage in costly aerial engagements. Unbeknown to him, by attacking the sector aerodromes of No. 11 Group he was also striking at the nerve centres of Fighter Command's defensive system. It was here that radar reports

could be translated into the effective deployment of forces. Advance warning was worth more than a hundred Spitfires and without it Britain faced the very real possibility of defeat.

However, it was extremely difficult for the Luftwaffe to score a direct hit on an operations room. They were inconspicuous single-storey brick buildings protected by blast walls in most cases, while at Tangmere the operations room was a concrete bunker. The Luftwaffe crews had no way of knowing that these buildings were far more significant than any aircraft hangar, nor were they capable of high-volume precision strikes once the Stukas were withdrawn from the Battle. Only the continued use of Erprobungsgruppe 210, the sheer volume of raids and a small measure of luck ensured that some attacks did cause real damage to the operational effectiveness of the command and control system.

On 30 August Biggin Hill endured a series of devastating attacks. The first raiders consisting of over 90 bombers crossed into British

The view from a German He 111 bomber on a mission against England escorted by Me 109 fighter planes on either 25 or 26 August 1940. (akg images, ullstein bild)

Previous page:
A page from the diary of 14-year-old Nigel Cameron who lived in Herne Bay and witnessed a number of dogfights over his Kentish seaside town throughout the summer months. (IWM Documents 1534)

airspace shortly before lunchtime. Although Park hastily scrambled almost all available fighters, a group of Ju 88s slipped through the net and successfully dropped some bombs on the airfield. Again, no lasting damage was done but towards the end of the afternoon wave after wave of enemy aircraft swept across the Channel. With so many plots to predict, 18 Ju 88 bombers once again avoided the defenders and struck Biggin Hill low and fast at 6pm. With no advance warning the effects were particularly devastating, with 39 ground staff killed and 26 wounded. The 500kg bombs had destroyed armouries, storerooms and staff accommodation. The shock waves from the explosion even buried the shelter of a group of WAAFs. Only one was pulled out alive. Battling against the shell shock and the deaths of many close colleagues, the ground staff nonetheless worked tirelessly to get the station running again.

However, this raid had simply been a portent of things to come. The following day the German raiders once again had Biggin Hill in their sights. This time they struck the operations room itself and for the first time since the start of the Battle of Britain a vital component of the defensive system went down. But this German success had occurred during one of the final raids of the day and the engineers worked tirelessly through the night to ensure that Biggin Hill was up and running again by the morning. On a positive note Park had called upon the Polish pilots of No. 303 Squadron to help with the defence of his sector station. The squadron had only become officially operational that day but the experienced, battle-hardened pilots were more than ready to take on the German pilots, at last in an equal contest. The following combat report illustrates the ruthless effectiveness of the Polish pilots, who easily showed what could be achieved when you got in close:

Flight A, Sqn 303 (Polish)

Number of enemy aircraft: 60 plus, Dornier 215s, Me 109s

Time: Approx 18.25 hrs

Place: East of Biggin Hill

Height of enemy: 14,000 feet

P/O Feric

I was Yellow 2. After about 15 minutes flying we saw about 70 E/A [enemy aircraft] to N.E. On the way towards them Yellow section met 3 Me 109s which did not see us as we had the sun behind us. The surprise was complete. Each of us took one E/A. A higher section of Me 109s began to descend on us. I gave a short burst at my Me 109 from 70 yards at fuselage and engine. The engine caught fire. The pilot baled out and E/A crashed in flames.

(Note: P/O Feric fired only 20 rounds from each gun)[103]

Biggin Hill had not been the only target. Before mid-morning Debden and North Weald had both been hit. Neither had sustained any permanent damage. Later in the day No. 12 Group also came under attack, with a bombing raid on Duxford, as did Eastchurch and Croydon airfields. That afternoon as Biggin Hill was being attacked a separate raiding party zoomed down on Hornchurch just as Alan Deere was taxiing off. His was one of three Spitfires caught on the ground as the bombs rained down, his aircraft skidding down the runway upside down with his helmet scraping along the ground. Miraculously none of the pilots were killed. But this day had seen Fighter Command suffer its heaviest casualties as it sought to halt the waves of German bombers. Forty aircraft were destroyed, nine pilots killed and 18 badly wounded, many of them with horrific burns. With the temporary exception of Biggin Hill, the system continued to function and to fight effectively. As the last hours of August faded away, Fighter Command waited anxiously to see what September would bring.

SEPTEMBER

Some members of the Luftwaffe felt a sense of disquiet as to how the Battle was progressing. Theo Osterkamp, the veteran Jagdflieger of Luftflotte 2, had experienced bitter defeat once before during the First World War and was disturbed by the losses the Luftwaffe was sustaining. From his perspective the attacks on the British airfields may have been reaping rewards but they were draining the air force of experienced pilots, which it could ill afford. Osterkamp submitted a report to the Air Inspector General, Erhard Milch, outlining his concerns. His reward was demotion and the threat of a court martial. Nor was everything well in the upper echelons of Fighter Command. As the Battle progressed, the relationship between Park and Leigh-Mallory had rapidly worsened. Park had hoped to call on No. 12 Group squadrons to protect his airfields while his own fighters were deployed to tackle the raiders. But on a number of occasions Park felt that these supporting fighters had been too slow in arriving and blamed Leigh-Mallory personally for the bombing of Debden and Hornchurch on 26 August. The relationship had deteriorated to the point where Park felt compelled to order his controllers to go through Fighter Command Headquarters rather

THE GUINEA PIG CLUB

Encased within their cockpits, strapped into the seats, and with a tank full of flammable petrol, fire was a common risk shared by all pilots. Some carried a loaded pistol to avoid what many considered a fate worse than death. Others flew with scarves, goggles and gloves to ensure that no piece of skin was left exposed. However all too often during the course of the Battle, and indeed for the rest of the war, pilots were badly injured as well as horrifically disfigured. Those that bailed out, often engulfed in flames, and landed on British soil could be treated at the Queen Victoria East Grinstead Hospital. Here something remarkable was taking place. Headed up by the New Zealand surgeon Sir Archibald McIndoe, a specialist burns unit was established. At the outbreak of the Second World War treatment centres were divided up and run on service lines. It is to the RAF's credit that early on they recognized not only McIndoe's genius as a surgeon, but that some of his more unorthodox treatments would be hugely beneficial to his patients. Known simply as 'The Boss' by staff and patients alike, McIndoe was one of the most gifted surgeons of his generation. Together with his cousin and former colleague on Harley Street, Sir Harold Gillies, they pioneered the development of the 'walking-stalk skin flap', where new skin was grown inside a tube attached on each end to the patient's body. Although it led to some of his patients likening themselves to elephant men, thanks to the long tubes often hanging from their faces, it was unique at the time in drastically helping to reduce the risk of infection.

Geoffrey Page photographed after receiving the Distinguished Flying Cross on his return to active service three years and several operations after he was badly burnt during the Battle of Britain. (Queen Victoria Hospital Museum)

Other simpler methods also reaped huge rewards, such as the practice of immersing patients in saline solution. McIndoe had noticed that burnt pilots who were rescued from the Channel healed more quickly than those that bailed out over land, and this relatively easy treatment would save countless patients. But, most unusually, McIndoe recognized that his patients were young men, just at the start of their lives, and would be devastated to discover that they were permanently scarred or horrifically disfigured. They would also have to face months, if not years, of painful surgery and treatment, which would require courage and determination to recover from. To counter any morbid thoughts or collapse in morale McIndoe strived to create a cheerful atmosphere. He hired the prettiest nurses, who were encouraged to flirt outrageously with the patients, barrels of beer were installed in the wards, and sing-alongs with the rudest lyrics possible were par for the course. Those patients who were well enough were encouraged to continue to wear their uniforms and were allowed to come and go as they pleased. McIndoe even roped in the residents of East Grinstead to assist in the process, and it became 'the town that did not stare', welcoming each new arrival with open arms, some pilots even staying as guests in local houses rather than as in-patients.

Not for them the usual occupational therapy of basket-making or embroidery. McIndoe knew that these were fighting men who would want to feel that they were still contributing to the war effort. So he set up a small satellite factory in the hospital grounds making aircraft instruments. Soon their output per man exceeded the parent company.

The patients themselves formed the 'Guinea Pig Club', an irreverent drinking society that met in one of the wooden sheds in the grounds of the hospital. A small entrance fee was charged and the Treasurer was elected on the grounds that his badly burnt legs encased in plaster would ensure that he did not run off with the club's funds. Later, at the suggestion of Geoffrey Page, a founding member and Battle of Britain pilot, it grew into a welfare society that provided funds for badly burnt pilots who required financial assistance. Not wanting to take themselves too seriously though, they called it the 'Society for the Prevention of Cruelty to Guinea Pigs'.

McIndoe's genius both as a surgeon and as a student of men ensured that many badly burned pilots, once thought of as the wreckage of the war, would be able to lead fulfilling lives. Quite a few married their nurses, many more returned to active service. One such example was Geoffrey Page. He had been shot down on 12 August over the English Channel. Burning petrol had splashed into the cockpit and he could smell his own burning flesh as he parachuted down into the icy waters. Fifteen operations later, remarkably Page returned to active duties flying Mustangs, American fighter aircraft. Page was the first chairman of the Guinea Pig Club and was just one of its success stories. It continues to meet annually although its numbers are steadily dwindling. All, however, can remember the words to their own unique anthem:

We are McIndoe's army,
We are his Guinea Pigs.
With dermatomes and peficles,
Glass eyes, false teeth and wigs.
And when we get our discharge
We'll shout with all our might:
'Per ardua ad astra'
We'd rather drink than fight

John Hunter runs the gas works,
Ross Tilly wields the knife.
And if they are not careful
They'll have your flaming life.
So, Guinea Pigs, stand steady
For all your surgeon's calls:
And if their hands aren't steady
They'll whip off both your ears

We've had some mad Australians,
Some French, some Czechs, some Poles.
We've had some Yankees,
God bless their precious souls.
While as for the Canadians –
Ah! That's a different thing.
They couldn't stand our accent
And built a separate wing

We are McIndoe's army ...[104]

Below: Sir Archibald McIndoe (1900–60). The Blond McIndoe Research Foundation at the Queen Victoria East Grinstead Hospital continues his pioneering work in the fields of reconstructive surgery and wound healing. (Queen Victoria Hospital Museum)

Left: McIndoe surrounded by patients and nurses during a typical hospital sing-along. (Queen Victoria Hospital Museum)

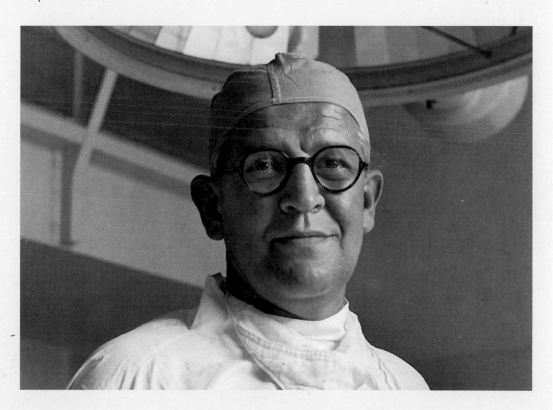

than approaching No. 12 Group directly if they wanted to ensure the timely arrival of supporting squadrons.

Leigh-Mallory in turn was increasingly unconvinced by the feasibility of Park's tactics. His views were endorsed by one of his own subordinates, Douglas Bader, the 30-year-old commander of No. 242 (Canadian) Squadron. Bader was a remarkable man. He had lost both his legs in a pre-war accident but had convinced his superiors to allow him to return to operational flying. No. 242 Squadron had been badly mauled during the Battle of France and suffered from low morale. By the sheer force of his inspirational personality he reinvigorated the pilots under his command so that they could return to operational duties. It should come as no surprise then that Bader was wildly enthusiastic about pursuing a more aggressive, attacking strategy through the deployment of 'big wings', designed to deliver a knock-out blow to the Luftwaffe. The 'big wing' theory could have been developed only outside of the frontline. As the Germans knew so well, amassing large formations of fighters and coordinating their movements takes a considerable amount of time. Such 'big wings' could not conceivably counter German raids until after they had made their bombing run; there simply wasn't enough time between the confirmation of a target by the plotters and getting a large formation airborne to a sufficient height. In the eyes of Park this left his precious airfields, and particularly his sector stations, dangerously exposed. Park had the unstinting support of his commander, but in some ways this was Dowding's great failure

Air Vice-Marshal Trafford Leigh-Mallory (1892–1944), commander of No. 12 Group, who clashed repeatedly with Air Vice-Marshal Keith Park at the height of the Battle of Britain. He replaced Park as Commander of No. 11 Group and eventually became head of Fighter Command. Prior to the D-Day invasions he lobbied successfully for a unified Allied air command to cooperate closely with the invading armies. Despite much opposition he was ultimately successful and was appointed Commander-in-Chief Allied Expeditionary Air Forces. With the Battle of Normandy drawing to a close he was appointed Air Commander-in-Chief of South East Asia Command but was killed when his transport plane crashed in bad weather. His replacement, ironically, was Keith Park. Today, Leigh-Mallory is often associated almost exclusively with the 'big wing' controversy and some of his later war successes have been unfairly overshadowed by this. (IWM CH 11943)

during the Battle of Britain; not so much in the respect of supporting Park's tactics, which were undoubtedly correct, but his failure to resolve the worsening relationship between two of his key commanders or to recognize the fact that No. 12 Group felt underused. Instead of convincing Leigh-Mallory that his policy would have merit once the threat to No. 11 Group lessened, Dowding allowed the debate to spiral into feuding and a very personal dispute. It is one of the few criticisms that can be levelled against Dowding throughout the course of the Battle.

Quite possibly Dowding simply did not have the time or the inclination to sort out his squabbling Group Commanders. He was more preoccupied with the dangerous shortage of experienced pilots. On 1 September Dowding was forced to realize that he could no longer afford the luxury of rotating squadrons out of No. 11 Group to rest and recuperate when necessary. Instead he was compelled to classify his squadrons as either A, B or C. 'A' would include all squadrons stationed in No. 11 Group, Duxford and Middle Wallop. They would be at the sharp end of the Battle until either the weather turned or one side buckled under the strain, whichever came first. Supporting them would be the 'B' squadrons, which was the rest of No. 12 Group as well as No. 10 Group. They would be kept at full operational strength and would support the 'A' squadrons when called upon to do so. The 'C' squadrons were those located in the quietest areas of the country and would essentially act as training units, to be promoted directly to 'A' squadrons as soon as the opportunity or need arose.

In the meantime the attacks on the airfields continued unabated. Biggin Hill was subjected to its usual late afternoon attack but this time was better prepared. When a lucky German strike ensured that the operations room was out of action, an emergency operations room had already been set up in the local village shop, proving at least Fighter Command's resourcefulness.

The first day of the month was a glorious summer's day and Kesselring made the most of the weather, ordering a number of raids in addition to the now normal Biggin Hill strike. Eastchurch, Debden and Kenley were hit again, as was the Fleet Air Arm base at

Detling. Despite this, and his own personal problems with Leigh-Mallory, Park remained convinced that No. 11 Group could take this punishing routine. When Churchill himself visited Park that afternoon to hear first-hand where things stood, the Prime Minister too came away convinced that the RAF would withstand the pressure thanks to Park's cool assessment of his pilots' abilities.

It had been another hard day of fighting for both sides. Lieutenant Josef Buerschgens had acted as Staffel Führer for 7/JG 26 during the attack on Kenley and later recalled the ferocity of the fighting in a sky crowded with fighters and bombers:

Our orders were to escort a Gruppe of bombers attacking Kenley. Flying at an altitude of about 6–7000m, we reached the target without being

With the intensification of the air battles throughout August and the daylight bombing campaign against London in September, many assumed that an invasion attempt was imminent before the weather turned. Here Home Guard members are shown training with an aircraft Lewis gun at a Weapon Training School in case they would be called upon to provide frontline service. (IWM H 4062)

attacked and only then were we engaged in aerial combat with British fighters which were more interested in the bombers and the Bf 110s. I had remained with the bombers when, immediately beneath me, a Bf 110 flying in a defensive circle was attacked by a Spitfire. It took no effort on my part to place myself behind the attacker so there in a row were the Bf 110, the Spitfire and then the Bf 109 flown by me. The gunner opened fire on the Spitfire and the Spitfire in turn tried to knock out the gunner. It was relatively easy for me to lay into the Spitfire in a continuous attack. At once smoke started to pour from the Spitfire who pulled away, diving steeply. During the attack, I had got rather close to the rear gunner of the Bf 110 who was still firing and I turned away to avoid ramming him. At this instant, I felt an impact by the side of my foot on the left of the cockpit, the engine cut out and the propeller began windmilling. My God! The gunner had taken me for an enemy fighter…Trailing fuel, I dipped my Bf 109 slightly and started gliding towards the French coast, hoping to reach the waters of the Channel where I might be picked up by a German rescue plane. The sun shone warm and bright and the seconds seemed like hours. I glided and glided whilst all around me furious battles were being fought. Some of our bombers which had been hit, fighters, enemies and friends fell, smoking, burning or disintegrating. Parachutes opened or didn't as the case might be. It was a gruesome yet thrilling spectacle. Never before had I been able to watch the fighting like now.

Gliding, I got nearer to the ground but could not reach the waters of the Channel. Near Rye, I finally disassembled my faithful Bf 109 into its many components. I regained consciousness in hospital, having suffered back and head injuries when I baled out.[105]

Buerschgens would spend the rest of the war as a POW. Others were more fortunate. Years later Hans-Ekkehard Bob, a fellow Messerschmitt 109 pilot, who served throughout the conflict, would claim that on some days in the late summer the British didn't have a single fighter aircraft that was capable of flying. In reality, the British would studiously avoid the vast swarms of fighters that would enter their air space, as per Park's instructions, unless they were escorting bombers. However, as Kesselring increased the number of fighters to serve as escorts for each bomber fleet, some British squadrons did indeed refuse to engage the Luftwaffe unless they had gained sufficient height. To attack too low was suicidal when there were so many enemy fighters in the air but this was no reflection on the determination of the defenders. As the early September days dawned clear and bright with the promise of yet more heavy fighting, it would have taken sheer guts on the part of the defenders to continue not only to battle against the attacking forces but their own exhaustion. A few couldn't take the pressure and were discreetly removed from the frontline, but the majority battled on. Courage came in many shapes and sizes. 'Ginger' Lacey, the second-highest scoring ace of the Battle, reportedly threw up before most combat sorties, while George Unwin recalled a different kind of heroism:

I never came across a lack of moral fibre in a Fighter Squadron … it was quite the opposite. I knew one chap who was scared stiff. A fellow named R—. Sergeant R— was in my squadron and he hated it but he wouldn't give in. He flatly refused, he should have been taken off, genuinely taken off and put on some other form… Now, I think that is courage of a different kind altogether but he was unfortunately killed in 1940. He was bound to be killed, bound to be killed, he really was. He should never have been allowed to carry on but there it is, he wouldn't let it be known.[106]

Their stoicism was having the desired effect. Despite some Luftwaffe fighter pilots' luck in not encountering any enemy defenders they were in the minority, as reflected in the declining strength of the German air fleets. The Luftwaffe had begun the Battle of Britain with over 900 fighter pilots available to call upon. By 1 September that figure had plummeted to just 735. In that same period, the number of British operational pilots had increased by almost the same margin. Of course, many of those pilots were inadequately trained, but in the battle of attrition there was still a clear winner. The final week of August until 2 September saw Fighter Command sustain its heaviest losses, but the production of fighters continued apace and Dowding's reorganization of his squadrons ensured that there was a ready pool of pilots to draw on. In contrast, the Luftwaffe was operating on a low level of reserves. Only as late as June had Hitler granted special priority to aircraft manufacture yet even the modest targets that were set for the aircraft industry failed to be met. Between June and September a grand total of 775 Me 109s were produced, compared to 1,900 fighters produced in Britain. Admittedly the German aircraft industry was required to produce large numbers of twin-engined fighters and other bombers, but it failed to recognize that more fighters would be required than any other aircraft type, particularly once Kesselring was forced to insist that over three-quarters of any raiding party should consist of fighters to counter the heavy losses sustained by the bombers. Germany had far greater access to raw materials and manpower than Britain, and Göring was no less bullying than Beaverbrook, so it is shocking that the Third Reich's aircraft industry failed to meet even its modest quotas. Reforms to the training of wartime pilots were also slow in coming. The Luftwaffe lost far fewer pilots than the British, thanks in part to their thorough pre-war training and previous combat experience. But these losses were perhaps more keenly felt when the flow of replacements was nothing more than a trickle. Most significantly, despite the sustained strikes at the very heart of its infrastructure, Fighter Command continued to shoot down more enemy planes than it lost. The total had dropped since the start of Eagle but then the Ju 87 had been temporarily withdrawn from service and there were no more Stuka parties for the British pilots to enjoy.

Kesselring continued his attacks regardless, with further raids launched on 2 September. The day had dawned with some mist and fog but soon gave way to brilliant, late summer sunshine. Once again there were four main stages of attack against the airfields. The first wave of enemy raiders crossed the Channel shortly before 8am, attacking Eastchurch, North Weald and, yet again, Biggin Hill. Seven squadrons were scrambled and a second smaller raiding party was forced to turn back. Two further large-scale raids followed in the afternoon and early evening. Biggin Hill was badly damaged again but continued to function. Eastchurch also took a pounding and was

The successful bomber pilot Werner Baumbach with his crew including bombardier, radio operator and gunner in front of their Ju 88 in the autumn of 1940. Baumbach had been one of the first pilots to be trained to fly the Ju 88 and flew a number of missions with Kampfgeschwader (KG) 30 throughout the Battle of Britain. He worked on a number of highly secret German bomber design teams and later commanded KG 200, the special-operations wing that flew covert operations including some with captured Allied aircraft. He was killed post-war in an air accident 1953. (akg images)

Flight Lieutenant Lawson and Flight Sergeant Unwin (with their backs to the camera) confer with No. 19 Squadron Commander, Squadron Leader B. J. E 'Sandy' Lane in September 1940. The fatigue and strain of flying continuously throughout the Battle of Britain is clearly visible on the young commander's face. He was just 23 at the time and would be shot down and killed two years later. (IWM CH 1366)

reduced to only one runway, which had to be used with caution. As was the norm, in both cases, ground staff worked tirelessly to ensure that these two stations would be fully functioning by the morning.

The following day Göring ordered his senior commanders to attend a conference at The Hague. Preparations for *Sealion* had been continuing but Hitler was disappointed with the lack of success on the part of the Luftwaffe. In the first place it was now clear that an

invasion would be necessary to subdue the stubborn British, despite Göring's earlier ambitions to be solely responsible for the destruction of Britain's resistance efforts. Preparations for *Sealion* were also no doubt hindered by the navy's reluctance to commit to an amphibious assault, which they knew was beyond their capabilities, and Hitler had been forced to postpone the launch date from 15 September to a probable start date of 21 September. But *Sealion* could not begin unless air superiority had been achieved over the south-east of England. This was clearly still a long way off and was Hitler's chief concern. Göring had just over two weeks to fulfil his Führer's wishes.

Kesselring, living up to his nickname of 'Smiling Albert', remained bullishly optimistic that Fighter Command was enduring unsustainable losses and was drastically short of fighters. He was pleased with the progress of the attacks on the airfields but was concerned that the British would simply retreat from the airfields around London to those beyond the range of German fighters. In Kesselring's eyes his bombers had simply been destroying airfields, of which the British had plenty. He remained ignorant of some of the success his Luftflotten had enjoyed against a number of the key sector stations and the risk this had posed to the British defensive system. Kesselring wanted to force the British fighters into the air in large numbers so that his more numerous and more experienced pilots could pick them off, causing final, truly debilitating losses. Only one place could inspire that kind of defence and it was not an aerodrome, it was the nation's own beating heart – London.

Sperrle disagreed. He was sceptical of the loss reports that both Göring and Kesselring seemed happy to accept, and preferred to continue the attacks on Fighter Command's infrastructure. However, the events of the past few days conspired against him. Throughout the Battle of Britain the RAF had been waging a war on two fronts. While Fighter Command struggled against the daily raids, Bomber Command was instructed to strike at Germany's military infrastructure and factories to prove that Britain was still capable of offensive action. By and large, Bomber Command's attempts had been disastrous, hugely costly in terms of lost manpower and for very little gain, not entirely dissimilar to the Luftwaffe's own attempts. Both sides had avoided wholesale attacks on major cities, keen to avoid the cycle of destruction that so many had predicted throughout the 1930s. However, on 15 August some German bombers had accidentally hit the outlying factories of Croydon, on the outskirts of London. Little damage was done and the incident was ignored. But on the night of 24/25 August a force of Heinkels had attempted to hit the oil terminal at Thameshaven. It was always going to be

difficult trying to locate a precise target in the inky-black skies and, not surprisingly the bombs fell across the residential quarter of the East End instead. In retaliation the War Cabinet approved the first raids on Berlin. In reality, civilian deaths had been on the rise steadily throughout the summer, even if deliberate German terror attacks were not authorized. In July 258 civilians had been killed. By the end of August that figure had risen to over 1,000 including 136 children. These figures would have played their part in the Cabinet's decision. On the night of 28/29 August British bombs hit a suburb of Berlin killing eight and wounding 21 others. Hitler lifted his veto on London and the capital was now fair game for Göring's Luftwaffe.

The Reichsmarschall himself was concerned about the effect the raids on Berlin would have on his political standing. For years he had trumpeted that no enemy bomber would ever attack Berlin. He could not risk becoming a laughing stock, and only swift, ruthless retribution

Joseph Goebbels, the German Propaganda Minister, inspects the bomb damage to Berlin following the RAF raid on the city on 25 August 1940. (IWM HU 76018)

would silence his critics. Several military commanders had already been pushing for a consolidated attack on the British capital. It was believed that the inhabitants would flee, as they had in France, blocking the roads and transport links, thereby preventing the free movement of the British Army. Sperrle was outvoted. The citizens of London would feel the full wrath of the Luftwaffe and in the process the RAF would be destroyed or the British government would be forced to the negotiating table. It would be a win–win situation for Göring.

7 SEPTEMBER – THE GOD OF FIRE

The German High Command made no secret of their intentions. On 4 September in front of a cheering crowd of mostly female factory workers and nurses Hitler laid down his challenge, each sentence punctuated with the cries of 'Heil! Heil!':

It is a wonderful thing to see our nation at war, in its fully disciplined state. This is exactly what we are now experiencing at this time, as Mr Churchill is demonstrating to us the aerial night attacks which he has concocted. He is not doing this because these air raids might be particularly effective, but because his Air Force cannot fly over German territory in daylight. Whereas German aviators and German planes fly over English soil daily, there is hardly a single Englishman who comes across the North Sea in daytime.

They therefore come during the night – and as you know, release their bombs indiscriminately and without any plan on to residential areas, farmhouses and villages. Wherever they see a sign of light, a bomb is dropped on it. For three months past, I have not ordered any answer to be given, thinking that they would stop this nonsensical behavior. Mr Churchill has taken this to be a sign of our weakness. You will understand that we shall now give a reply, night for night, and with increasing force.

And if the British Air Force drops two, three or four thousand kilos of bombs, then we will now drop 150,000, 180,000, 230,000, 300,000 or 400,000 kilos, or more, in one night. If they declare that they will attack our cities on a large scale, we will erase theirs! We will put a stop to the game of these night-pirates, as God is our witness. The hour will come when one or the other of us will crumble, and that one will not be National Socialist Germany. I have already carried through such a struggle once in my life, up to the final consequences, and this then led to the collapse of the enemy who is now still sitting there in England on Europe's last island.[107]

That same day the bombers streamed in to attack British aircraft factories, the Hurricane plant at Brooklands bearing the brunt of the attack with 700 casualties. But this was simply the prelude. The seventh of September would mark the start of the main event. Code-named Operation *Loge* after the god of fire, Göring announced on German radio that he would be taking charge of proceedings himself. In reality Kesselring and his immediate subordinates had already done all of the planning. Nonetheless, Göring's personal train

Opposite:
One of Paul Nash's last works for the Air Ministry was a watercolour showing the bombing of Berlin on 25 August 1940 by Whitley bombers from Bomber Command. (IWM ART LD 827)

Below:
Following RAF Bomber Command's attack on Berlin Hitler addresses a crowd of factory workers, nurses and other relief workers on 4 September 1940, assuring them that the Luftwaffe will prevail and that Churchill's Britain will be crushed mercilessly. (akg images)

6.48pm on 7 September 1940 and a
Heinkel III bomber is photographed
over the Isle of Dogs. (IWM C 5422)

pulled into the Pas-de-Calais just as the Air Ministry formally issued Invasion Alert No. 1 ('Attack Imminent') to all of the relevant commands. Shortly before 4pm the first 'hostile' raid was picked up and plotted. Then suddenly the radar screens lit up as wave after wave of enemy planes crossed the Channel. It was a remarkable sight – almost 350 bombers drawn from five different Kampfgeschwader accompanied by 617 Me 109s and 110s. Nothing had ever been seen like this before. The gathering formations were two miles high, staggered between 14,000 and 23,000 feet.

Within half an hour every squadron within a 70-mile radius of the capital was either airborne or waiting to be scrambled.

Despite Hitler's threats, Fighter Command expected a mass attack on the vulnerable No. 11 Group airfields. Instead of splitting up to attack several different airfields simultaneously the vast formation, consisting of virtually every available attack aircraft in France, advanced towards London. Too late the mistake was realized and as Park frantically ordered the squadrons to attack the first bombs were already raining down on the docks and factories along the Thames. As the air-raid sirens screamed their warning, people were initially slow to move into the shelters, reluctant to abandon the September sunshine. This soon changed once the initial bombs found their mark, and for the first time since the start of the war London was ablaze.

Park had instructed his squadrons to scramble in pairs, with Hurricanes focusing on the bombers and the Spitfires dealing with the fighter escorts. However, such a vast formation proved impossible to break up and the British defenders were incapable of preventing the wholesale attack. Park's initial restraint was understandable. It was standard practice to hold off deploying forces until the exact size and direction of each raid was determined. Now

Top:
Czech pilots of No. 310 Squadron enjoy a brief moment of respite on 7 September 1940. (IWM CH 1299)

Bottom:
Burning oil tanks at Purfleet on the Thames following a German air raid on 7 September 1940. (akg images, ullstein bild)

A dogfight over England on 18 September 1940 leaves its mark on the British skies. (IWM H 4219)

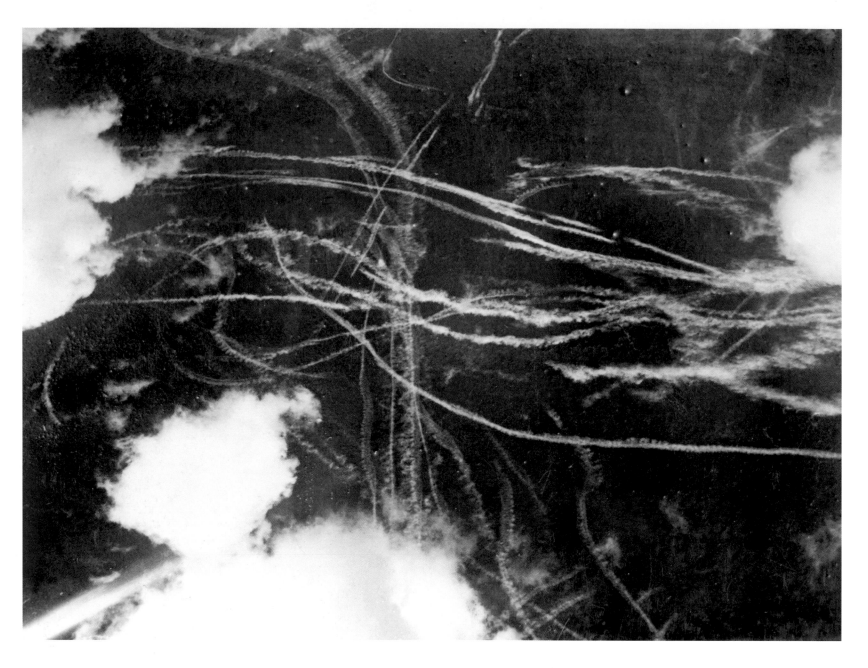

the Luftwaffe had thrown the rulebook out of the window. The situation was not helped by the fact that Bader scrambled a 'big wing', which arrived too late to help prevent the initial attacks, and in the confusing mêlée with hundreds of aircraft in the skies it was unable to operate effectively. Moreover, it caused the relationship between Park and Leigh-Mallory to deteriorate still further.

For months pilots had existed in this surreal situation where the war was being fought thousands of feet in the air but life went on as normal on the ground. Edward Morris, a pilot with No. 79 Squadron, recorded his thoughts on the incongruity of the situation throughout that Spitfire Summer:

Once one had broken off the engagement and was heading for home, often at low level to escape the attentions of enemy fighters, the incongruity of this type of warfare became apparent. It was commonplace to fly over four white clad tennis players or even a village cricket match on these lovely summer afternoons. There were many stories of those who had force landed or baled out, a friend of mine landed his shot-up Spitfire, wheels up, on a golf course fairway to get an icy reception from some elderly members and a ticking off from the Secretary for ruining the surface.[108]

Now for the citizens of Greater London there was no escape from the realities of war. Four hundred and forty-eight lives were lost during the bomb attacks of 7 September. Once the great German armada had turned for home, the late-arriving British squadrons had been able to inflict some damage, with 38 German bombers and fighters shot down. But it had come at the price of 28 aircraft; the British would need to be better prepared next time.

There was no way the Luftwaffe could maintain this kind of momentum on a daily basis. Over the next couple of days only limited raids were launched and the weather had finally begun to turn, grounding aircraft on at least one occasion. Night-time raids, however, continued apace. There was little Fighter Command could do about such attacks as it was still without an effective night fighter. This was the start of the Blitz and London would be bombed consecutively every night for the next 57 days. The great attack of 7 September itself had not yielded any definitive result, although Kesselring would undoubtedly have taken heart from the Luftwaffe's performance. Another test was required.

Top:
Winston Churchill visited the 'blitzed' East End on 8 September 1940 to see for himself the destruction caused and to assess the mood of the people. (IWM H 3978)

Bottom:
The squadron mascot greets Sergeant Furst of No. 310 Squadron (Czechoslovakia) on his return to Duxford after a successful sortie on 7 September 1940. (IWM CH 1296)

15 September – Battle of Britain Day

A weather-induced pause allowed Dowding and Park to take stock of the situation. Both were heartily relieved that the Germans had seemed to have moved away from their attempts to destroy Fighter Command's infrastructure. This would not only give them the breathing space that they so desperately required, but more importantly both foresaw it as a crucial strategic error on the part of the Luftwaffe. Rather than teetering on the brink of defeat, both men could sense the opportunity for a British victory. The pause in hostilities caused by the weather meant that Dowding even had

Opposite:
Residents of one bombed-out London suburb pile the furniture they have managed to salvage in the road. The resourcefulness of the London population in the face of such adversity ensured that the British government was not forced to sue for peace. (IWM CP 10637)

Left:
The outbreak of war had heralded a huge wave of evacuations of children from major cities. Almost two-thirds had returned home by mid-1940. However, with the bombing of London at the start of September a second round of evacuations began. (IWM D 2593)

Others chose to stick it out in home-made shelters. Here Doris and Alan Suter are shown entering their own Anderson shelter, which was situated in their back garden. It was for a media piece entitled 'British Working Class Family in Wartime'. (IWM D 778)

a couple of days to realign his forces and was able to once again rotate squadrons.

On 9 September with the weather improving the raiders gathered in substantial numbers again and this time Park was prepared. The Luftwaffe approached in a pincer movement, with two separate raiding parties approaching London via Dover and Beachy Head. Park had scrambled his fighters early and they were positioned well in advance of the capital. Instead of burning London the first raiding party was forced to offload their bombs on Canterbury, while the second formation was so badly broken up by the British attacks that it scattered, showering the surrounding towns and countryside with

its arsenal as it began a desperate retreat. Although some of the squadrons scrambled failed to intercept the enemy, particularly as the weather worsened, overall the day had been a British success. Despite high RAF losses – a total 17 planes and six pilots – the Luftwaffe had failed to strike at their intended target. Indeed, German losses were even higher for no real gain, with 24 aircraft lost in combat and ten pilots killed.

With the weather worsening there was time to refine tactics yet further. Leigh-Mallory met with Douglas Bader and decided that the lack of success with the 'big wing' had been due to insufficient numbers. The wing would now be increased from three squadrons to five. It is not clear on what basis they came to such a decision. In contrast, Park pored over combat reports from his pilots and decided to issue more specific instructions over the course of the next five days to ensure greater success against the attacking Luftwaffe. He recommended head-on attacks as they had proven results as well as flying as cohesive squadrons. An old combat hand himself, he also reminded his pilots not to follow the stricken enemy down to guarantee a kill; the point was to attack as many aircraft as possible. 'Sailor' Malan, the high-scoring commander of No. 74 Squadron, would have agreed. It is said that he preferred for a damaged German bomber to make it back to France so that their colleagues could witness the full horror of the dead and dying crews on board. For all the mythology of 'knights of the air' Fighter Command was, virtually from the start, a ruthless organization. As a Flying Officer in No. 85 Squadron during the Battle of France, Count Czernin noted in his after-action report that after shooting down a German bomber he made several attacks on the downed crew as they attempted to escape, displaying a ruthlessness that would stand him in good stead during a later career as an SOE agent.

Many would have been motivated by the loss of their colleagues or a sense of patriotism to defend their homeland from the threat of a Nazi invasion. With the daylight bombings of London, everyone's worst fears of the Nazi war machine had been realized. Denis Wissler, Count Czernin's young colleague in No. 85 Squadron, would comment in his diary after 7 September that the Jerries were 'complete swines' and 'God Damn and blast Hitler'.[108] Now the British pilots would fight with renewed vigour to protect their friends, their families, their homes and their country from obliteration. Their opportunity would come on 15 September as Göring authorized one final attempt to destroy Fighter Command.

For once the weathermen had got the prediction right and the day dawned clear and bright. Churchill had chosen to visit Uxbridge again and so was present as the drama began to unfold. The first raid was spotted shortly after 11am. Park chose to respond by scrambling Nos. 92 and 72 Squadrons. As the German fighters and bombers met to form up, the markers on the plotting board came thick and fast. Two squadrons would not suffice if this was Kesselring's main thrust. Squadrons were scrambled from Kenley, Debden, Northolt, North Weald, Hornchurch and Middle Wallop. Throughout south-east England phones rang in dispersal huts to rouse the pilots who had been idling away the hours since coming on duty at first light. The squadrons were not to be deployed en masse. Instead two were situated well forward, over Canterbury, another four patrolled over Biggin Hill and a further two were held slightly in the rear as support.

But this was not in fact the main attacking force. Kesselring had amassed all that Luftflotte 2 had to offer, just short of 500 bombers, supported by virtually the same number of Me 109s, together with 120 Me 110s. Instead of using his numerical superiority to bludgeon London with one attack, Kesselring decided to launch a preliminary raid to tire the defenders before launching his main assault. Just 25 Dorniers made up this initial bombing force but they were protected by over 100 Me 109s. Joining them were 21 specially adapted Me 109s, each carrying a 550lb bomb. Following on from the success of Erprobungsgruppe 210, they were designed to make a low-level, fast attack before joining the rest of the fighter escort. When they too were picked up by radar, Park, unsure whether they posed a threat or not, decided to scramble yet more fighters. This time he turned to No. 12 Group, officially calling on the Duxford wing. For the first time since the start of the Battle of Britain there were now greater numbers of defenders than there were attackers. As the Dorniers and their fighter escorts crossed over into Britain the British squadrons began to swarm around them like a pack of hunting dogs. Slowly the fighter escorts were stripped away as they became embroiled with the attacking Spitfires and Hurricanes. With admirable determination, the Dorniers, bunched tightly together to offer each other protection, maintained their formation and continued on their flight path towards London, despite having already lost one of their number. It must have been with horror that the Dornier crews witnessed something astonishing as Bader's wing swept into view. There were now so many British planes crowding the skies that they were forced to take turns attacking the crippled Dorniers. A total of six were shot down, one abandoned by its crew, which plummeted towards the heart of London and crashed into Victoria Station, although it was inaccurately reported at the time that it had attempted to bomb Buckingham Palace.[109] In contrast, the 21 fighter-bombers were left well alone, and failing to encounter any

Flight Lieutenant J. H. 'Ginger' Lacey of No. 501 Squadron in the cockpit of his Supermarine Spitfire Mark I. Between May and October 1940 he would claim 23 victories. (IWM CH 2793)

British defenders easily succeeded in attacking their target of a railway station and scattering bombs over Dulwich and Norwood.

The 254 Hurricanes and Spitfires that had been deployed in the attack returned to their bases to rearm and refuel. Just as they were doing so, Kesselring's main thrust was forming up over Calais. This would consist of 114 bombers and an incredible 340 Me 109s supported by 20 Me 110s. Kesselring had gone one better than Göring's recommendations for fighter escorts, and there was an astonishing four fighters to every one bomber. With so many fighters, Kesselring allowed some of them to fly higher and faster than the bombers, and it was these aircraft that would pose the greatest danger to the British defenders.

At Uxbridge, Park, with Churchill at his elbow, watched the plots begin to take shape. Convinced that once again London was the target, Park, the consummate strategist, decided to refine his tactics once more. Instead of deploying the majority of his squadrons well forward he would lull the attacking raiders into a false sense of security with smaller attacks, and just as their fighter escorts were beginning to run low on fuel he would cut through the formation with his main attack. It was a gamble, but he reckoned that Kesselring was risking everything he had, so it was a chance Park was willing to take. Shortly after 2pm the first British defenders made contact. There were just 27 of them so it was fortunate that they had the element of surprise and the sun to their rear. They claimed 14 for only one loss before the majority of the vast formation had even registered that it was under attack. As it neared London, Park increased the number of attacks as he scrambled every squadron within No. 11 Group. The Poles of No. 303 Squadron now tore into

Pilots of No. 19 Squadron gather at their satellite base, RAF Fowlmere, after a sortie. Standing fourth from the left in the bottom picture, and first right in the top image, is Squadron Leader 'Sandy' Lane. The system of satellite airfields ensured that even if the main base came under attack then there were alternative airstrips with limited facilities that could be used. The real danger came if a Sector or Group Command HQ suffered a direct hit but with so many potential targets to choose from the Luftwaffe did not always attack these more important airfields. With the Luftwaffe unable to gauge any means of success with the attacks on airfields, London became the primary target. (IWM CH 1370, IWM CH 1364)

the attack, supported by No. 602 Squadron. Yet more escorts peeled off to counter these attacks. But the German bombers had successfully breached the first line of defence and ploughed on, straight into the welcoming arms of Nos. 213 and 607 Squadrons. The vast formation had now split into three loose groups, but all were still aiming for their original target of the Royal Victoria and West India Docks, despite their bruising encounters with the first British fighters. But between them and the docks were the bulk of Park's defences – 185 fighters. Drawn from 19 different squadrons they too entered the fray, attacking each of the three German columns. The fighter escorts became scattered as they twisted and turned, trying to engage the British fighters. But just as Bader's 'big wing' swung into view, shortly before 3pm, most of the petrol lights within each Me 109 had flickered on. As the British defenders from the Duxford Wing dived into the attack, the German bombers desperately scanned the ground below for their designated target. Thickening cloud obscured most of the city directly beneath them. The pilots of Kampfgeschwader 2, now with just a few fighters to protect them and unable to find their target, were forced to turn for home. Just one lone Hurricane was there at the time to witness an entire German formation forced to flee without fulfilling their objectives. Group Captain Stanley Vincent was the Station Commander of RAF Northolt. A First World War veteran he enjoyed the occasional 'lone defence' sortie. This day was no different and undaunted by the thought of flying solo when the sky was virtually dark with Luftwaffe aircraft he filed the following combat report:

Number of enemy aircraft: Approx. 18 bombers, 20 fighters (Do 215s and Me 109s)

Time of attack: 1500

Place: Near Biggin Hill

Height of enemy: 19,000ft

Enemy casualties: One Do 215 damaged

When at 19,000 ft near Biggin Hill I saw a large formation of enemy bombers, escorted by Fighters in the South East, and when flying towards it saw a formation of 18 Do 215s approaching from the South, escorted by 20 Me 109s. The bombers were in Vics of 3 sections in line astern – Fighters 2 to 3,000 ft above and in no apparent formation. There were no other British fighters in sight, so I made a head on attack on the first section of the Bombers opening at 600 yds and closing to 200 yds. I saw the De Wilde ammunition hit the e/a.

On breaking away I noticed that five of the Bombers were continuing northwards together with apparently all the fighters, whilst thirteen of the Bombers had turned right round and were proceeding due south. I made further attacks on the retreating Bombers, each attack from climbing beam, and I could see the De Wilde ammunition hitting in each attack. In one instance I could see De Wilde hit the main part of the fuselage and the wing group. One Dornier left the formation and lost height. With no ammunition left I could not finish it off. I last saw the Bomber at 3,000 ft dropping slowly and still traveling south.[111]

Desperately the now unprotected bombers sought to make their way back to the coastline where they would be met by new fighter

Two Spitfires of No. 616 Squadron with their flaps down come in to land at Fowlmere, Cambridgeshire, after a sortie in September 1940. (IWM CH 1454)

Gruppen to escort them back over the Channel. Many did not make it, scattering their bombs over Dartford, Bromley and West Ham as they fled from the attackers.

As the weather worsened and no further big raids appeared on the radar screens, the pilots of Fighter Command could finally relax. Göring could not. Incensed by the lack of success, he ordered a second massed attack. The listeners in Hut 3 of Bletchley Park also received the order, as Frederick Winterbotham later recalled:

> The Ultra, which came from Göring, really almost burnt the paper. They were to turn round, refuel their aeroplanes and go back and bomb London. Churchill had been down with Keith Park and said, 'What reserves have you got?'
>
> Keith Park said, 'Perhaps you'd better ask the Commander-in-Chief, sir.'
>
> So the Commander-in-Chief was telephoned at Stanmore and asked, 'What reserves have you got?' And Dowding's remark, 'I have no reserves, sir, every aeroplane is in the sky' ... that put old Churchill in his place.[112]

The situation was not as dire as all that. There were of course reserves in No. 12 Group and throughout the rest of the country. Nonetheless, if a second raid had followed immediately after the first and had been directed against British airfields, nearly all the squadrons in No. 11 Group would have been caught on the ground as they refuelled. But Park had banked on Kesselring not having any reserves either, as well as the weather worsening in the afternoon. He was right on both accounts. Park's decisions were undoubtedly risky, but then battles are not won by the timid.

During the course of the day the RAF had lost 29 aircraft and 12 pilots had been killed. In contrast, the Luftwaffe had lost 56 aircraft and

Ground crew at a German air base celebrate the victorious return of a returned fighter pilot. With their pilot losses steadily increasing throughout September for little discernible effect on their opponents there would be little cause to celebrate as the month drew to a close. (akg images, ullstein bild)

136 men were either dead or POWs. At the time, however, the press trumpeted the fact that the British pilots had claimed an astonishing 185 enemy aircraft. Dowding and Park knew this was not the case. Indeed, considering the sheer number of British planes deployed their kill-ratio was not as high as it had been in the past, when fewer defenders had scored an equivalent number. But whatever the final numbers there was a sense of jubilation in the air. The British pilots knew full well that they were countering everything that the Germans had and enjoying much success. Across the Channel the mood was despondent. For three months now the German crews had been deluded by promises that Fighter Command was on its last legs, indeed, that the British were down to their last 50 Spitfires. Yet again and again the defenders had pressed home their attack, in increasing numbers and with a greater determination than before.

Sketch of Josef František by the war artist Cuthbert Orde on 19 September 1940. Josef František was the leading Allied ace of 1939–40, with 31 confirmed victories: three over Poland, 11 over France and a remarkable 17 during just six weeks in the Battle of Britain. Although Czech, he served with the legendary 303 (Polish) Squadron until he was killed in a flying accident on 8 October, just three weeks after this sketch was completed. (IWM ART LD 421)

Flight Lieutenant Eric Lock, sketched by Orde in July 1941, one year after the Battle of Britain, in which he was the most successful British-born pilot, with 16 and a half confirmed enemy kills. For this and other aerial victories in 1941 he received the DSO, DFC and Bar. He had first flown on his 14th birthday when his father had bought him a flight during one of Alan Cobham's Flying Circuses. His last flight was 3 August 1941, when he went missing over Calais. His body was never recovered. (IWM ART LD 2363)

Flight Lieutenant Alan Deere DFC and Bar, No. 54 Squadron, sketched by Orde in May 1941. Deere had what would have been referred to as a 'good war', and decided to remain in the RAF post-1945 until his eventual retirement in 1977 with the rank of Air Commodore. He passed away in 1995 and his ashes were scattered by a Spitfire over the River Thames. Although by birth a Kiwi, Deere came to love his adopted country, remarking in an interview for the IWM several decades after the Battle of Britain: 'I consider myself privileged to have been there, to fight for this country… I'd a hectic round, so to speak, but it was all worthwhile.' (IWM Sound 10478) (IWM ART LD 2364)

THE BATTLE DRAWS TO A CLOSE

The majority of German pilots knew that they had lost. The evidence was in the sheer number of British pilots that came up to attack them. Even Bader's Duxford Wing, with its questionable tactical value, was a huge psychological blow to the Luftwaffe pilots. It was less obvious to the German High Command, or indeed to Fighter Command. Göring was thrilled with the idea of massed British formations; this, after all, was what they had wanted all along. But time was running out for Göring. It was already mid-September, and the glorious sunshine that had prevailed for most of the summer months could not last. With the weather turning there would be fewer opportunities for the Luftwaffe to exploit. Hitler's patience was also wearing thin. He had never been wholeheartedly committed to the idea of an invasion of Britain. His thoughts were already drawn eastward to Russia. Göring's failure to achieve air superiority in time for an amphibious assault simply confirmed the

26 September 1940 and the Heinkel He IIIs of KG 55 have just bombed the Supermarine aircraft factory in Southampton when they are picked up by Pilot Officer J. D. Bisdee of No. 609 Squadron. (IWM CH 1826)

Left:
A second still from a camera gun taken from the Supermarine Spitfire Mark I of No. 609 Squadron flown by Pilot Officer R. F. G. Miller on 25 September 1940. This shows a Heinkel He III receiving hits in the port engine from Miller's machine guns. Miller himself was killed two days later when he collided head on with a Messerschmitt Me 110. (IWM CH 1830)

Right:
A third still from another No. 609 Squadron Spitfire, this time flown by Pilot Officer M. E. Staples, showing a Messerschmitt Bf 110 banking steeply to port as it tries to avoid Staples's gunfire. This aircraft may have belonged to Erprobungsgruppe 210, the fighter-bomber unit that earned some notable successes throughout the course of the Battle. (IWM CH 1834)

inevitable. The launch date had already been postponed several times; now, in the light of these substantial German losses, *Sealion* was postponed indefinitely on 17 September 1940. Nonetheless, Göring would be allowed to continue his attacks as and when opportunities arose. Nor were the invasion preparations totally abandoned. Instead they were simply placed on hold until a more suitable opportunity could arise in 1941. With the invasion barges still clogging the ports and harbours along the coastlines of France and Holland, Fighter Command was reluctant to lower its guard.

They were right not to do so. Several attempts were made to destroy the Supermarine factory in Southampton and, thanks to the damage caused, production lowered considerably. It did not matter much. There were fewer days now when the weather allowed for

serious action, and Fighter Command had sufficient Spitfires to see them through.

The twenty-seventh of September was one such day. As was the norm, a number of smaller raids were launched in the morning, designed to distract the defenders from the main attempt. Both these and the bombing raid made on London failed horribly. Once again the German pilots had the uncomfortable experience of being outnumbered by the defenders and they were badly mauled as a result. The Luftwaffe lost 57 aircraft that day, the same as it had on 15 September. It had only succeeded in shooting down 29 defenders and had not hit a single one of its targets. The writing was on the wall. Göring could no longer rely on daylight attacks to destroy Fighter Command. Instead it was the Luftwaffe that was being slowly decimated. Sporadic daylight raids continued with lessening intensity throughout the final months of the year. As late as 8 November, young Pilot Officer Denis Wissler could note in his diary with regret that he had missed a fabulous 'Stuka party', where his squadron had claimed 15 for no loss to themselves. So too did the Germans continue to claim their quota of enemy pilots. Just three days after making his final diary entry Denis Wissler was killed in combat. He was just 20 and newly engaged.

The official end date for the Battle of Britain is 31 October 1940, as stipulated in the Air Ministry pamphlet on the subject published in 1941. In reality war is not so clear-cut and there was significant overlap. For the British government, and indeed for the British public, the Battle of Britain was fought to thwart the much-anticipated invasion. Hugely significant then was a Ultra signal, which confirmed the dismantling of some of the invasion preparations, that Group Captain Winterbotham received and passed on to the Prime Minister himself:

A Spitfire pulls away after an unsuccessful attack on a Do 17 in December 1940. As the autumn turned into winter daylight attacks became increasingly scarce. (Bundesarchiv Bild 146-1969-094-18)

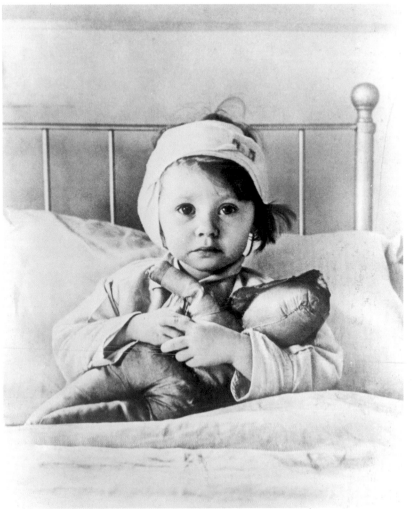

Left:
The highly successful Me 109 pilot Captain Helmut Wick. He had been awarded the Knight's Cross with Oak Leaves by the time he was shot down and killed on 28 November 1940. (Bundesarchiv Bild 1011-404-0512-17)

Right:
Aged just three, little Eileen Dunne was injured during an air raid in September 1940. The photograph of her in bed taken by Cecil Beaton at Great Ormond Street Hospital for Sick Children was widely publicized and became one of the enduring images of the Blitz. (IWM MH 26395)

I sent that signal straight through to Churchill and that very evening he ordered a conference down in the room under the Foreign Office. I was commanded to go along with my boss to explain it to the Chiefs of Staff. It was one of the most extraordinary moments of my life.

Down there were all the Chiefs of Staff, the Prime Minister, General Ismay, my chief and me. Churchill said, 'Well, gentlemen, we'd like to know what this signal really means.'

I was called upon because I'd studied the whole thing. I pointed out that if these loading bays were dismantled it meant that they would not have proper air support and that in fact Hitler had given up the idea of invasion. So Churchill looked at me, then he turned to the Chief of Air Staff. 'May I have your views?' he said and Cyril Newall said, 'That is entirely our view. With the dismantling of these, the invasion is off.'

Churchill sat back, smiled, pulled out a big cigar and lit it. He said, 'Well, gentlemen, let's go and see what is happening upstairs.'

There was a terrific blitz going on upstairs. The whole of Carlton House Terrace was in flames, and the bombs were dropping all around. Churchill came up smoking his cigar and put on his tin hat. In front of the underground offices was a concrete screen, and everybody tried to prevent him walking out because there was so much metal flying about. But he went out and I can still see him today with his hands on his stick, smoking his cigar. 'My God,' he said, 'we'll get the buggers for this.'[113]

92 EAST INDIA SQUADRON

DESTROYED 129
PROBABLE 60
DAMAGED 70
TOTAL 259

AFTERMATH

❝ *I do not regard the situation as having passed beyond our strength... Hitler will have to break us in this Island or lose the war.* **❞**

Winston Churchill to the prime ministers of the Dominions, 15 June 1940

AS AUTUMN STRETCHED INTO WINTER, the Luftwaffe did not diminish its attempts to obliterate the cities and towns of Britain. This was the Blitz and it would not lessen until May 1941. The British people did not abandon their homes, flee from the factories, or beg their government to negotiate a peace deal, all of which the German High Command had expected them to do. Indeed, none of the nightmares envisaged during the 1930s came true, except that is for the horrific loss of life and the wholesale destruction of communities. By the end of the war 60,000 British men, women and children had been killed by German air attacks. In addition two million homes had been destroyed with over 46,000 tons of high explosive and 110,000 incendiary bombs dropped. But Churchill had his vengeance, and 600,000 German civilians were killed as the Allies too tried to force the Third Reich to surrender.

As the British people took refuge in their home-made shelters or slept on the platforms of Tube stations, this battle of Churchill's 'few' had irrevocably become a people's war.

For Dowding the Battle had been won but his war was over. He was officially retired on 25 November 1940. He had been due for retirement long before war had even been declared and he had conducted his brilliant defence of Britain with the knowledge that he could be removed from his post at any time. Park, his loyal and brilliant deputy, was also moved aside to make way for a new order at Fighter Command, and his old nemesis Trafford Leigh-Mallory replaced him as Controller of No. 11 Group. Meanwhile, the pilots that had survived still had a long war ahead of them and not all of them would see it through to the end. With such a long and arduous journey ahead, just how significant was their victory in the summer of 1940?

The British fought the Battle as if it was the prelude to the invasion of their island, and to prevent the fate that had already befallen nearly all of Western Europe. Since the conclusion of the war, however, there has been much debate over how serious Hitler's intentions were with regards to invasion. Certainly he faced opposition to the idea from some of his most senior commanders. When Admiral Raeder, his Commander-in-Chief of the Navy, met with Hitler on 11 July to discuss the preliminary plans for invasion, Raeder made it abundantly clear that he regarded the idea as pure folly because of the extreme risk attached to it, and much preferred

Opposite:
February 1941 and the pilots and non-operational officers of No. 92 Squadron pose proudly at RAF Manston with the squadron scoreboard reflecting their 130th enemy aircraft destroyed. Squadron Leader Johnny Kent, formerly of No. 303 Squadron, is shown propping up the board. (IWM CH 2538)

the idea of a trade blockade and bomb attacks to break the will of the British public. Nonetheless, Hitler allowed plans for invasion to develop on the condition that air supremacy could be achieved. When Hitler finally abandoned *Sealion*, he did so again because the air question had been settled, and not in Germany's favour. Other considerations including Raeder's opposition and Hitler's own yearning for the East played their part, but a German victory in the Battle of Britain would have delivered the knock-out blow that would have made invasion conceivable, if not perhaps guaranteed. Once summer became autumn, and the treacherous waters of the Channel became more dangerous than usual, Hitler reverted to Raeder's original scheme. If invasion could not be considered at the present time, then there was always the possibility that economic ruin and bombing would force the British government to the negotiating table instead. With the invasion of Soviet Russia in the following spring the moment passed. In 1940, with Britain left without a formal ally and her army humiliated and poorly equipped thanks to Dunkirk, the German High Command must have recognized that here was their best opportunity for a successful invasion. That they failed to do so would be one of the costliest strategic errors of the war. The maintenance of British sovereignty ensured that she would later become a giant floating base for the Allied armies before the invasion of Europe four years later. Indeed, it is extremely doubtful whether the United States would have been able to wage a successful campaign in Western Europe when separated by 3,000 miles of ocean.

The Blitz was a victory of the spirit, but it did not yield the strategic gains that victory in the Battle of Britain secured. This was the first military defeat for the Third Reich since 1939. No one thought it could be done. In the late June of 1940, General Maxime Weygand, Commander-in-Chief of the French armed forces, predicted that 'in three weeks, England will have her neck wrung like a chicken'. At the end of July, Joseph Kennedy, the US

Crowds gather in the Elephant & Castle Tube station on 11 November 1940. Tube stations throughout London became heavily crowded as people sought shelter as soon as the air-raid warnings were sounded. (IWM HU 672)

Ambassador to Britain, informed the State Department that the German Luftwaffe had the power to put the RAF 'out of commission'. Dowding's fighter boys and his own brilliant defensive system proved the doubters wrong and with it won the admiration of the world. In particular it inspired the American President, Franklin D. Roosevelt. Not one to back a lame horse, it is debatable whether Roosevelt would have offered any support to Britain if it had lost the Battle of Britain, whether or not it subsequently survived an invasion attempt. American support was crucial. Spitfires were costly to produce, as were battleships, destroyers and tanks; no amount of Beaverbrook appeals could prevent the British Treasury haemorrhaging money. Roosevelt extended the long arm of friendship and credit across the Atlantic and secured Britain's survival.

This mattered, not just for Britain, but for the whole of Western Europe. If Hitler had not faced any further opposition from the British in North Africa, in the Mediterranean or in the Atlantic then he would have been free to redirect all his energies and resources towards the East. He might still have lost. Either way, a war fought exclusively between the forces of Nazism and Stalinism could not have any real winners. Indeed, a war fought on two fronts at least ensured that eventually it was Britain and America who secured freedom for huge swathes of the Continent, including, somewhat ironically, for part of Germany.

Britain could not have won the war alone. It was impossible without the support of her dominions and territories throughout the world, and indeed without American money and, later, American manpower. But for almost a year until Hitler's invasion of Russia,

Top:
A standard inscription on a bombed London shop that perfectly captures the so-called 'Blitz spirit'. Of course, it was not simply the capital that was bombed. Major industrial centres the length and breadth of the country became the target of the Luftwaffe throughout the winter of 1940/1. No one in the targeted cities was immune, bombs rained on the East End as well as Buckingham Palace, but some areas undoubtedly suffered more than others. (IWM HU 659)

Bottom:
A wrecked bus stands among a scene of devastation in the centre of Coventry after a major Luftwaffe air raid on the night 14/15 November 1940. (IWM H 5593)

Britain and her Empire struggled on alone. The Battle of Britain was arguably her most important strategic victory during that time. It was the springboard for all later successes – for her endurance during the Battle of the Atlantic and her breakthrough victory at El Alamein in 1942. It was a huge morale boost not only for her people but for Britain's High Command as well. As Churchill once said, they just had to KBO – 'Keep Buggering On'.

Churchill's famous speech on 20 August 1940 helped mythologize the Battle while it was still being fought. Most pilots treated his lauding of them with a touch of irreverence. George Unwin later recalled that his squadron commander maintained that the debt of so many owed to so few referred to unpaid mess bills. But it did irrevocably change the public's perception of this small band of warriors. It seems part of the British national culture that they prefer the underdog, the plucky hero snatching victory from the jaws of defeat, a David securing victory against Goliath despite the overwhelming odds. A small band of amateur pilots suits this stereotype.

In fact, they were anything but. When Britain fought for her survival in the summer of 1940 she could call upon a core of hard-bitten, professional fighting men who were first-rate pilots. This was a battle that Britain was uniquely prepared for and one that she was more than capable of winning. Thanks to Dowding's elaborate defence system and Park's masterful tactics, not to mention the steadfastness of the men and women of Fighter Command, they concluded 1940 tired and weakened but undoubtedly triumphant. It is often assumed that Britain came closest to losing the Battle during the attacks on the airfields and was saved only by the good fortune of the Luftwaffe switching to bombing London. This theory pays too much credit to the Luftwaffe and too little to the RAF. In reality, although the Luftwaffe scored some direct hits against key airfields throughout the month of August, runways were repaired and sites rebuilt, and the aircraft continued to land, refuel and take off. Despite 40 concentrated attacks on airfields between 28 August and 5 September, only two ever became unfit for flying for more than 24 hours. Only one airfield, Manston, was ever abandoned, and it was of no real strategic value. Some sector stations and radar stations were hit, but none went down for any significant period of time. Dowding and Park protested loudly about attacks on airfields and the dangers this could create, but this was largely for the benefit of the Air Ministry and their colleague at No. 12 Group, Trafford Leigh-Mallory, to ensure better protection for those airfields in the frontline. Throughout this critical phase of the Battle the Luftwaffe kept hammering home the attack for no real gain. What if they had stayed the course and not been diverted by the thought of London? Quite simply, it is likely that they would have lost the battle of attrition themselves. There was no infinite supply of men and machines on that side of the Channel either, and the Germans were losing them at a far faster rate. Besides, would they have really hit

St Paul's Cathedral, the heart of London, surrounded by smoke and fire. (Topfoto)

enough of the key operations rooms? This again was not guaranteed – after all, they did not really know what they were targeting. To have won the Battle the Luftwaffe would have needed to know what they were up against – the world's finest defensive system developed by brilliant commanders and using cutting-edge technology gathered together in an elaborate system involving sector stations and command rooms of which the Luftwaffe had no

understanding. It made Göring look positively amateurish. This was modern warfare, and skilful pilots, of which the Luftwaffe had plenty, could not triumph alone.

Together, the Dunkirk evacuation, the Battle of Britain and the Blitz defined Britain during her finest hour and with it a nation at war. Of the three, only the Battle was an actual military victory and yet it has never been widely celebrated on an annual basis. The

Fighter Command's success during the Battle of Britain did not mean the end of its role in the war. Five long years of tough fighting were ahead but undoubtedly the Battle was a unique rallying point for prospective recruits. Here one is shown at the Euston Combined Recruits Centre in 1941 in front of a poster of Hurricanes with the caption 'Mightier Yet'. (IWMCH 1645)

fifteenth of September is officially recognized as Battle of Britain Day but it is unlikely that many members of the public are even aware that such a date exists. There are no large-scale annual commemorations like there are on Armistice Day and for many years the RAF itself was reluctant to commemorate an event that was associated with just one Command. Most of the airfields of No. 11 Group are grown over and many of the operations rooms abandoned. For years the Battle of Britain did not even have an official memorial in London itself. Finally in 2000, 60 years after the Battle was fought, an appeal was launched to create a memorial on London's Embankment to honour all who served. Today a giant bronze plinth stands alongside the Thames, that great meandering river that was the visual marker for so many German bombers. It depicts every aspect of the Battle, from pilots scrambling, to the WAAFs plotting, the Observer Corps watchmen to the anti-aircraft gunners and the aircraft factory workers. It is a fitting tribute to the brave men and women who participated. But they deserve much more than simply a physical memorial. They should be honoured and remembered every year, not just on anniversaries, because without them Britain, Europe, if not the world, would be a very different place.

★ ★ ★

I climbed again. After about ten minutes, saw two more Dorniers, well below me, flying along together in very tight formation, wings overlapping.

Good, I was ahead of them, and down I went in the good old head-on dive, and it got results!

They seemed surprised to see me, for they wobbled and separated so violently that their wings touched, and a chunk came off one wing-tip. They both lost height, and I gave them a quick burst each for luck. One was almost on his back as he went into the cloud-layer, the other seemed to be out of control too.

I followed them through. We were now just off our coast.

Three Luftwaffe heroes: Mölders and Galland discuss tactics watched by Theo Osterkamp in April 1941. (Bundesarchiv Bild 183-B14349, Bild 183-B12018)

The first went head-long into the 'drink', there was an almighty splash, and he disappeared.

The second was spinning. A piece off one wing, he spiralled crazily down into the water. It reminded me of chestnut leaves in the autumn, fluttering down onto the school playing field. He hit, exploded, and petrol and oil burned fiercely on the surface of the sea. The flames died away, only a few bits of wreckage remained floating.

I remember seeing another Dornier explode, and burn – let me see, when was it? Why, only that very morning. It was still Sunday, September 15th. The day had been a year.

I flew to the coast, and set a course for home.

Passing low over fields and villages, rivers and towns, I looked down at labourers working, children at play, beside a big red-brick schoolhouse, a bomb crater two streets away; little black heads in the street, turning to white blobs as they heard my engine and looked up.

I thought of workers in shops and factories, of stretcher-parties and A.R.P wardens. I hoped the 'All Clear' had gone. I was tired, I'd done my best for them. [114]

The British had not won the Battle on 15 September, even though today it is officially recognized as 'Battle of Britain Day'. Rather they had proved conclusively that it could not be won by the Luftwaffe. The real British victory had come every day, every time a squadron was scrambled against overwhelming numbers, every time a new Spitfire rolled off the production lines, every time the WAAFs had stayed at the posts as the bombs rained down above them, every time the ground crews worked through the night repairing runways or every time a novice pilot forced down his nerves and engaged in his first dogfight. It had been a summer of endurance, of ordinary people caught up in extraordinary times. They had done their best for us; then, and now, it was enough.

Fighter pilots were feted throughout the country following the successful conclusion of the Battle of Britain. Here a Fleet Air Arm pilot signs a captured tail section of a downed Luftwaffe aircraft. The Fleet Air Arm provided valuable assistance to the RAF by protecting vulnerable convoys. (Topfoto)

NOTES

PREFACE

1.   Churchill, 4 June 1940, following the evacuation of Dunkirk.

INTRODUCTION

2.   Edith Kup (née Heap)
IWM Documents 507 88/2/1

3.   Edward James Morris
IWM Documents 8231 99/7/1

4.   Churchill, 3 September 1939, following the declaration of war.

5.   'The end of the year 1939 left the war still in its sinister trance ...', *The Second World War Volume 1: The Gathering Storm*, Churchill, W. S., p.494; 'Bore War' was the popular name among the British public. 'Phoney War' was also used, but was a predominantly American expression.

6.   Quoted in Manchester, William, *The Last Lion: Winston Spencer Churchill: Alone 1932–1940*, p.619

FIGHTER COMMAND

7.   At the time, not all the RFC squadrons were equipped with aircraft and some were instead equipped with balloons to serve as part of the aerial defence.

8.   Quoted in Bishop, Patrick, *Fighter Boys: Saving Britain 1940*, p.31

9.   Quoted in 'The bomber will always get through', *Air Force Magazine* [date to come]

10.   Rosemary Horstmann
IWM Sound 10871

11   Christopher Foxley-Norris
IWM Sound 10136

12.   Elizabeth Quayle
IWM Sound 10609

13.   Jean Mills
IWM Sound 11885

14.   Diana Pitt Parsons
IWM Sound 9948

15.   Rosemary Horstmann
IWM Sound 10871

16.   Petrea Winterbotham
IWM Sound 7463

17.   Diana Pitt Parsons
IWM Sound 9948

18.   Petrea Winterbotham
IWM Sound 7463

19.   Ibid.

20.   Ibid.

21.   Group Captain Frederick Winterbotham
IWM Sound 7462

22.   Jackie Moggridge
IWM Sound 8668

23.   Edward James Morris
IWM Documents 8231 99/7/1

24.   Percival Legget
IWM Sound 27075

25.   Quoted in Bishop, Patrick, *Fighter Boys: Saving Britain 1940*, p.44

26.   Quoted in Ward, Arthur, *A Nation Alone: The Battle of Britain – 1940*, p.61

27.   Jeffrey Quill
IWM Sound 10687

28.   Pilot Officer James Goodson, an American pilot with No. 43 Squadron IWM Sound 11623 and quoted in Levine, Joshua, *Forgotten Voices of the Blitz and the Battle for Britain*, p.129

29.   George Unwin
IWM Sound 11544

30.   Quoted in Bishop, Patrick, *Fighter Boys: Saving Britain 1940*, pp.51–52

31.   Hillary, Richard, *The Last Enemy*, p.15

32.   Pilot Officer Archibald Winskill, No. 72 and later No. 603 Squadrons IWM Sound 11537

33. Rupert Parkhouse
    IWM Sound 15476

34. George Unwin
    IWM Sound 11544

35. Alan Deere
    IWM Sound 10478

36. William Strachan
    IWM Sound 10042

37. Kent, J., *One of the Few*

38. Cyril Bamberger
    IWM Sound 27074

39. Alan Deere
    IWM Sound 10478

40. George Unwin
    IWM Sound 11544

41. Flying Officer Peter Brothers
    IWM Sound 10218

THE LUFTWAFFE

42. Hans von Seeckt, *Gedanken eines Soldaten* (Berlin: Verlag fur Kulturpolitik, 1929), translated in Corum, J., *The Luftwaffe: Creating the Operational Air War, 1918–1940*, p.54.

43. See Corum, J., *The Luftwaffe: Creating the Operational Air War, 1918–1940*, pp.102–103 for further details.

44. Werner Roll
    IWM Sound 12563

45. Ernest Wedding
    IWM Sound 26960

46. See Weal, John, *Ju 88 Kampfgeschwader on the Western Front*, pp.10–13, for full account.

47. Quoted in Deighton, Len, *Fighter: The True Story of the Battle of Britain*, p.20

48. Hans-Ekkehard Bob
    IWM Sound 26965

49. Ibid.

50. As later recalled by Group Captain Frederick Winterbotham, Deputy to the Chief of Secret Intelligence Service with responsibility for Ultra messages.
    IWM Sound 7462

51. Hans-Ekkehard Bob
    IWM Sound 26965

52. Ernest Wedding
    IWM Sound 26960

53. Wolfgang Falck
    IWM Sound 11247

54. Hans-Ekkehard Bob
    IWM Documents 788 91/1/1

55. Wolfgang Falck. This is personal recollection and some statements contained within are not strictly accurate.
    IWM Sound 11247

56. Once war broke out on the Eastern Front the number of points necessary to receive an award was increased to prevent a flood of applications.

57. Wolfgang Falck
    IWM Sound 11247

BLITZKRIEG

58. Hugh Ironside
    IWM Sound 13101

59. Quoted in Manchester, William, *The Last Lion: Winston Spencer Churchill: Alone 1932–1940*, p.680

60. All quotes attributed to Pilot Officer Denis Wissler are taken from his diary now held by the Imperial War Museum.
    IWM Documents 786 91/41/1

61. Flying Officer Peter Brothers
    IWM Sound 10218

62. AC 71/17/15

63. Pilot Officer Denis Wissler
    IWM Documents 786 91/41/1

64. The Venerable Guy Mayfield
    IWM Documents 14311 06/12/1

65. Flying Officer Peter Brothers
    IWM Sound 10218

66. Churchill 19 May 1940

67. Sergeant Major Martin McLane
    IWM Sound 10165

68. George Unwin
    IWM Sound 11544

69. Ibid.

70. Hugh Dundas
    IWM Sound 10159

71. Roland Beamont
    IWM Sound 10128

SPITFIRE SUMMER

72. R. Pountain
    IWM Documents 14379 06/11/09

73. Churchill, 18 June 1940

74. The Venerable Guy Mayfield
    IWM Documents 14311 06/12/1

75. Roland Beamont
    IWM Sound 10128

76. Churchill later referred to this comment in a speech addressing the Canadian parliament in Ottawa on 30 December 1941 in which he stated: 'When I warned them [the French] that Britain would fight on

alone whatever they did, their generals told their Prime Minister and his divided Cabinet, "In three weeks England would have her neck wrung like a chicken." Some chicken! Some neck!' The comment went down doubly well because 'neck' was Canadian slang for 'nerve'.

77. Flying Officer Peter Brothers
IWM Sound 10218

78. Domarcus, Max (ed.), Hitler's Speeches and Proclamations 1932–45: The Chronicle of a Dictatorship, trans. Chris Wilcox, p.2040

79. www.seftondelmer.co.uk

80. As later recalled by Group Captain Frederick Winterbotham, Deputy to the Chief of Secret Intelligence Service with responsibility for Ultra messages.
IWM Sound 7462

81. George Unwin
IWM Sound 11544

82. Ibid.

83. Flying Officer Pete Brothers
IWM Sound 10218

84. Group Captain Frederick Winterbotham
IWM Sound 7462

85. Flying Officer Geoffrey Page
IWM Sound 11103

86. Pilot Officer Denis Wissler
IWM Documents 786 91/41/1

87. Goss, C., The Luftwaffe Fighters' Battle of Britain, pp.21–23

88. Flying Officer Peter Brothers
Quoted in Holmes, T., Hurricane Aces 1939–40, pp.73–74

89. Translation of original document courtesy of the Battle of Britain Historical Society.

90. George Unwin
IWM Sound 11544

91. Such 'Funkstationen mit Sonderanlagen' were clearly marked on Luftwaffe target maps. Martini was well aware of their significance to the British defences but had little understanding of how they worked. See Deighton, Len, Fighter, pp.157–8

92. Flight Lieutenant Hugh Beresford was later killed on 7 September after having seen almost daily action throughout the month of August and was credited as being an inspirational commander. He crashed near Elmy, Kent and was officially posted as missing in action. The crash site was finally discovered and excavated in the late 1970s and he was buried with full military honours in 1979. He had been just 24 at the time of his death.
After-action report: IWM Documents 4175 83/15/4

93. Hans-Ekkehard Bob
IWM Documents 788 91/1/1

94. Although Dundas has identified the Luftwaffe bombers as Dorniers, they were in fact Junkers Ju 88s from KG 30.
Interview: IWM Sound 10159

95. Roland Beamont
IWM Sound 10128

96. Hans-Ekkehard Bob
IWM Sound 26965

97. Alan Deere
IWM Sound 10478

98. Pilot Officer Ronald Brown
IWM Sound 12404

99. Nigel Cameron
IWM Documents 1534 06/80/1

100. Churchill, 20 August 1940, speech to the House of Commons

101. Pilot Officer Denis Wissler
IWM Documents 786 91/41/1

102. Alan Deere
IWM Sound 10478

103. IWM Documents 4175 83/15/4

104. Quoted in Mayhew, E. R., The Reconstruction of Warriors: Archibald McIndoe, the Royal Air Force and the Guinea Pig Club

105. Goss, C., The Luftwaffe Fighters' Battle of Britain, pp.111–112

106. George Unwin
IWM Sound 11544

107. Hitler, 4 September 1940

108. Edward James Morris
IWM Documents 8231 99/7/1

109. Pilot Officer Denis Wissler
IWM Documents 786 91/41/1

110. This supposedly deliberate attempt on the lives of the King and Queen horrified the British press and public. Buckingham Palace had already been directly hit on 13 September, with a bomb causing considerable damage to the Royal Chapel. This famously caused Her Majesty Queen Elizabeth to comment that she 'could finally look the East End in the eye'. The popularity of the monarchy soared as a result.

111. De Wilde ammunition, named after its Belgian inventor, was the incendiary bullets used by the RAF.
Group Captain Stanley Vincent
Combat report: IWM Documents 4175 83/41/1

112. Group Captain Frederick Winterbotham
IWM Sound 7462

113. Ibid.

AFTERMATH

114. This was an account of the Battle of Britain published as part of an anthology of ten such accounts entitled Ten Fighter Boys in 1942. The pilots were from No. 66 Squadron and by the time the book was in print five pilots had already been killed, including the author of this particular account, Crelin 'Bogle' Brodie.

APPENDICES

APPENDIX 1

FIGHTER COMMAND STRENGTH: (AIR 22/296)

1940	Establishment	Strength	Deficiency
15 June	1,456	1,094	-362
6 July	1,456	1,259	-197
13 July	1,456	1,341	-115
20 July	1,456	1,365	-91
27 July	1,456	1,377	-79
3 August	1,558	1,434	-124
10 August	1,558	1,396	-162
17 August	1,558	1,379	-179
24 August	1,558	1,377	-181
31 August	1,558	1,422	-136
7 September	1,558	1,381	-177
14 September	1,662	1,492	-170
21 September	1,662	1,509	-153
28 September	1,662	1,581	-81
5 October	1,714	1,703	-11
12 October	1,714	1,752	+38
19 October	1,700	1,737	+37
26 October	1,727	1,735	+8
2 November	1,727	1,796	+69
9 November	1,727	1,829	+102
16 November	1,701	1,763	+62
23 November	1,749	1,728	-21
30 November	1,763	1,768	+5
7 December	1,599	1,744	+145
14 December	1,655	1,786	+131
21 December	1,655	1,801	+146
28 December	1,655	1,809	+154

APPENDIX 2

WEEKLY OUTPUT OF AIRCRAFT: (AIR 22/293)

Week ending	Beaufighter	Defiant	Hurricane	Spitfire
6 April		5	35	14
13 April	1	3	38	17
20 April		3	41	13
27 April		6	40	14
4 May		3	34	15
11 May		5	41	12
18 May		4	40	14
25 May		4	59	17
1 June		8	87	22
8 June		2	79	22
15 June		7	67	25
22 June	2	8	75	21
29 June		13	68	26
6 July		12	65	32
13 July		12	57	30
20 July	1	11	67	41
27 July	4	14	65	37
3 August	3	13	68	41
10 August	5	10	64	37
17 August	5	11	43	31
24 August	5	8	64	44
31 August	5	3	54	37
7 September	5	11	54	36
14 September	6	10	56	38
21 September	4	6	57	40
26 September		10	58	34
5 October		12	60	32
12 October	4	11	55	31
19 October	6	8	55	25
26 October	9	16	69	42
2 November	3	10	56	41

APPENDIX 3

CASUALTY RATES/LOSSES TO FIGHTER COMMAND BY WEEK (AIR 22/262)

Week [running Monday to Sunday]	Lost	Damaged
1–7 July	3 Blenheims 1 Hurricane 3 Spitfires	2 Hurricanes
8–14 July	16 Hurricanes 7 Spitfires	6 Hurricanes 2 Spitfires
15–21 July	6 Defiants 10 Hurricanes 6 Spitfires	5 Hurricanes
22–28 July	4 Hurricanes 12 Spitfires	1 Hurricane 6 Spitfires
29 July–4 August	4 Hurricanes 4 Spitfires	nil
5–11 August	3 Blenheims [1 trainer] 33 Hurricanes 12 Spitfires	3 Hurricanes 10 Spitfires
12–18 August	29 Hurricanes 10 Spitfire 76 aircraft unidentified	5 Hurricanes 8 Spitfires
19–25 August	4 Defiants 20 Hurricanes 23 Spitfires	1 Hurricane
26 August–1 September	7 Defiants 81 Hurricanes 47 Spitfires	10 Hurricanes 6 Spitfires
2–8 September	4 Blenheims 74 Hurricanes 52 Spitfires	34 Hurricanes 31 Spitfires
9–15 September	59 Hurricanes 28 Spitfires	20 Hurricanes 15 Spitfires
16–22 September	12 Hurricanes 7 Spitfires 7 aircraft unidentified	9 Spitfires
23–29 September	46 Hurricanes 32 Spitfires	23 Hurricanes 24 Spitfires

APPENDIX 4

FIGHTER COMMAND ORDER OF BATTLE, 8 JULY 1940 (AIR 16/635)

	Squadron	War Station	Type of Aircraft
No, 10 Group	87	Exeter	Hurricane
	213	Exeter	Hurricane
	92	Pembrey	Spitfire
	234	St Eval	Spitfire
No. 11 Group	43	Tangmere	Hurricane
	145	Tangmere	Hurricane
	601	Tangmere	Hurricane
	FIU Unit	Tangmere	Blenheim
	64	Kenley	Spitfire
	615	Kenley	Hurricane
	245	Hawkinge	Hurricane
	111	Croydon	Hurricane
	501	Croydon	Hurricane
	600	Manston	Blenheim
	79	Biggin Hill	Hurricane
	610	Gravesend	Spitfire
	32	Biggin Hill	Hurricane
	54	Rochford	Spitfire
	65	Hornchurch	Spitfire
	74	Hornchurch	Spitfire
	56	North Weald	Hurricane
	25	Martlesham	Blenheim
	151	North Weald	Hurricane
	1	Northolt	Hurricane
	604	Northolt	Blenheim
	609	Northolt	Spitfire
	236	Middle Wallop	Blenheim
No. 12 Group	19	Duxford	Spitfire
	264	Duxford	Defiant
	85	Debden	Hurricane
	17	Debden	Hurricane
	29	Digby	Blenheim
	611	Digby	Spitfire
	46	Digby	Hurricane
	23	Wittering	Blenheim
	266	Wittering	Spitfire
	229	Wittering	Hurricane
	66	Coltishall	Spitfire
	253	Kirton-in-Lindsey	Hurricane
	222	Kirton-in-Lindsey	Spitfire
No. 13 Group	41	Catterick	Spitfire
	219	Catterick	Blenheim
	152	Acklington	Spitfire

FIGHTER COMMAND ORDER OF BATTLE, 8 JULY 1940

	Squadron	War Station	Type of Aircraft
	72	Acklington	Spitfire
	249	Leconfield	Hurricane
	616	Leconfield	Spitfire
	603 A	Turnhouse	Spitfire
	141	Turnhouse	Defiant
	602	Drem	Spitfire
	603 B	Montrose	Spitfire
	3	Wick	Hurricane
	504	Wick	Hurricane
Non-Operational Squadrons			
10 Group	238	Middle Wallop	Hurricane
	1 (Canadian)	Middle Wallop	Hurricane
11 Group	257	Hendon	Hurricane
12 Group	242	Coltishall	Hurricane
13 Group	73	Church Fenton	Hurricane
	605	Drem	Hurricane
	607	Usworth	Hurricane
	263	Grangemouth	Hurricane

APPENDIX 5

FIGHTER COMMAND ORDER OF BATTLE,
3 NOVEMBER 1940 (AIR 16/635)

	Squadron	War Station	Type of Aircraft
No. 9 Group	312 (Czech)	Speke	Hurricane
	611	Ternhill	Spitfire
	29	Ternhill	Blenheim
No. 10 Group	79	Pembrey	Hurricane
	87 (half)	Bibury	Hurricane
	504	Filton	Hurricane
	60	Middle Wallop	Spitfire
	604	Middle Wallop	Blenheim
	238	Middle Wallop	Hurricane
	56	Boscombe Down	Hurricane
	152	Warmwell	Spitfire
	601	Exeter	Hurricane
	87 (half)	Exeter	Hurricane
	234	St Eval	Spitfire
	247 (half)	Roborough	Gladiator
No. 11 Group	25	Debden	Blenheim and Beaufighter
	73	Castle Camp	Hurricane
	17	Martlesham	Hurricane
	229	Northolt	Hurricane
	61	Northolt	Hurricane
	302 (Polish)	Northolt	Hurricane
	257	North Weald	Hurricane
	249	North Weald	Hurricane
	46	Stapleford	Hurricane
	264	Hornchurch	Defiant
	41	Hornchurch	Spitfire
	603	Hornchurch	Spitfire
	222	Rochford	Spitfire
	141	Gravesend	Defiant
	74	Biggin Hill	Spitfire
	92	Biggin Hill	Spitfire
	66	West Malling	Spitfire
	421 (half)	West Malling	Hurricane
	605	Croydon	Hurricane
	253	Kenley	Hurricane
	501	Kenley	Hurricane
	219	Redhill	Blenheim and Beaufighter
	145	Tangmere	Hurricane
	213	Tangmere	Hurricane
	422 (half)	Tangmere	Hurricane
	602	West Hampnett	Spitfire
	23	Ford	Blenheim
No. 12 Group	303 (Polish)	Leconfield	Hurricane
	616	Kirton-in-Lindsey	Spitfire
	85	Kirton-in-Lindsey	Hurricane
	151	Digby	Hurricane
	1	Wittering	Hurricane
	266	Wittering	Spitfire
	29 (half)	Wittering	Blenheim
	72	Coltishall	Spitfire
	64	Coltishall	Spitfire
	242	Duxford	Hurricane
	310 (Czech)	Duxford	Hurricane
	19	Duxford	Spitfire
No. 13 Group	607	Turnhouse	Hurricane
	65	Turnhouse	Spitfire
	232 (half)	Drem	Hurricane
	263 (half)	Drem	Hurricane
	1 (Canadian)	Prestwick	Hurricane
	32	Acklington	Hurricane
	610	Acklington	Spitfire
	600 (half)	Acklington	Blenheim
	43	Usworth	Hurricane
	54	Catterick	Spitfire
	600 (half)	Catterick	Blenheim
	245	Aldergrove	Hurricane
No. 14 Group	3	Castleford	Hurricane
	111 (half)	Dyce	Hurricane
	111 (half)	Montrose	Hurricane
Non-Operational Squadrons			
9 Group	308 (Polish)	Baginton	Hurricane
12 Group	306 (Polish)	Church Fenton	Hurricane
	307 (Polish)	Kirton-in-Lindsey	Defiant
	71 (Eagle)	Church Fenton	Buffalo
13 Group	263 (half)	Drem	Whirlwind

APPENDIX 6

GERMAN LOSSES DURING THE BATTLE OF BRITAIN

LUFTWAFFE OPERATIONAL AIRCRAFT LOSSES JULY–SEPTEMBER 1940

Type of aircraft	Operational strength 29 June 1940	Losses due to enemy action	Losses not due to direct enemy action	Total
Single-engine fighters	1,107	398	79	518
Twin-engined fighters	357	214	9	235
Bombers	1380	424	127	621
Dive-bombers	428	59	10	88

Murray, W, *Luftwaffe Strategy for Defeat 1933–45*, p.50

AIRCRAFT AND CREW LOSSES – AUGUST 1940

	Aircraft written off	Pilots killed	Captured	Injured	Uninjured	Missing
Me 109	229	57	3	41	47	84
Me 110	123	48	2	6	19	48
Do 17	75	22	2	14	10	26
He 111	98	36	1	9	15	34
Ju 88	104	33	4	5	17	44
Ju 87	62	20	1	5	9	28

Murray, W, *Luftwaffe Strategy for Defeat 1933–45*, p.53

LUFTWAFFE SINGLE-ENGINE FIGHTER PILOT STRENGTH

	Date
	01-Jun-40
906	01-Aug-40
869	01-Sep-40
735	01-Nov-40

Overy, R, *The Battle*, p.162

of Britain: Then and Now, After the
, 1987

Dowding and the First Victory, 1940,

Perspectives: Behind the scenes of the
ur Press (London), 1994
gles, Weidenfeld and Nicolson

e Battle of Britain – 1940,
997

9–41, Osprey Publishing (Oxford),

r on the Western Front, Osprey

: The Battle of Britain and the rise of
 Press (London), 1990

BIBLIOGRAPHY

UNPUBLISHED SOURCES

IMPERIAL WAR MUSEUM

Bamberger, Cyril, IWM Sound 27074

Beamont, Roland, IWM Sound 10128

Bob, Hans-Ekkhard, IWM Documents 788 91/1/1

Bob, Hans-Ekkhard, IWM Sound 26965

Boddington, M., IWM Documents 7078 77/85/1

Brothers, Flying Officer Pete, IWM Sound 10218

Brown, Pilot Officer Ronald, IWM Sound 12404

Cameron, Nigel, IWM Documents 1534 06/80/1

Deere, Alan, IWM Sound 10478

Dundas, Hugh, IWM Sound 10159

Falck, Wolfgang, IWM Sound 11247

Foxley-Norris, Christopher, IWM Sound 10136

Horstmann, Rosemary, IWM Sound 10871

Ironside, Hugh, IWM Sound 13101

Kup, Edith (neé Heap), IWM Documents 507 88/2/1

Legget, Percival, IWM Sound 27075

McLane, Sergeant Major Martin, IWM Sound 10165

Mayfield, Guy The Venerable, IWM Documents 14311 06/12/1

Mills, Jean, IWM Sound 11885

Moggridge, Jackie, IWM Sound 8668

Morris, Edward, IWM Documents 8231 99/7/1

Page, Flying Officer Geoffrey, IWM Sound 11103

Parkhouse, Rupert, IWM Sound 15476

Pitt Parsons, Diana, IWM Sound 9948

Pountain, R., IWM Documents 14379 06/11/1

Quayle, Elizabeth, IWM Sound 10609

Quill, Jeffrey, IWM Sound 10687

Roll, Werner, IWM Sound 12563

Strachen, William, IWM Sound 10042

Unwin, George, IWM Sound 11544

Vincent, Group Captain Stanley (combat report),
    IWM Documents 4175 83/41/1

Wedding, Ernest, IWM Sound 26960

Wilkins, R. T. (collection of private papers including combat
    reports), IWM Documents 4175 83/15/4

Winskill, Pilot Officer Archibald, IWM Sound 11537

Winterbotham, Group Captain Frederick, IWM Sound 7462

Winterbotham, Petra, IWM Sound 7463

Wissler, Denis, IWM Documents 786 91/41/1

NATIONAL ARCHIVES, KEW

AIR 16/635 Orders of battle and operational strength of
    RAF squadrons

AIR 20/3543 Aerodrome repairs July–August 1940

AIR 20/4174 Daily state of operational aircraft and crews in
    Fighter Command (July 1940–1945)

AIR 22/262 Daily return of casualties to RAF aircraft (June–September 1940)

AIR 22/293 Aircraft production (1940–44)

AIR 22/296 Statistics relating to RAF personnel June 1940–1945

ROYAL AIR FORCE MUSEUM, HENDON

AC 71/17/15

PUBLISHED SOURCES

ARTICLES

'The bomber will always get through', *Air Force Magazine*, Vol. 91, No. 7, July 2008

Nasson, Bill, *A Flying Springbok of Wartime British Skies: A. G 'Sailor' Malan*, University of Stellenbosch, 16 August 2009

BOOKS

Addison, Paul and Crang, Jeremy (ed.), *The Burning Blue: A New History of the Battle of Britain*, Pimlico (London), 2000

Bishop, Patrick, *Fighter Boys: Saving Britain 1940*, Harper Perennial (London), 2004

Brown, Malcolm, *Spitfire Summer: When Britain Stood Alone*, Carlton Books in association with the Imperial War Museum (London), 2003

Bungay, Stephen, *The Most Dangerous Enemy*, Aurum Press (London), 2001

Churchill, Winston S., *The Second World War: Volume I: The Gathering Storm*, Houghton Mifflin Company (New York), 1985

Clayton, Tim and Craig, Phil, *Finest Hour*, Hodder & Stoughton (London), 1999

Corum, James S., *The Luftwaffe: Creating the Operational Air War, 1918–1940*, University Press of Kansas (Lawrence, Kansas), 1997

Deighton, Len, *Fighter: The True Story of the Battle of Britain*, Vintage (London), 2008

Domarcus, Max (ed.), *Hitler's Speeches and Proclamations 1932–45: The Chronicle of a Dictatorship*, trans Chris Wilcox, Bolchazy-Carducci Publishers (Wauconda, Il.)

Domarcus, Max (ed.), Hit[...] The Chronicle of a [...] Bolchazy-Carducci [...]

Douhet [include from OL[...]

Forbes, Athol and Allen, H[...] (London), 1942 and 200[...]

Glancey, John, *Spitfire: A Bi[...]*

Goss, Christopher, *The Luft[...]* Publishing (Manchester)[...]

Hillary, Richard, *The Last E[...]*

Holmes, Tony, *Hurricane Ace[...]* 1998

Kaplan, Philip, *Spitfire: The [...]* (Great Britain), 2008

Kaplan, Philip and Collier, [...] Blandford (London), 199[...]

Kent, Johnny, *One of the Few[...]*

Kershaw, Alex, *The Few: The [...] Everything to Save Britain [...]* (Philadelphia), 2006

Levine, Joshua, *Forgotten Voice[...]* Ebury Press in associatio[...] (London), 2007

Manchester, William, *The Las[...] 1932–40*, Little Brown an[...]

Mayhew, E. R., *The Reconstru[...] Royal Air Force and the Gui[...]*

Murray, Williamson, *The Luftw[...]* Brassey's (Washington), 199[...]

Overy, Richard, *The Battle: Su[...]*

Overy, Richard, *Why the Allies[...]*

Page, Geoffrey, *Tale of a Guinea[...]*

Price, Alfred, *Battle of Britain D[...]* Jackson (London), 1990

Price, Alfred, *The Hardest Day:[...]* Cassel (London), 1988

INDEX

References to illustrations are shown in **bold**.

Admiralty 126–127 *see also* Royal Navy
Air Council 26, 27, **105**
Air Ministry 28, 38, 50, 87, 88, 178, 184
  and fighter development 34–35, 36, 37, 39
  Invasion Alert No. 1 ('Attack Imminent') 165
Air War 1936: The Destruction of Paris 59
American support 183
Anglo-German Naval Agreement (1935) 12
Ark Royal, HMS 66
Armstrong Whitworth Whitley **163**
Atcherley, F/O Richard **39**
Atlantic, Battle of the (1940–45) 184
Avro 504N **21**
awards for pilots 76–77, 114, **117**

Bader, Sqn Ldr Douglas 45, **97**, 135, 156, 166, 170, 171, 173
Baldwin, Stanley 23, 24
Balfour, Harold 87
Ball, Capt Albert, VC **43**, 43
Bamberger, Cyril 49
Barcelona, bombing of 23, **25**
'Barking Creek, Battle of' (1939) 116
Barratt, Air Marshal 86
Baumbach, Werner **160**
Bayne, Flt Lt 149
Beamont, P/O Roland **16**, 94–95, 102, 137–138, **139**
Beaton, Cecil **179**
Beaverbrook, Lord 108–109, 110, 183
Belfast, raid on 134
Beresford, Flt Lt Hugh 131–132
Berlin, raids on **161**, 161, **163**
Bisdee, P/O J. D. **176**
Bletchley Park 32, 109, 113, 174
Blitz, the 181, **182**, 182, **183**, **184**, 185 *see also* London, first major raid
Blitzkrieg 15, 16, 83–97 *see also* Poland, invasion of
  Dunkirk 90, 92–95
  France, Battle of 83–90, **85**
Bob, Hans-Ekkehard 69, 72, 73, 74–75, 77, 134, 140, 158
Boddington, Sqn Ldr Michael **81**
Boeing B-17 61
bomber development, Luftwaffe 61, 63–66
  Dornier Do 17: 63, 66
  Heinkel He 111: 65–66

Junkers Ju 87 Stuka 64–65
Junkers Ju 88: 66
Bootham, Flt Lt John 38
Boulogne harbour **110**
Boulton Paul Defiant 122, **123**
Brand, Quintin 48
Brauchitsch, FM Walther von **111**
Bristol Beaufighter 134
Britain
  declares war on Germany **10**, 10–11
  defence of 83, 85–86, 87–88
  fighter aircraft, repair of 110
  fighter aircraft funding and production **108**, 108–109, **109**, 110
  planned invasion 104, **110**, 177, 178–179, 182
Britain, Battle of (1940) 17, 97–179
  Adlerangriff (Eagle Attack) **128**–133, **130**, **131**
  Adlertag ('Eagle Day' – 13 August) **133**, 133–134, **134**
  Battle of Britain Day (15 September) 169–175, 185–187
  Black Thursday (15 August) 134, 136–141, **137**
  draws to a close 176–179
  hardest day (18 August) 140–146, **142**
  Operation *Loge* 163, 165–167
  preparing for 97–99, 101–105, 109–110
  victory claims 122–123, 139, 141, **145**
British Army 94
  Territorial Army 13
British Chiefs of Staff 85
British Expeditionary Force 83, 85, 90, **91**, 92, 93, 94, 98
Broadhurst, Harry 51–52
Brodie, Crelin 'Bogle' 186–187
Bromley 174
Brooklands aircraft factory raid 163
Brothers, Flt Lt Peter **49**, 52–53, 86, 89–90, 102–103, 112, 118, **122**
Brown, P/O Ronald 143
Buerschgens, Lt Josef 157–158
Bulman, George 37

Cameron, Nigel 148, **150**
Camm, Sydney 35–36, **36**
Canadian Air Force, Royal 44, 146–147
  No. 1 Sqn **45**
Candlish-Henderson, Cpl Elspeth, MM **143**
Canterbury, raid on 170
Castle Bromwich, raid on 134

Chamberlain, Neville 9, **10**, 10, **11**, 24, 85, 90
Channel battles (Kanalkampf) 109, 110, 111, 113–115, 117–119, 122–124, 126–127
  and pilots ditching 124, 126
Charterhouse, Somerset **136**
children, evacuation of **9**, **169**
Chundall, Charles **91**
Churchill, Winston **6**, 9–10, 30, 97, **104**
  after outbreak of war 11, 13
  and air power 19
  and American support 47
  argues for strategic rearmament 21
  and Battle of France 85, 86–87, 88, 89, 90
  and defence of Britain 83, 90, 99, 101
  forms national government 85
  'Never in the field of human conflict...' speech **15**, 148–149, 184
  speech to prime ministers of Dominions 181
  vengeance 181
  visits Keith Park at Uxbridge 157, 171, 172, 174
  'We shall fight on the beaches...' speech 99, 101
civilian casualties 161, **179**, 181
Civilian Repair Organisation 110
Cobham, Alan, and 'Flying Circus' 41, 43, **48**, 73, **175**
Command of the Air, The 23, **24**
Condor Legion 23, **70**, 70–71, **71**, **78**, 80
convoys, attacks on 113, 114, 118, 126–127
Croydon, raid on 161
Curtiss F8C Helldiver 64
Curtiss P-36 74–75
Czernin, F/O Count 170

Daily Express 105
Daimler-Benz DB 601 engine **41**, 63, **68**, 68–69, **69**, 70
Dartford 174
David, P/O Dennis **16**
Deere, Wg Cdr Alan 44, 45, 50, 142, **144**, 149, 153, **175**
Deichmann, Oberst Paul 132
Delmer, Sefton 105
Dessau, Junkers plant **56**
Deutsche Jungvolk 75
Dornier 63
  Do 17: 63, **66**, 66, 71, 115, 133, **142**, **178**, 186–187
  Do 215: 63
Douhet, Gen Giulio 23, **24**, 59, 64

Dowding, AC[...]
26–27, 29, [...]
and Cham[...]
and defenc[...]
and defenc[...]
fighter de[...]
125, 18[...]
and form[...]
and Keith[...]
and Leigh[...]
and Lond[...]
and oper[...]
and Polis[...]
reorganiz[...]
strategy [...]
and Ultr[...]
and WA[...]
Dundas, G[...]
Dundas, Jo[...]
Dunkirk **9**[...]
182, 18[...]
Dunkirk (t[...]
Dunne, Ei[...]

East Grins[...]
155
Eben Ema[...]
Edwards-J[...]
El Alamei[...]
Empire A[...]
Enigma c[...]
Epenstein[...]
Eurich, R[...]

Falck, W[...]
Feric, P/[...]
fighter de[...]
Luftwa[...]
Me[...]
RAF [...]
Fink, O[...]
Fiske, B[...]
Focke-W[...]
Fokker [...]
Fokker [...]
Foxley-[...]
*Foyleba[...]

France, Battle of (1940) 16–17, 52–53, 74–75, 83–90, **85**, **86**, **89**, 92, 99, **100**, 110
Francke, Gefr Carl 66
František, Josef 47, **175**
Freeman, Wilfred 39
French air service (Armée de l'Air) 84, 89–90
Furst, Sgt **167**

Galland, Adolf 77, 112, **135**, 135, **186**
Gamelin, Gen Maurice 15
George VI, King 30, **34**
German air arm (Luftstreitkräfte) (WWI) 55, 56, 57, 58
  Bombengeschwader No. 3: **56**
German air force (Luftwaffe) 17, 55–80 see also Condor Legion
  bomber crews **133**, **141**, **151**, **160**
  bombers see bomber development, Luftwaffe
  and Dunkirk 90, 92, 93, 94
  Erprobungsgruppe 210: 130, 132, 138–139, 151, 171, **177**
  Fallschirmjäger (parachute and glider troops) 73
  Fighter Command as target 146–149, 151–153
  fighters see fighter development, Luftwaffe
  Flugzeugführerschule A/B (flight schools) 78
  'freie Jagd' ('free hunting') fighter sweeps 114
  High Command 130, 133, 140, 141
  and invasion of Norway 13, 15, **16**
  Jagdgeschwader (fighter units) 97; 7/JG 26: 157–158; JG 51: **63**, 114, 118–119, 123; JG 52: 139; JG 53: 131
  Jagdverband 44: 135
  Jagdwaffe (fighter arm) 67, 76
  Kampfgeschwader (bomber units) 97; KG 1: 142, 143–144; KG 2: 132, 173; KG 27: **136**; KG 30: **160**; KG 51: 131; KG 55: **176**; KG 76: 142–143
  Luftflotten (air fleets) 97; Luftflotte 2: 71, 97, 98, 101, 111, 114, 139, 141, 146, 151, 171; Luftflotte 3: 97, 98, **102**, 111, 114, 139, 141, 144–145, 146; Luftflotte 5: 97, 114, 136–137, 139
  night attacks 134, 167
  origins 16, 55–59; sports aviation (Luftsportsverband) 58–59, **75**, 75; 'Training Inspectorates' 58, 60
  pilots see pilots, Luftwaffe
  and planned invasion of Britain 104, 105, 109
  preparations for Battle 97–98
  strategy for Battle 130
  strength before Battle of Britain 109–110
  strength before Battle of France 84
  tactics, pairs **76**, 77, **79**, 80
  Zerstörergeschwader (heavy fighter units) 97; ZG 76: **68**
German Air Staff, Imperial 55
German Armed Forces, Supreme Command (OKW) 104, 111
German armed forces awards system 76–77
German army 9, 15, 56, 85
  Armoured Corps, XIXth 92–93
  infantry officers and men **59**, **69**

strength before Battle of France 84–85
German High Command 98, 163, 176, 181, 182
German Nationalsozialistische Fliegerkorps (NSFK) **75**, **76**
German navy (Kriegsmarine) 12, 13, **16**, 56, **110**, **111**, 160
Germany
  aircraft production in 160
  Britain declares war on **10**, 10–11
  glider training in 58–59, **75**, 75, **76**
  planned offensive in the West by 13, 15
  radar research in 28
Gillies, Sir Harold 154
Gloster Gauntlet **44**
Gloster Gladiator **17**
Goebbels, Joseph **161**
Göring, Reichsmarschall Hermann 55, 60, 66, 67–68, 71, 72–73, **72**, **73**, **74**, 98, 160, 185
  and Adlertag ('Eagle Day') 133
  and Battle of France 84, 93
  battle-winning scenario 105, 109, 113, 123, 126
  and Channel battles 122, 123
  final attempt to destroy Fighter Command 171, 174
  and Galland 77
  and Operation Loge 163
  plans 160, 161
  and preparations for Battle 97, **98**
  and raids on Berlin 161, 163
  revises strategy on Black Thursday 139–140, 142
  and strength of Luftwaffe 109, 110, 111
  The Hague conference 160
  withdraws Stukas 146
Gort, Lord 85
Gosport, raid on **131**
Gotha G IV 55, **56**, 57
Grice, Richard 151
Guderian, Gen Heinz 92–93
Guernica, bombing of 23, **71**, 71
Guinea Pig Club **154**, 154–155, **155**

Halahan, Sqn Ldr Patrick 'Bull' 88–89, **89**
Halifax, Lord 9, 10, 85
Hawker 35
  Brooklands aircraft factory 163
  Hart 49, **52**
Hurricane **19**, 26, 35–37, **36**, 49–50, 69, **97**, **119**, **165**, **167**; and Battle of France **37**, **84**, 85, 86, 88–89, **89**, 90, 92, 94–95, **95**; Channel battles 113, 114; Mark I **100**; 'OK 1' **125**, 125; production 108–109, 110, 118, 128, 141, 147; prototype **35**, 37
Heap, Edith 10, **121**
Heinkel 64, 67
  He 51: 78
  He 111: **16**, 55, 65–66, **71**, 71, **136**, **137**, **151**, **164**, **176**, **177**
  passenger planes 59
Herne Bay 148, **150**

Higgs, F/O Tom 118, 119
Hillary, Richard 43, 44
Hitler, Adolf **11**, 13, 16, 68, 75, 76, **111**, 176
  and Battle of France 92–93
  British opposition 183
  destruction of RAF directive (No. 17) 126, 130
  and Göring 72, 73
  hopes for peace settlement with Britain 98, 103, 104–105, **105**
  'Last Appeal to Reason' speech 104–105, **105**
  and planned invasion of Britain 104, 113, 160, 161, 181, 182
Hitler Jugend (Hitler Youth) **75**, 75
Home Guard **157** see also Local Defence Volunteers
Horstmann, Rosemary 25, 29
House of Commons 10, 11, 23, 90, 99, 101, 148–149
Houston, Lady **38**, 38

intelligence, Ultra 32, 73, 113, 126, 174, 178–179
  see also Enigma codes
Iraq, British bombing in 23
Iron Cross awards 76–77
Ironside, Hugh 83–84
Ismay, General 179

Jeschonnek, Hans 104
Jodl, Gen Alfred 104, **111**
Johnson, Amy 41
Jones, Taffy 53
Junck, Werner 123
Junkers 57, 63, 64, 67
  Dessau plant **56**
  Ju 52: **13**, 61, **63**
  Ju 87 Stuka 12, **56**, 64–65, **65**, 66, 71, 84, 111, 113, 114, 144, 146, 160
  Ju 88: **56**, 64, 66, **160**
Junkers, Prof Hugo **56**, 57

Karinhall estate 139
Keitel, FM Wilhelm **111**
Kellet, Ronald 48
Kennedy, Joseph 102, 182–183
Kent, Sqn Ldr Johnny 48, **49**, 51, **181**
Keough, P/O Vernon 'Shorty' 46, **47**
Kesselring, FM Albert 98, 101, **101**, 111, 139, 141, 146, 151, 157, 159, 160, 161, 163, 167
  and 15 September raid on London 171, 172
Kiel harbour 28
Knauss, Dr Robert 59, **60**, 61

Lacey, Flt Lt J. H. 'Ginger' 159, **171**
Lane, Sqn Ldr B. J. E. 'Sandy' **160**, 172
Lawson, Flt Lt **160**
Legget, Percival 36
Leigh-Mallory, AVM Trafford 125, 147, 153, **156**, 156, 157, 166, 170, 181, 184
Lindbergh, Charles 41

Local Defence Volunteers 99 see also Home Guard
Lock, Flt Lt Eric **175**
London
  Carlton House Terrace 179
  Central Telegraph Office **57**
  East End 9, **164**, **167**
  Euston Combined Recruits Centre **185**
  first bombing of 139
  Isle of Dogs **164**
  Norwood 172
  as planned target 161, 163
  raids: first major (7 September) **164**, 165–166, **165**, **167**, 167
  9 September 170
  15 September 171–175
  27 September 177
  residents **169**
  St Paul's Cathedral 47, **184**
  as target in First World War 55, **57**
  West Ham **66**, 174
London Gazette 114
Lufthansa 57, **59**, 60, **63**

MacDonald, Ramsay, government of 38
McIndoe, Sir Archibald 154, **155**, 155
McLane, Sgt Maj Martin 90
Malan, D. F. 116
Malan, Grp Capt Adolf 'Sailor' 112, **116**, 116, 147–148, 170
Mamedoff, P/O Andrew 46, **47**
Manstein, Gen von 13
Mantle, Leading Seaman Jack, VC 114, **117**
Martini, Genmaj Wolfgang 130
Mayfield, The Venerable Guy 88, 101
Messerschmitt 67
  Me 108 'Taifun' ('Typhoon') 67, **115**
  Me 109: 52–53, 67, 68–69, 71, **77**, 84, 102, 112, 115, 117, 118, 134, **147**, **151**; Me 109B **69**; Me 109E **69**; prototype 67, **68**, 68
  Me 110: **68**, 70, **83**, 84, **87**, **112**, 114, 138, **177**
  Me 262: **67**, 135
Messerschmitt, Prof Wilhelm 'Willy' 67, 67, 68
Meuse, River 86, 92
Milch, FM Erhard 57, 58, 60, 61, **63**, **67**, 67, 68, 101, 153
Miles Master 50
Miller, P/O R. F. G. **177**
Mills, Jean 27
Mitchell, Reginald J. **38**, 38, 39, 40, **41**, 67
Moggridge, Jackie 32
Mölders, Werner **76**, 80, 123–124, **124**, 135, **186**
Morris, Edward 10–11, 166–167
Morrison, Edward James 32, 34
Mortimer, Sgt Joan, MM **143**
Munich Agreement (1938) 9, **11**

Narvik 13, 15, **16**
National Aviation Day Displays 43

National Physical Laboratory 28
Nazi party 57, 58, 60, 75, 78
    Sturmabteilung (SA – 'Brownshirts') 72, 73
New Zealand, RAF recruits from 44, **45**, 45, 48, 50
Newall, ACM Sir Cyril 26, 27, 85, 86, **105**, 179
Nicholson, Wg Cdr James, VC **117**
night attacks 134, 167
Night of the Long Knives (1934) 73
Normandy invasion (1944) 94
Norway, invasion of 13, 15, **16**, **17**

Observer Corps 24, 29, **34**, 132, 142, 186
Operation *Barbarossa* 73
Operation *Loge* 163, 165–167
Operation *Seelöwe* (Sealion) 104, **110**, **111**, 160–161, 177, 178–179, 182
Orde, Cuthbert **175**
Orpen, Sir William **22**
Osterkamp, 'Onkel' Theo **63**, 114, **115**, 118, 123–124, 153, **186**

Page, F/O Geoffrey 43, 114, **154**, 155
Paris **83**, **87**
Park, AVM Keith 48, 92, 118, 123, 125, **125**, 145
    and airfield attacks 184
    and Biggin Hill raids 152, 153
    and Channel battles 126
    and Dowding 156–157
    and Leigh-Mallory 153, 156, 166, 181
    and London raids 165, 169, 170, 171, 172, 174, 175
    strategy for Battle 129
    tactics 147, 159, 184
Parker, Rupert 49
Parkhouse, Rupert 44
Paszkiewicz, Flt Off 48
pilots, American 46–47
pilots, Czech 47, **49**
pilots, Luftwaffe 73–78, 80, 103, **129**, **174**
    motivation 75–77
    recruitment 73–77
    training **78**, 78, 80, 160; gliders 58–59, **75**, 75, **76**; Russian secret flying schools 58, 75, 78, **81**
pilots, Polish 13, **46**, 47, 48, **49**
pilots, RAF **7**, 41, 43–53, **52**, **97**, **119**, 128, **129**, 158, **172**, **181**
    Commonwealth 44–46
    foreign **46**, 46–48
    recruitment 41, 43–44, **44**, **45**, 48
    shortages 118, 157
    training **46**, 49–53, **53**, 147, 148; blind flying 49; formation-style flying 50–51, **51**; gunnery 50, 51–52
Pitt Parsons, Diana 27–28, 31
Poland, invasion of 9, 12–13, **13**
Polish Air Force 12, 47

Portland, raids on **113**, 113–114, **117**, 133, 137–138
Portsmouth, raids on **130**, **131**, 131, 141
Purfleet, raid on **165**

Quayle, Elizabeth 27
Quill, Jeffrey 39

radar, development of 26–27, 28
radar, German 'Freya' mobile 113, 114
radar stations 27–29, 30, 31, 32, 34, 113, 142
    attacks on 130–132, 140, 144
    Chain Home **28**, 28, **33**, **34**, 140, 141, 144
    Chain Home Low 28, **33**, 138, 144
Raeder, Adm Erich 104, 181–182
Rapallo Treaty (1922) 58
Reichstag **105**, 105
Reynaud, Paul 85
Richey, Paul 101
Richthofen, Manfred von 72, **74**, 74
Roll, Werner 64–65
Rolls-Royce
    Derby production plant **41**
    Merlin engine **41**
    PV engine 36
    R-Type engine 38
Roosevelt, Franklin D. 183
Royal Air Force (RAF)
    Advanced Air Striking Force **37**, 83, 84, **85**, 85, **86**, 86, 87, 88–89, **89**, 90, 94–95, 99, **100**
    Andover Staff College 19
    Bomber Command 16, 21, 161
    bombing concept, strategic 23–24
    Coastal Command 21
    Cranwell air academy 19, **20**, 20, 49
    Duxford wing 171, 173, 176
    Elementary and Reserve Flying Training Schools 49, 50
    Elementary Flying Training School, 4: 46
    Elementary Flying Training Schools 50, **53**
    Fighter Command 10, **15**, 15, 16, 17, 19–53; Channel battles 113; Dowding's defence system 24–25, 27–29, 32, 34, **50**, 116, 125, 183, 184; Dunkirk 90, 92, **93**, 93, **94**, 94, 99, 102, 128; formed 21; Headquarters, Bentley Priory 24, **28**, **29**, 30, **32**, 32, **33**; as Luftwaffe target 146–149, 151–153; operations in preparation for Battle of Britain 102–103; origins 19–21; strategy for Battle of Britain 129; strength before Battle of Britain 110
    Fighting Area Attacks 51
    Flying Training School, 9: 49
    formations 50–51, **51**, 92, **127**, 147–148; 'big wing' 125, 147, 156, 166, 170
    ground crews **100**, 100, 187
    groups: No. 10 Group 24, 48, **50**, 133–134, 157; No. 11 Group 24, 31, 48, **50**, 90, 92, **99**, 118, 125, 128, 136, 141, 142, 144–145, 146, 149, 153, 156,

157, 172, 174, 181, **186**; No. 12 Group 24, **50**, 136, 144–145, 153, 156, 157, 171, 174; No. 13 Group 24, **50**, 136
    Halton Technical Training School 19
    Operational Training Units 50, 147
    operations rooms 25, 27, **28**, **29**, 30, 31, **33**, **99**, 142, 151, 153, 157, 184–185, 186
    Service Flying Training Schools 50
    squadrons: auxiliary 20 *see also* Royal Auxiliary Air Force; No. 1 Sqn 88–89, **89**; No. 17 Sqn **44**, 138; No. 19 Sqn **40**, 40, **43**, 51–52, 92, 101, **128**, **160**, **172**; No. 32 Sqn 118–119, **119**, 139, 143; No. 43 Sqn 144; No. 54 Sqn 142, 149; No. 56 Sqn 116, 118–119; No. 57 Sqn **52**; No. 64 Sqn **140**; No. 66 Sqn 186–187; No. 72 Sqn 171; No. 73 Sqn **86**; No. 74 Sqn 116, 118–119, 133; No. 79 Sqn 10–11, 32, 34, 115, 166–167; No. 85 Sqn 86, 88, **121**, 149, 170–171; No. 87 Sqn **16**, **84**, 94–95, 102, 137–138; No. 92 (East India) Sqn **136**, 171, **181**; No. 111 Sqn **19**, 118–119, 122, 133, 134, 136, 139, 142–143; No. 141 Sqn 122; No. 145 Sqn 134; No. 152 Sqn 132; No. 213 Sqn 137, 173; No. 234 Sqn **81**, 137, 144; No. 242 (Canadian) Sqn 45, **97**, 156; No. 257 Sqn 131–132; No. 264 Sqn 122, **123**; No. 302 (Polish) Sqn 146; No. 303 (Polish) Sqn 48, **49**, 147, 153, 172–173; No. 310 (Czech) Sqn **49**, 146, **165**, **167**; Oxford University Air 20, **21**; University Air 20
    Training Command 21, 50
Royal Auxiliary Air Force **23**
    No. 601 (County of London) Sqn **23**, 41, 46–47, **126**, 144; No. 602 Sqn 144, 173; No. 607 Sqn 173; No. 609 Sqn 46, **47**, 132, 134, 136, **176**, **177**; No. 610 Sqn **127**; No. 616 (South Yorkshire) Sqn 93–94, 136, **173**
Royal Flying Corps 16, 19, 26, 55–56, 112, 125
Royal Navy 12, 13, 15, 66, 99, 104, **110** *see also* Admiralty
    and Dunkirk 90, **91**, 93
    Fleet Air Arm **187**
Rundstedt, Gen Gerd von 93
Russia 13, 58, 76

Schneider Trophy **38**, 38, **39**, **41**, 67
Seeckt, Col Gen Hans von 58, **59**
Sinclair, Rt. Hon. Sir Archibald 85, **105**
Sopwith Camel 35
Southampton, raids on 133, **176**, 177
Spanish Civil War (1936–39) 16, 23, **25**, 35, 66, **70**, 70–71, **71**, **78**, 80
Speer, Albert 67
Sperrle, FM Hugo 71, 80, 98, **102**, 111, 139, 141, 161, 163
Spitfire Funds **108**, 109
Staples, P/O M. E. **177**
Strachan, William 46

Striberny, Lt Albert 115, 117–118
Sudetenland 71
Supermarine 38
    S.5 38
    S.6 **39**
    S.6B 38, **39**, 39
    Southampton aircraft factory **176**, 177
Spitfire 26, 34, 38–40, **40**, 49–50, 69, **100**, 112, **140**, **178**, **181**; and Channel battles 113; Mark I **43**, **177**; Mark II **41**, 43; production **108**, 108–109, **109**, 110, 118, 128, 141, 147; prototype 39, **40**
    Type 224: 39

Ten Rules of Air Fighting 147
Tobin, P/O Eugene 'Red' 46, **47**
Trenchard, Hugh, Lord 20, **22**, 23, 26
Turner, Sgt Helen, MM **143**

Udet, Col Ernst 64, 67, 68
Ultra intelligence 32, 73, 113, 126, 174, 178–179 *see also* Enigma codes
Unwin, Flt Sgt George 40, 44, 51–52, 92, **97**, 112, **128**, 128–129, 159, **160**, 184
US Army Air Corps 61

Versailles, Treaty of (1919) 56–57, 60, 75
Vickers 39–40 *see also* Supermarine
Victoria Cross 76, 114, **117**
victory claims 122–123, 139, 141, **145**, 175
Vincent, Grp Capt Stanley 173
Voase-Jeff, Flt Lt Robert **16**

War Cabinet 9, 15, 85, 87, 161
War of 19—, The 59
Warrington-Morris, Air Cdre A. D. 29
Watson, Peter 101–102
Watson-Watt, Sir Robert Alexander 26–27, 28, 30, **32**
Wedding, Ernst 66, 74
Wever, Lt Gen Walther **61**, 61, 63, 68, 71, 101
Weygand, Gen Maxime 102, 182
Wick, Hptm Helmut **79**, **179**
Winskill, P/O Archibald 43, 73
Winterbotham, Grp Capt Frederick 32, 113, 174, 178–179
Winterbotham, Petrea 30, 31
Wissler, P/O Denis 86, 88, 115, **121**, 149, 170–171, 178
Women's Auxiliary Air Force 30–31, **143**, 152, 186, 187
    plotters 25, 27, 30, 31, **33**, **99**, 131, 142
    radar operators 25, 27–28, 30, 32, **34**
    Y service radio 'eavesdroppers' 29, 31
Women's Royal Naval Service 31
World War, First 16, 19, 41, **43**, 43, 55–56, **56**, **57**, **58**, 58, **72**, 72, 125
Wright Brothers 19

Zeppelin bombing unit 55